SCHUMANN
SOLO PIANO LITERATURE

A Comprehensive Guide:

Annotated and Evaluated
with Thematics

Edited by
Carolyn Maxwell
William DeVan

Assistant Editors
Charles Shadle
Joan Forsyth

MAXWELL
MUSIC
EVALUATION

ACKNOWLEDGEMENTS

Charles Shadle--Historical Information and Prefaces
     to the reviews of Op. 1 through 26
Elizabeth Harris--Cover Design
Kenneth Andrus--Production

Contributers
Christine Armstrong
William DeVan
Joan Forsyth
Mary Mosher Humm
Gayle Kliever
Charles Shadle
Dennis Varley

Published by Maxwell Music Evaluation Books
1245 Kalmia, Boulder, Colorado 80302

First printing, 1984

Printed in the United States of America.

ISBN 0-912531-01-0

TABLE OF CONTENTS

CONTENTS BY OPUS NUMBER ii

GERMAN TITLES IN ALPHABETICAL ORDER iii

ENGLISH TITLES IN ALPHABETICAL ORDER v

FOREWORD vii

SCHUMANN PIANO MUSIC CRITIQUES 1

INTRODUCTION TO THE SONATAS 67

BIBLIOGRAPHY......................... 327

INDEX OF GERMAN TITLES................. 328

INDEX OF ENGLISH TITLES................ 330

CONTENTS BY OPUS NUMBER

Opus 1: Variationen über den Namen
                    Abegg........................... 1
Opus 2: Papillons 5
Opus 3: Studie nach Capricen von
                    Paganini 13
Opus 4: Intermezzi 18
Opus 5: Impromptus über ein Thema
                    von Clara Wieck.................. 23
Opus 6: Davidsbündler Achtzehn
                    Charakterstücke 30
Opus 7: Toccata 43
Opus 8: Allegro 45
Opus 9: Carnaval 47
Opus 10: Sechs Concert-Etuden nach
                    Capricen von Paganini 62
Opus 11: Grosse Sonata, No. 1 69
Opus 12: Phantasiestücke 76
Opus 13: Etuden in Form von
                    Variationen 85
Opus 13: Symphonische Etüden
                    Anhang zu Op. 13 96
Opus 14: Dritte Gross Sonate, No. 3 100
Opus 14: Scherzo
                    Anhang zu Opus 14 109
Opus 15: Kinderscenen 111
Opus 16: Kreisleriana 123
Opus 17: Phantasie 129
Opus 18: Arabeske 136
Opus 19: Blumenstück....................... 138
Opus 20: Humoreske 140
Opus 21: Novelletten 142
Opus 22: Zweite Sonate, No. 2................. 148
Opus 22: Presto
                    Anhang zu Op. 22 155
Opus 23: Nachtstücke 159
Opus 26: Faschingsschwank Aus Wien........... 163
Opus 28: Drei Romanzen.................... 171
Opus 32: Scherzo, Gigue, Romanze
                    und Fughette 175

CONTENTS BY OPUS NUMBER

Opus 56: Studien fur den
Pedal-Flügel 178
Opus 58: Vier Skizzen fur den
Pedal-Flügel 183
Opus 60: Sechs Fugen über den
Namen BACH.......................... 186
Opus 68: Clavierstücke für die
Jugend................................ 191
Opus 68: Sketches for Opus 68................. 243
Opus 72: Vier Fugen 253
Opus 76: Vier Märsche 256
Opus 82: Waldenscenen 260
Opus 99: Bunte Blätter 270
Opus 111: Drei Phantasiestücke............... 280
Opus 118: Drei Clavier-Sonaten für
de Jugend 283
Opus 124: Albumblätter 291
Opus 126: Sieben Stücke in
Fughetten Form 309
Opus 133: Gesänge der Frühe................. 314
WoO 4: Kanon über "An Alexis" 319
Theme in Eb with Five Variations 321
Etüden in Form Freier Variationen
uber ein Thema von Beethoven 325

TABLE OF CONTENTS—GERMAN TITLES

Albumblätter, Op. 124 291
Allegro, Op. 8 45
Arabeske, Op. 18 136
Blumenstück, Op 19 138
Carnaval, Op. 9 47
Clavierstücke für die Jugend, Op. 68 191
Sketches for Op. 68 243
Davidsbündler Achtzehn
Charakterstücke, Op. 6 30
Drei Clavier-Sonaten für de Jugend,
Op. 118 283

iv

TABLE OF CONTENTS—GERMAN TITLES

Drei Phantasiestücke, Op. 111 280
Drei Romanzen, Op. 28 171
Dritte Gross Sonate, Op. 14 100
    Anhang zu Opus 14 109
Etüden in Form von Variationen,
    Op. 13 85
    Anhang zu Opus 13 96
Etüden in Form Freier Variationen
    uber ein Thema von Beethoven 325
Faschingsschwank Aus Wien, Op. 26 163
Gesänge der Frühe, Op. 133 314
Grosse Sonata, Op. 11 69
Humoreske, Op. 20 140
Impromptus über ein Thema von Clara
    Wieck, Op 5 23
Intermezzi, Op. 4 18
Kanon über "An Alexis", WoO 4 319
Kinderscenen, Op. 15 111
Kreisleriana, Op. 16 123
Nachtstücke, Op. 23 159
Novelletten, Op. 21 142
Papillons, Op. 2 5
Phantasie, Op. 17 129
Phantasiestücke, Op. 12 76
Scherzo, Gigue, Romanze und
    Fughette, Op. 32 175
Sechs Concert-Etuden nach Capricen
    von Paganini, Op. 10 62
Sechs Fugen über den Namen BACH,
    Op. 60 186
Sieben Stücke in Fughetten Form,
    Op. 126 309
Studien für den Pedal-Flügel, Op. 56 178
Studien nach Capricen von Paganini,
    Op. 3 13
Theme in Eb, with Five Variations,
    No Opus number 321
Toccata, Op. 7 43

TABLE OF CONTENTS--GERMAN TITLES

Variatinen Über den Namen Abegg, .
Op. 1 1
Vier Fugen, Op. 72 253
Vier Märsche, Op. 76 256
Vier Skizzen fur den Pedal-Flügel,
Op. 58 183
Waldenscenen, Op. 82 260
Zweite Sonate, Op. 22................... 148
Anhang zu Op. 22 155

TABLE OF CONTENTS--ENGLISH TITLES

Album for the Young, Op 68 191
Sketches for Op. 68 243
Album Leaves, Op. 124 291
Allegro, Op. 8 45
Arabesque, Op. 18 136
Canon, "To Alexis", WoO 4 319
Carnaval, Op. 9 47
Carnival Jest from Vienna, Op. 26 163
Colored Leaves, Op. 99 270
Davidsbundler Eighteen Character
Pieces, Op. 6 30
Etudes in the Form of Variations
(Symphonic Etudes) Op. 13 85
Supplement to Op. 13 96
Fantasy, Op. 17 129
Fantasy Pieces, Op. 12 76
Supplement to Op. 12 84
First Grand Sonata, Op. 11 69
Flower Piece, Op. 19 138
Forest Scenes, Op. 82 260
Four Fugues, Op. 72 253
Four Marches, Op. 76 256
Four Sketches for Pedal Piano, Op. 58 183
Humoresque, Op. 20 140
Impromptus on a Theme by Clara Wieck,
Op. 5.................................... 23

TABLE OF CONTENTS—ENGLISH TITLES

Intermezzi, Op. 4 18
Kreisleriana, Op. 16 123
Night Pieces, Op. 23 159
Novelettes, Op. 21 142
Papillons, Op. 2 5
Scenes from Childhood, Op 15 111
Scherzo, Gigue, Romance and
    Fughette, Op. 32 175
Second Sonata, Op. 22....................... 148
    Supplement to Op. 22 155
Seven Pieces in Fughetta Form,
    Op. 126 309
Six Concert Etudes Based on Caprices
    of Paganini Op. 10 62
Six Etudes for the Pedal-Piano,
    Op. 56 178
Six Fugues on the Name BACH, Op. 60.......... 186
Songs of the Morning, Op. 133 314
Studies on Paganini Caprices, Set I,
    Op. 3................................... 13
Theme in Eb Major and Five
    Variations 321
Third Great Sonata, Concerto without
    Orchestra, Op. 14....................... 100
    Supplement to Op. 14 109
Three Fantasies, Op. 111.................... 280
Three Romances, Op. 28 171
Three Sonatas for the Young, Op. 118 283
Toccata, Op. 7 43
Variations on the name Abegg, Op. 1 1

FOREWORD

The piano works of Robert Schumann (1810-1856) provide the pianist with a large body of challenging and rewarding literature. Especially in the shorter character pieces, the performer finds works that embody the essense of musical romanticism. The present volume Schumann: Solo Piano Literature is a complete survey of the piano works of Robert Schumann.

Schumann's penchant for providing descriptive titles to his compositions is particularly important in reviewing these works because of constant allusion to literary or imaginary personalities. Pertinent historical and biographical information is given at the beginning of many evaluations. It cannot be stressed too strongly that many of Schumann's compositions are far more difficult to perform than a quick personal perusal might suggest. Tone color, rhythmic and textural subtlety, and rapid shifts of mood are all critical factors in performing these works successfuly. Special attention is given to works in which spontaniety of performance combined with secure structural understanding is essential.

In this book, titles are given in the original language, followed by an English translation. All German indications are translated into English. In cases where a composition exists in more than one version (notably Opuses 5, 6, 13, and 14) Schumann's revised editions have been used for evaluation. Supplements to Opuses 12, 13, 14, and 22 have been included.

The table of contents is organized into three sections. The first is categorized by opus numbers. The second and third sections list the titles alphabetically in German and English respectively. All German titles, the number of measures, and metronome markings are generally taken from the three Dover Volumes, as these are the most accessible and complete sources. At the end of the book there are two indices: a complete index in German followed by another in English.

Sonatas and large compositions such as the Fantasy, Opus 17, are reviewed by movements (a separate thematic is provided for each movement). The thematics or incipits are the first few measures of each composition or movement, and are included for identification purposes only. Following the thematic example, the salient features of the work are reviewed. After each evaluation the reader will find the tempo indication, the length, and a summary of the most important technical features of the piece. Measure numbers refer only to the number of printed bars; second endings are included, but repeats and da capos are not considered.

Graded levels are included for every composition, and are determined by technical, rhythmical, and musical content. The following levels are suggestions only.

Elementary
Advancing Elementary   - Elementary School

Early Intermediate
Intermediate   - Junior High School
Advancing Intermediate

Advancing Intermediate
Early Advanced   - High School
Advanced

Advanced
Difficult   - University or Artist
Very Difficult

Contributors to Schumann: Solo Piano Literature are musicians on the staff of Maxwell Music Evaluation Books.

All available sources are listed with each opus, as well as each individual composition or movement. A bibliography has been included to give the reader sources for additional information. Schumann: Solo Piano Literature is a comprehensive reference guide for teachers, students, and performing artists of all levels who wish to familiarize themselves with the piano works of Robert Schumann.   --William DeVan

VARIATIONEN ÜBER DEN NAMEN ABEGG, Advanced
F Major, Opus 1 (Variations on the the Name Abegg)
"Theme sur le nom Abegg Varie pour le pianoforte"
(1831)

Schumann's first published composition, the Abegg
Variations, was completed in January of 1830, and
publication by Kistner followed in 1831. The theme,
based on the pitches A.B.(Bb) E.G.G., derives from the
name of a casual acquaintance of the composer, Meta
Abegg. In a characteristic flight of fancy Schumann
dedicated the work to the now metamorphosed "Pauline,
Contesse d'Abegg." Unusual features typical of
Schumann such as syncopation, irregular accentuations,
and inventive figurations, are already in evidence. The
use of an original theme as a source of motives rather
than as an inflexible structural formula is also
characteristic of Schumann, but otherwise quite rare at
the time. However, certain elements of these
variations reveal the influence of such popular
composers of the era as Hummel (1778-1837) and
Moscheles (1794-1870). Schumann was soon to remove
all vestiges of this "salon" idiom from his style, and
indeed, when this work was published, the composer
eliminated half of the original number of variations as
being too virtuosic.

Note: The following editions contain Opus 1 in its
    entirety.

BOETTICHER, Wolfgang: Schumann Klavierwerke, Band
    II (Henle).
SAUER, Emil: Complete Works of Robert Schumann,
    Volume 3 (Peters #2300C).
SCHUMANN, Clara: Piano Music of Robert Schumann,
    Series I (Dover).
SCHUMANN, Clara: Robert Schumann--Complete
    Works, Volume 1 (Kalmus #3923/Belwin).
SHEALY, Alexander: Schumann--His Greatest Piano
    Solos (Ashley).

Thema (Theme)

The clever and engaging theme is presented by the right hand in octaves, while the left hand provides a simple repeated chordal accompaniment. The B section is essentially only a retrograde of the A, and this attractive waltz is based entirely on sequential repetition of the initial motive.

        Tempo: Animato ♩ = 108
        Length: 32 measures
        Technique: octaves

Variation 1

Variation 1 contains sparkling figurations and the upper registers of the instrument are used to great effect. The development of the opening semitone was used as a motive in the first and second variations.

        Tempo: ♩ = 104
        Length: 25 measures
        Technique: octaves, broken octaves, sustained
           and moving notes, brilliant figuration,
           dexterity

Variation 2

The second variation is of moderate difficulty and emphasizes a syncopated pattern, with the left hand crossing over the right.

> Tempo: ♩ = 112
> Length: 25 measures
> Technique: hand-crossing, melody and
>   accompaniment in same hand, octaves,
>   clarity of voicing

Variation 3

This brilliant variation is marked "corrente," and contains sparkling right hand passagework. Again, the upper registers are effectively exploited.

> Tempo: ♩ = 80
> Length: 25 measures
> Technique: constant RH 16th note triplet
>   figuration, LH octaves and wide leaps

Cantabile, Ab Major

The Cantabile section introduces a new, expressive

quality. The continuous trill against a melodic line, all in the right hand, calls for well-developed finger independence. The Ab tonality, 9/8 meter, and relaxed tempo form a welcome contrast to the other variations.

  Tempo: Cantabile ♪ = 126

  Length: 19 measures

  Technique: octaves, sustained and moving
    notes, trill and melody in the same hand,
    brilliant scale and arpeggio passages

Finale Alla Fantasia

  The buoyant finale in 6/8 meter is pervaded by lilting dance rhythms. Scintillating bravura figurations create an aura of spirited elegance. The gradually released chord, a favorite device of Schumann's, is featured. The entire set is rewarding to play. It is less subtle and musically sophisticated than many of the composer's works, and is generally quite accessible. Of moderate length, this work has proven pedagogical value, which never obscures its inherent charm.

  Tempo: Vivace ♩. = 80

  Length: 105 measures

  Technique: octaves, broken octaves, scales,
    scalar passages, sustained and moving notes,
    voicing, bravura

PAPILLONS, Opus 2 Advanced
(Butterflies) (1832)

Schumann clearly associated Papillons with the
novel Flegeljahre, by Jean Paul Richter (1763-1825), an
important early exponent of romanticism, who was the
literary hero of Schumann's youth. The composer's
elaborately wrought and effusive prose style, as well as
his aesthetic viewpoint, owe much to this author. The
penultimate Chapter 63 of Flegeljahr is entitled "Der
Larventanz," (which may be translated as either Masked
Ball or Dance of the Larvae) and is directly related to
Papillons. Schumann selected specific incidents from
the text and matched them to the numbers of the suite.
The novel is concerned with the convoluted relationship
of two brothers, Walt and Vult Harnish. As examples of
the divided consciousness, they are clearly the
antecedents of Schumann's own Florestan and Eusebius.

However, in spite of the programmatic associations
of Papillons, the work was composed over a lengthy
period of time, with constant revision, and much of the
musical material derives from widely disparate
sources. Papillons was eventually completed in 1831,
and was published by Kistner the following year. With a
vivid literary impetus, revolutionary formal and
harmonic structures, and passionate romanticism,
Papillons is Schumann's first major creative
achievement, and contains many elements that are
prophetic of his later masterpieces.

Note: The following editions contain Opus 2 in its
    entirety. Other sources are listed with each piece.

BOETTICHER, Wolfgang: Schumann Klavierwerke,
    Band III (Henle).
LIPSKY, Alexander: Robert Schumann Album I for Piano
    (Kalmus #3930/Belwin).
SAUER, Emil: Complete Works of Robert Schumann,
    Volume 3 (Peters #2300C).
SCHUMANN, Clara: Piano Music of Robert Schumann,
    Series I (Dover).

SCHUMANN, Clara: Robert Schumann--Complete
Works, Volume 1 (Kalmus #3923/Belwin).

Introduzione, D Major

A fleeting wisp of an introduction announces the
opening of the Ball. This single brief phrase and its
echo are presented in unison octaves. In the earlier
sketches for the work this section was much longer, and
bore a marked resemblance to Weber's "Aufforderung
zum Tanz" (Introduction to the Dance), Op. 65.
Tempo: Moderato
Length: 6 measures

No. 1, D Major

The theme of this memorable first Waltz was
particularly significant to Schumann. It plays a
prominent role as Florestan's motive in both Carnaval,
Op. 9, and Die Davidsbündler, Op. 6.
Tempo: ♩ = 120
Length: 16 measures
Technique: sustained and moving notes, RH
octave melody, firm sense of direction
throughtout, sensitive rhythmic flexibility

No. 2, Eb Major/Ab Major

An explosive flourish of arpeggios and interlocking octaves introduces this whimsical movement. A delicate scherzo ensues with left hand broken tenths.

Tempo: Prestissimo ♩ = 116
Length: 12 measures
Technique: arpeggios, interlocking octaves, broken 10ths

No. 3, F♯ Minor

This briskly emphatic march features accented octaves in both hands. The final strain is an ingenuous and effective canon at the octave.

Tempo: ♩ = 120
Length: 28 measures
Technique: octaves, hand independence

No. 4, F♯ Minor

Light and breathless right hand octaves are exploited in this charming miniature. Careful dynamic gradation will heighten the air of elfin grace.

Tempo: Presto ♩. = 108
Length: 49 measures
Technique: octaves, rolled chords

No. 5, Bb Major

The fifth Papillon is an ingratiating interplay between soprano and bass voices with subdued inner accompaniment figures. This movement derives from the Trio of the seventh of the youthful Acht Polonaisen, WoO 20, which Schumann designated Op. 3, but never subsequently published.

Tempo: ♩ = 80
Length: 26 measures
Technique: voicing, melody and
      accompaniment in same hand, octaves

No. 6, D Minor

The protean character of this movement taxes the performer with rapid shifts of tempo and character. Light chords and octaves enliven this volatile piece.

Tempo: ♩ = 152
Length: 42 measures
Technique: octaves, sustained and moving
      notes, *pianissimo* chords

No. 7, F Minor/Ab Major

The limpid opening measures in F Minor create an atmosphere of simple beauty. At the modulation to Ab Major a single motive is worked into a paragraph of outstanding lyric charm.

Tempo: Semplice ♪. = 58
Length: 24 measures
Technique: rolled chords, sustained and moving notes, voicing, cantabile touch

No. 8, C♯ Minor/Db Major

The influence of Schubert is apparent in this sweeping little landler, and indeed, on several occasions Schumann took delight in convincing his friends that it was an actual work by the Viennese master. The exuberant vitality of this dance invites a characteristic rhythmic lilt.

Tempo: ♩ = 132
Length: 32 measures
Technique: repeated chords, rolled chords, octaves, voicing

No. 9, Bb Minor

This delicate work commences with a brilliant gesture based on a descending figure. The difficult staccato four-voice contrapuntal texture of much of the material is utterly disarming when performed at the prescribed *pianissimo* dynamic level.

Tempo: Prestissimo ♩. = 112
Length: 41 measures
Technique: voicing, staccato, repeated notes,
    finger facility

No. 10, C Major

The opening recalls the ascending scalar motive of the preceding movement, and the "Piu Lento" section appropriates a prominent theme from the sixth "Papillon." The lengthier conclusion is characterized by an expressive and tender melodic line, accompanied by a flowing, if oddly accentuated, arpeggio figure. This attractive waltz appears to parody certain elements of Weber's "Aufforderung zum Tanz," a work which must have been in Schumann's thoughts during the composition of Papillons. Subtle rubato and close attention to phrase structure will accentuate this fascinatingly diverse movement.

Tempo: Vivo ♩. = 108; Piu Lento ♩ = 138
Length: 82 measures
Technique: octaves, chords, melody and
    accompaniment in same hand, arpeggios

No. 11, D Major

This brilliant and evocative piece is an extremely effective potpourri based on material from the early set of polonaises for piano duet. The fiery rhythms, syncopations, and metric eccentricities of the Polish dance pervade this work. The touching middle section in G Major is both buoyant and ethereal. Precise rhythmic accuracy will convey the enchanting mood of this delicate theme. After a recapitulation the movement rushes to a humorous *pianissimo* conclusion.

Tempo: Piu Lento—in tempo vivo ♩ = 112
Length: 67 measures
Technique: octaves, grace notes, finger
    facility

No. 12 Finale, D Major

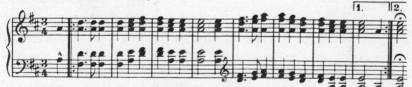

DEXTER, Harry: The Young Pianist's Schumann
    (Hansen).

A theme in horn-fifths, suggested in several previous movements, bursts forth as the famous Grossvater Tanz---the climax of the Ball. This well-known folk tune was often used to signal the close of a night of dancing and festive revelry. The melody, so often quoted by Schumann, may symbolize the restraining influence of mature inhibitions on the madcap gaiety of youth. Its triumphant progress is interrupted by a vulgar gaffaw in duple meter. This melody was used to similarly humorous effect in J.S. Bach's recitative "Nu, Miecke" from the Peasant Cantata, "Mer hahn ein neue OberKeet," BWV 212. The Grossvater Tanz returns, and the opening theme of the first Papillon is counterpointed against it. Over a pedal point D, the gay swirl of the waltz begins to dissipate in a shower of fleeting melodic fragments. Now the clock chimes six, and the Papillons disperse through a "disappearing chord" into the pale light of dawn.

    Tempo: Piu Lento
    Length: 90 measures
    Technique: octaves, contrapuntal textures,
        syncopation

STUDIEN NACH CAPRICEN VON PAGANINI, <u>Difficult</u>
Opus 3 (Studies on Paganini Caprices, Set I) (1832)

On Easter Day of 1830 Schumann attended a concert by the great violinist Paganini (1782-1840). Like
his contemporaries, Schumann was overwhelmed by the
seemingly diabolical technical feats with which
Paganini, a stellar actor and musician, amazed all of
Europe. The newly inspired Schumann strove for corre-
sponding levels of virtuosity in his own playing, and
certain elements of Paganini's style and attitude began
to appear in the youthful composer's sketches. Paganini
jealously guarded his compositions (the foundation of his
repertoire), and the fiendishly difficult "Caprices," Op.
1, were among the few works the virtuoso published.

In 1832 Schumann arranged six of the twenty-four
"Caprices" as piano etudes.   He was extremely
interested in the etude genre, and had often
contemplated composing a complete "school" of
pianism.   During the first decades of the nineteenth
century, the etude occupied an ambiguous position
between the purely technical exercise, and the difficult
but expressive character pieces which Chopin was to
publish as Opus 10 in 1833. Schumann's Paganini Etudes
are clearly less developed pianistically and musically
than the studies of Chopin or the "Etudes d'execution
transcendante d'apres Paganini of Liszt," yet they were
composed at an earlier point in the evolution of the
genre. Schumann's <u>Studien nach Capricen von Paganini</u>
consist of literal transcriptions of the original
"Caprices" by Paganini with enriched harmonic and
pianistic figurations and idioms.   Schumann worked
diligently on these compositions, and considered them
an important milestone in the development of his
compositional technique.   The Studien are
representative of the brilliant and virtuosic aspects of
the composer's earlier works. The first edition, published by Hofmeister in 1832, is prefaced by a set of
preparatory exercises and a lengthy and informative
essay on piano performance. Schumann took the pedagogical precaution of supplying much of the fingering.

The redoubtable Carl Czerny found the collection worthy of inclusion in his "Art moderne du doighter," No. 10, where it was published under the title, "Six Amusements en form d'Etudes pour le Pianoforte d'apres les Caprices de Paganini, dedies aux professeurs avec avant-propos et Exercises preparatif par Robert Schumann." The Studien exhibit a quaint musical charm, and their historical importance is undeniable as part of a series of works culminating in the great Symphonic Etudes, Op. 13.

Note: The following editions contain Opus 3 in its entirety.

SAUER, Emil: Complete Works of Robert Schumann, Volume 4 (Peters #2300D).
SCHUMANN, Clara: Piano Music of Robert Schumann, Series I (Dover).
SCHUMANN, Clara: Robert Schumann--Complete Works, Volume 1 (Kalmus #3923/Belwin).

No. 1, A Minor

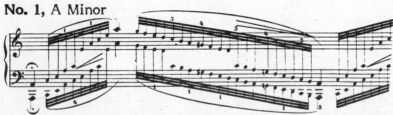

This etude derives from the fifth of the Paganini "Caprices." The opening and closing sections display flourishes of sweeping arpeggios and rapid chromatic scales. The central "agitato" makes use of scales and arpeggios, as well as sustained and moving notes. In general, this etude lies well under the hand. A fiery performance will create a sparkling effect.

> Tempo: Agitato
> Length: 57 measures plus cadenzas
> Technique: scales and arpeggios (hands together), melody and accompaniment in same hand, fast broken chord figuration, leaps, articulation, finger independence

No. 2, E Major

In rondo form, this attractive etude is pervaded by bucolic charm. The ninth "Caprice" is the source of this work, and Paganini instructs that the first phrase should imitate the flute, while its consequent mimics the hunting horn. Significantly, both the original version and Schumann's arrangement feature horn fifths. Schumann's simple accompaniment figures are designed to heighten the rustic dance-like character of this work. The A Minor episode contains numerous scales and trills which will benefit from a pristine clarity. Though eschewing the exquisite pianism of Liszt's fine setting of this "Caprice," the work is sprightly and elegant.

  Tempo: Allegretto
  Length: 111 measures
  Technique: leaps, double note passages, scales,
    rapid broken chord figuration in close
    proximity

No. 3, C Major

Schumann omits the "Presto" middle section and eventual recapitulation of Paganini's eleventh "Caprice." The large stretches in the left hand may be easily rolled. The brevity of this miniature and its contrasting lyrical nature make it most effective when played as part of a set.

Tempo: Andante
Length: 29 measures
Technique: long melodic lines, trills, legato
    octaves, inner voices, careful pedal,
    warm cantabile tone

No. 4, Bb Major

A nonchalant charm characterizes Schumann's version of the thirteenth "Caprice." In simple ternary form, the opening section displays portamento double thirds, often combined with difficult leaps. The center section, in G Minor, contains widely spaced accompanimental figures, as well as many broken tenths. Lightness of touch and an effortless facility will enhance this etude.

Tempo: Allegro
Length: 56 measures
Technique: double 3rds, wide leaps, broken
    octaves, syncopation, finger facility

No. 5, Eb Major

Fast repeated notes abound in this sprightly and engaging etude in ternary form. The contrasting C Minor section contains several quick right hand leaps with many dynamic changes. This etude, a literal transcription of the nineteenth Caprice, might serve as an effective encore.

Tempo: Lento - Allegro assai
Length: 66 measures
Technique: rapid repeated notes, rapid register
   changes, wide RH leaps, fast figuration,
   scales, sudden dynamic changes

No. 6, G Minor

   This etude is based on Paganini's sixteenth
"Caprice." An unusual feature of the work is the
occasional use of the "Caprice" theme as an
accompanimental figure. In these passages the high
register makes it difficult to embue the theme with the
proper clarity. The many double-stemmed notes are
marked with sforzandos.

Tempo: Allegro molto
Length: 53 measures
Technique: rapid arpeggiated figuration with
   inner accents, legato melody within thick
   texture, sudden dynamic changes, wide
   LH leaps, broken octaves

INTERMEZZI, Opus 4 (1832)   <u>Advanced</u>

The <u>Intermezzi</u>, Op. 4, occupy an important position in the catalogue of Schumann's works. The composer described this work as "extended Papillons," crediting the extra length to his study of counterpoint and the influence of Bach. Unlike <u>Papillons</u>, Op. 2, in which each section is little more than an epigrammatic vignette, the <u>Intermezzi</u> are extended character pieces. However, like their smaller prototypes, Schumann clearly intended that the work be performed in its entirety. Perhaps the rather ambiguous position of this collection between the youthful vigor of <u>Papillons</u> and the mature mastery of <u>Carnaval</u>, Op. 9, has contributed to its virtual oblivion. The musical material is less immediately appealing than many of the composer's later works, yet the <u>Intermezzi</u> contain many excellent and characteristic passages, and are certainly of more than mere historical interest.

With the exception of No. 4, the <u>Intermezzi</u> are in simple song form with trio (Schumann labels the central trio "Alternativo," a term taken from older dance music). The passionate but whimsical nature of the set is reflected in the original title, "Pieces phantastiques." Though the <u>Intermezzi</u> were designed for Clara Wieck (1819-1894), the 1832 Hofmeister publication is dedicated to the minor Bohemiam composer and violinist, J. W. Kalliwoda (1801-1866).

Note: The following editions contain Opus 4 in its entirety.

BOETTCHER, Wolgang: Schumann Klavierwerke, Band III (Henle).

SAUER, Emil: Complete Works of Robert Schumann, Volume 3 (Peters #2300C).

SCHUMANN, Clara: Piano Music of Robert Schumann, Series III (Dover).

SCHUMANN, Clara: Robert Schumann--Complete Works, Volume 1 (Kalmus #3923/Belwin).

I. A Major

A brief but compelling sequence of introductory chords prefaces this highly contrapuntal movement. The canonic treatment of the material is particularly effective, and the entire composition will benefit from careful voicing and linear definition. The "Alternativo," marked "Piu vivo," is a light and vivacious respite from the solemn imitative sections that enclose it.

> Tempo: Allegro quasi maestoso
> Length: 118 measures
> Technique: double dotted rhythms, sudden
>   dynamic changes, double note passages,
>   voicing

II. E Minor

This wild, tempestuous piece contains many elements, such as syncopation, hand-crossing, and sudden tempo changes, that are characteristic of the mature Schumann. The tender and lyrical middle section bears the quotation, "Meine Ruh' ist hin" from Gretchen's spinning song in Goethe's "Faust." This reference to "Faust" is appropriate to the quality of fervid romantic passion that permeates the entire intermezzo.

> Tempo: Presto a capriccio
> Length: 204 measures
> Technique: arpeggiated figuration, hand-
>   crossing, syncopation, wide hand stretches,

fast octaves, sudden dynamic contrasts, endurance

III. A Minor

Sensitive voicing, articulation, and careful definition of phrase structure will enhance this light and humorous scherzo. In the "Alternativo," a rapid tempo and rhythmic syncopation create some technical difficulties.

    Tempo: Allegro marcato
    Length: 165 measures
    Technique: legato and staccato in same hand,
        sudden dynamic changes, full chords,
        syncopation, articulation

IV. C Major

This short lyrical piece is primarily a transcription of the song "Hirtenknabe," to a text by Ekert, which Schumann composed in 1828. The little ritornello figure and the coda derive from a rejected movement of Papillons, and an unpublished piano quartet. An effective performance will utilize a strong sense of rhythmic sweep.

    Tempo: Allegretto semplice
    Length: 18 measures
    Technique: widely spaced chords, octaves,
        rapid LH figuration, sustained and moving
        notes

V. D Minor

As in the second intermezzo, Schumann's unique and entirely idiomatic mature style is presaged in this attractive movement. The opening accompaniment figuration is particularly suggestive of similar passages in the composer's later works. A warm cantabile, and sensitivity to the many subtle transformations of atmosphere, color, and tempo will heighten the expressive qualities of this intermezzo.

     Tempo: Allegro moderato
     Length: 207 measures
     Technique: legato melody with detached
        accompaniment in same hand, staccato
        octaves, inner voices, sudden mood changes

VI. B Minor

Rapid arpeggiated triplet figurations are featured in this fiery Allegro. Much of the musical substance originated as part of an unpublished Piano Quartet in C Minor of 1829, and measures 44-46 and their subsequent reprise contain an allusive reference to the A.B.E.G.G. theme of Op. 1. The delicate, elfin-like "Alternativo" is particularly charming, and is based on an early sketch for the tenth movement of Papillons. The movement forms an effective but abrupt conclusion to this unusual and seldom performed set of Intermezzi.

Tempo: Allegro
Length: 135 measures
Technique: arpeggios, cross-rhythms, long
melodic line, staccato chords and running
8th notes, syncopation, voicing

IMPROMPTUS ÜBER EIN THEMA VON   Advanced
   CLARA WIECK, C Major, Opus 5 (1833)
   (Impromptus on a Theme by Clara Wieck)

Schumann composed the Impromptus über ein
Thema von Clara Wieck in 1833, as a birthday tribute to
Friedrich Wieck (1785-1873). The work was published at
his brother's printing house so it would arrive in time for
Friedrich's birthday, and also by Hofmeister in that
same year. The Impromptus were drastically revised in
1850, at which time the original eleventh section was
deleted, a new variant replaced the third section, the
pieces were renumbered, and the appellation "Romanza"
was removed from the Thema. This more familiar
second version is generally considered superior to the
first. The title of the work is quite misleading; the
Impromptus are an elaborately structured set of
variations, rather than a collection of tenuously related
character pieces. Not only is a theme subjected to
variation procedures but a distinctive ground bass is also
employed. The use of this structural pattern, almost
certainly inspired by Beethoven's "Eroica Variations,"
Op. 35, provides a strong chaconne-like formal unity. In
this respect the Impromptus represent a considerable
technical advance over the A.B.E.G.G. Variations, as all
traces of the virtuosic "salon" style have vanished.
Unfortunately, the musical substance of the Impromptus
lacks the genial elegance and imaginative fantasy of the
composer's more characteristic works, and in spite of
occasional flashes of genius, this atypical opus is,
understandably, seldom performed. As a historically
important example of Schumann's experimentation with
the variations genre, the Impromptus create an
interesting link between the A.B.E.G.G. Variations and
the refined grandeur of the Symphonic Etudes.

Note: The following editions contain Opus 5 in its
     entirety.

SAUER, Emil: Complete Works of Robert Schumann,
    Volume 3 (Peters #2300C).

SCHUMANN, Clara: Piano Music of Robert Schumann,
    Series III (Dover).
SCHUMANN, Clara: Robert Schumann--Complete
    Works, Volume 1 (Kalmus #3923/Belwin).

Ziemlich langsam

The introduction consists of a simple bass melody featuring prominent falling fifths. This unadorned melodic line functions as a ground bass, and is the harmonic model for the entire work The motivic fifths permeate and direct the Impromptus.

> Tempo: Ziemlich langsam (Rather slowly)
> Length: 16 measures

Thema (Theme)

The graceful and unaffected theme derives from a Romance by the thirteen year old Clara Wieck, on which she also wrote variations dedicated to her mentor and confidant, Schumann. This theme is grafted onto the opening bass melody, and is built of four simple yet lyrical phrases. A constant four-part texture is maintained, and the wide distances between the bass and tenor voices may be bridged by rolling these intervals.

> Tempo: none indicated
> Length: 16 measures
> Technique: voicing, wide intervals

No. 1

The first variation is a brief and straightforward presentation of the ground bass in octaves accompanied by chords in the right hand.   The numerous harmonic suspensions are the only noteworthy feature of this prosaic movement.

    Tempo: none indicated
    Length: 18 measures
    Technique: careful pedal to keep RH chords
       distinct

No. 2

In this impromptu the left hand presents the ground bass, though in an accompanied form, while the right hand introduces new melodic material.   The theme eventually appears in the guise of an inner voice.

    Tempo: Lebhafter (Livelier)
    Length: 32 measures
    Technique: melody as an inner voice, wide
       hand stretches, phrasing

No. 3

The third variation features sprightly staccato figuration. Less dependent than many of its companions on either the theme or the ground bass, this rather difficult miniature possesses much of Schumann's inherent charm.

> Tempo: Sehr präcis (Very precisely)
> Length: 16 measures
> Technique: staccato chords, leaps, wide hand
> stretches, 2-note phrasing

No. 4

The ground bass reappears, but here a lilting melody in 6/8 meter is superimposed above it. A regularity of structure renders this variation less effective than the metrical intricacies might suggest.

> Tempo: Ziemlich langsam (Rather slowly)
> Length: 16 measures
> Technique: good singing tone in lower register

No. 5

Variation five is an energetic and rhythmically vital treatment of the thematic material. Constant use of the rhythmic pattern ♪ 𝄾 ♩ ♩ , and sequential melodic patterns build considerable drive and momentum.

> Tempo: Lebhaft (Lively)
> Length: 34 measures
> Technique: long melodic line, repeated figures,
> melody and accompaniment in same hand

No. 6

The sixth impromptu is a bravura etude in rapid right hand chords and octaves with accented syncopations, against a rhythmic left hand accompaniment. Though generally centered in A Minor, this attractive variation repeatedly cadences in C Major.

Tempo: Schnell (Fast)

Length: 22 measures

Technique: repeated octaves and chords, leaps, syncopation

No. 7

In this undistinguished variation the left hand theme is ornamented by leaping grace notes. The right hand provides a gentle broken chord accompaniment.

Tempo: Tempo des Themas
(Tempo of the theme)

Length: 16 measures

Technique: wide hand stretches, tonal control within a limited range, pedal control

No. 8

Hammered staccato octaves and chords mark this flamboyant variation. The melodic material is strikingly developed, and this virtuosic work generates considerable rhythmic impetus.

Tempo: Mit grosser Kraft
(With great strength)
Length: 16 measures
Technique: constant wide leaps, repeated
octaves and chords in the *fortissimo* range,
hand-crossings

No. 9

In this engaging variation the theme and a repeated interval accompaniment, are presented by the right hand, while the left hand leaps over the right to weave pointillistic bass and soprano melodies. The piece is an excellent etude in hand-crossing technique.

Tempo: none indicated
Length: 18 measures
Technique: repeated notes, simultaneous
melodies, hand-crossing, syncopation

No. 10

The tenth variation is the longest and most elaborate of the Impromptus. An informal ABA structure, three times the length of the other variations, is followed by a coda. The opening section features a ground bass, which is punctuated by chordal outbursts. This section gives way to an ingenious, if overworked, five part fugue, in which the prominent fifths of the ground bass provide the subject, while fragments of the theme form the countersubject. This fugue originated as a contrapuntal study labelled "Fugue No. 3" in Schumann's sketchbook of 1831/32. Prior to the composition of the Impromptus, the composer had also adapted this fugue in a draft for the Finale of the unfinished Symphony in G Minor of 1832. The opening material is recapitulated, and sweeps along to the coda. The coda makes a noble attempt at apotheosis, with the ground bass in a four-octave unison restatement. This is followed by the final appearance of the theme, which quietly and effectively concludes the Impromptus.

Tempo: Lebhaft (Lively)
Length: 176 measures
Technique: repeated chords, wide leaps,
    parallel 6ths within one hand, awkward hand
    movements, octaves, wide hand stretches,
    wide dynamic range

DAVIDSBÜNDLER ACHTZEHN
CHARAKTERSTÜCKE, Opus 6
Difficult
(Davidsbundler Eighteen Character Pieces)
or "Die Davidsbündler" (1837)

Though a prolific and respected composer, it was as a critic and editor that Schumann exercised the most immediate influence on his contemporaries. Born into a familiy of marked literary abilities, Schumann often wielded his pen in the services of the parental publishing firm. Schumann's first important work as a critic came in 1831 with the publication of an essay in the "Allgemeine Musicalische Zeitung." This review, perhaps Schumann's most famous, provides an ecstatic critique of Chopin's Variations, Op. 2 on "La ci darem al mano," from Mozart's Don Giovanni. In this essay Schumann introduces three fanciful characters, Florestan, Eusebius, and a wise mediator, Master Raro. This trio discusses in a rich romantic prose, ultimately derived from Schumann's literary hero Jean-Paul, the merits of Chopin's composition. Master Raro, based initially on Frederich Wieck (Schumann's piano teacher and future father-in-law) was a character of profound integrity who was able to synthesize and moderate the poetic effusions of Florestan and Eusebius. In these two personages, Schumann presents the distinct and contradictory elements of his own nature. Florestan is a brilliant and impulsive extrovert, while the thoughtful and dreamy Eusebius is the typical introvert. This constant dialogue of polarities, traces of which appear as early as Papillons, Op. 2, establish Schumann as the most essentially "romantic" composer of his era.

By 1833 Schumann and several friends had begun to meet informally to discuss aesthetic and artistic concerns. This group gradually organized with the goal of establishing a musical journal in which an ongoing effort would be made to cultivate German romantic music of the most advanced kind. Schumann soon assumed leadership of this endeavor and became the editor and most important contributor to the Neue Zeitschrift fur Musik. At the center of the publication was a mysterious secret society, the Davidsbündler. The progressive Davidsbündler was fanatically devoted to the tenet of high romanticism and strove at all times to overthrow the Philistines--bastions of bourgeoise tastelessness and complacency. The use of the term Philistine to denote the culturally ignorant or reactionary did not originate with Schumann, but he did popularize it. The Davidsbündler was among the most selective of organizations, and in later years Schumann admitted that its membership could be found exclusively in his imagination. Certainly the characters of the Davidsbündler were originally based on actual people: Florestan and Eusebius were Schumann himself, Master Raro--Wieck, and Jonathan--the pianist Ludwig Schunke. Soon these figures developed literary identities of their own. Through the imaginative vehicle of the Davidsbündler, Schumann and the Neue Zeitschrift fur Musik were able to perpetuate a constant state of seige, leveled against all that was contemptible in the contemporary musical scene. The Davidsbündler played a prominent role not only in Schumann's critical writing but also in his musical compositions. These compelling characterizations were immediately absorbed as part of the vast apparatus of simile and metaphor which was so essential to Schumann's creative process. As early as Carnaval, Op. 9, published in 1837 but commenced in 1834, the Davidsbündler appear as musical portraits. Though written after Carnaval, the Davidsbündler, Op. 6 has an earlier opus number. This seems to have been a simple case of expediency in terms of publication.

Composed in 1837, the Davidsbündler was published by Friese in 1838 in two volumes of nine pieces. The first edition lacks the composer's name, and the collection is described as the work of Florestan and Eusebius. The work is in the form of an integrated collection of brief and fantastic character pieces, a genre Schumann cultivated with particular success. The title of the first edition was "Davidsbündlertanze," though the revised edition of 1851 modifies the title to the shorter Die Davidsbündler. There are a number of important disparities between these versions. Several small musical changes were made, yet the primary differences involve the deletion of various epigrams and mottos. The earlier version opens with the following proverb:

"Along the way we go
In mingled joy and woe
In joy, though glad, be grave
In woe, though sad, be brave."

This, as well as the curious prose fragments connected to No. 9 and No. 10, was deleted from the later edition. Each movement of the "Davidsbündlertanze" was also initialed F. or E., signifying that the piece represents the contribution of either Florestan, Eusebius, or the two in collaboration. These initials do not appear in Die Davidsbündler. Schumann made a decisive break with musical tradition by using German rather than the Italian tempo and expression markings.

Schumann's creative imagination was perhaps more dependent on extra-musical associations than was that of any other major composer, and it is characteristic that he felt certain reservations about making this fact public. Throughout his later career Schumann disguised the often intensely personal content and relationships within his music, and his letters testify to the fact that many of his works contain elaborate hidden scenarios. In the famous review of Berlioz's Symphony Fantastique the composer writes:

It seems as if men stand somewhat in awe
of the workshop of genius; they do not care
how to use the causes, tools, and mysteries
of creation; just as nature herself seems to
exhibit a certain delicacy in covering her
roots with earth. Therefore let the artist
also lock the door upon himself and his
griefs; we should gain too deep an insight
if every work revealed to us the causes of
its existence."

Surely it is for this reason that Schumann removed the mottos and captions from Die Davidbündler.

At one point Schumann wrote to a friend that the Die Davidsbündler were "dances of death, gnomes and spirits." However, it is known that the composer most closely associated the work with his upcoming marriage to Clara. It is possible to consider the work as an evocation of a "Polterabend," the evening of dancing and gaiety that precedes the wedding morning. This seems particularly germaine in light of the original title, which makes direct reference to the work as a sequence of dances.

Die Davidsbündler is unquestionably one of Schumann's finest compositions, and the composer himself preferred it to the infinitely more popular "Carnaval." Less obviously unified by motivic and thematic relationships than the earlier work, it is still ingeniously conceived and structurally coherent. Perhaps the great length and emotional demands of this great work have prevented it from achieving a more prominent position in Schumann's oeuvre. Die Davidsbündler reveals Schumann at the height of technical mastery and imaginative freedom.

Note: The following editions contain Opus 6 in its entirety. Other sources are listed with each piece.

BOETTICHER, Wolfgang: Schumann Klavierwerke, Band III (Henle).
SAUER, Emil: Complete Works of Robert Schumann, Volume 2 (Peters #2300B).
SCHUMANN, Clara: Piano Music of Robert Schumann, Series I (Dover).
SCHUMANN, Clara: Robert Schumann--Complete Works, Volume 1 (Kalmus #3923/Belwin).

Note: The initials F., E., and F. und E. derive from the Davidsbündlertanze of 1838, and signify the contribution of Florestan, Eusebius, or the two in conjunction.

I. G Major F. und E.

The opening musical motto, a quotation from the Mazurka of Clara's "Soirees musicales," Op. 6, provides a stirring introduction to this vital movement. Unusual motivic figures, usually beginning on the third beat of the measure, create a sense of restlessness which may be emphasized with subtle rubato. This motive provides much of the source material for the other pieces. "Clara's motto" is also prominent. A refined legato will enhance the elegant yet spirited character of this waltz.

> Tempo: Lebhaft (Lively) ♩ = 160
> Length: 73 measures
> Technique: wide leaps, arpeggios, wide hand
>   stretches, syncopation, wide dynamic range

II. B Minor E.

This introspective movement benefits from a gentle non-percussive touch, combined with an extreme sensitivity to the constant rhythmic interplay of 6/8 and 3/4 meters. Careful accenting of the downbeats will prevent a "thumpy" sound.

> Tempo: Innig (Heartfelt, tender) ♩ = 138
> Length: 26 measures
> Technique: syncopation, wide leaps, tone
>   control, voicing, important "held" notes

III. G Major F.

The humor is evident in the crisp staccato opening. Measure 17 contains a reference to the theme from Papillons which later occurs in Carnaval. The faster middle section contains a direct reference (measure 55) to the "Promenade" from Carnaval, Op. 9. This spirited movement concludes with several measures of delicate right hand arpeggio figuration.

      Tempo: Mit Humor (With Humor) ♩. = 60
          Schneller (Faster)
      Length: 94 measures
      Technique: staccato chords, wide leaps,
          octaves, wide hand stretches, arpeggios

IV. B Minor F.

Constant syncopation pervades this fantastic and disquieting miniature. The lyricism of the inner voices is heightened by resourceful voicing.

      Tempo: Ungeduldig (Impatient) ♩. = 80
      Length: 48 measures
      Technique: syncopation, tone control, leaps,
          pedal control, legato control, hands in
          close proximity

V. D Major E.

The fleeting, almost incorporeal nature of this piece will be revealed by an adroit legato execution in conjunction with delicate pedalling to produce an effect of total effortlessness.

> Tempo: Einfach (Simply) ♩ = 116
> Length: 58 measures
> Technique: LH leaps, legato scales, pedal
> control, tonal control within limited
> dynamic range

VI. D Minor F.

This fiery and impetuous movement is among the most difficult of Die Davidsbündler. The proper clarity of the notated left hand articulation is quite taxing at this tempo, especially for small hands. The center section, in D Major, features staccato octaves, and may be enlivened by careful voicing.

> Tempo: Sehr rasch (Very quickly) ♩. = 132
> Length: 100 measures
> Technique: rapid staccato octaves, hand
> independence, syncopation, awkward LH
> passages, arpeggios

VII. G Minor E.

Vibrant yet delicate tone, as well as a lengthy, slow-moving line are the primary pianistic features in this piece. The expressive depths of this imaginative work are revealed at the hands of an experienced and thoroughly accomplished musician.

      Tempo: Nicht schnell (Not fast) ♩ = 92
      Length: 60 measures
      Technique: thin texture, arpeggiated figures,
         widely spaced rolled chords, sudden dynamic
         contrasts, long legato lines, tonal control,
         pedal control

VIII. C Minor F.

This inventive piece has an interesting irregular phrase structure. A bar form of three 7-measure phrases is capped by an unexpected five measure close. An excellent staccato etude, this boisterous piece will benefit from precise rhythmic detailing.

      Tempo: Frisch (Brisk) ♩ = 100
      Length: 26 measures
      Technique: awkward LH leaps, fast staccato
         chords, texture changes

IX. C Major

The epithet originally appended to this volatile movement reads, "Here Florestan kept silence, but his lips were quivering with emotion." A breathless intensity marks this luminous composition. The sforzandos, when attacked with gusto, contribute greatly to the propulsive drive of this marvelously crafted movement.

Tempo: Lebhaft (Lively) ♩ = 112

Length: 32 measures

Technique: wide leaps, melody in thumb, sudden dynamic changes, difficult skips in LH, voicing

X. D Minor F.

This tempestuous piece is an excellent example of one of Schumann's favorite devices, the superimposition of duple onto triple meter. The melody is set in high relief and all subordinate figures are subdued. Certain brief turns of phrase remind one of "Aufschung" from Phantasiestücke, Op. 12, an equally tumultuous work that delights in similar metrical ambiguities.

Tempo: Balladenmässig, Sehr rasch ♩. = 80
(In ballad style, Very fast)

Length: 63 measures

Technique: syncopation, melody and accompaniment in same hand, long melodic line

XI. D Major E.

AGAY, Denes: An Anthology of Piano Music--The
Romantic Period--Vol. III (Yorktown).

The engaging simplicity of this brief work is a
particularly welcome contrast to the fiery movements
that surround it. A legato and cantabile approach will
contribute to the tone of guileless purity.

Tempo: Einfach (Simply) ♩ = 80
Length: 25 measures
Technique: cantabile, long melodic line,
melody in thumb, pedal control, voicing

XII. E Minor F.

AGAY, Denes: An Anthology of Piano Music--The
Romantic Period--Vol. III (Yorktown).

This capricious scherzo reveals a jovial spon-
taneity. The humorous aspects will be highlighted when
the dynamics and pedal markings are implemented.

Tempo: Mit Humor (With Humor) ♩ = 104
Length: 24 measures
Technique: wide leaps, melody in thumb, fast
staccato execution, sudden dynamic
changes, articulation, singing tone

XIII. B Major F. und E.

    This movement opens wildly with violent and fast chords and wide leaps. The central section provides a chorale-like atmosphere which may be further enhanced by a sauve legato touch and a careful delineation of phrase structure. The *pianissimo* coda is an effective contrast to the fury of the opening material.

        Tempo: Wild und Lustig (Wild and Gay) ♩ = 114
        Length: 123 measures
        Technique: fast octaves with wide leaps, long
            melodic line, fast chord changes

XIV. Eb Major E.

    Among the loveliest of Die Davidsbündler, this extraordinary work is characterized by a warm and tender lyricism. Sensitive pedalling will create an ethereal and seamless structure.

        Tempo: Zart und singend
           (Tenderly and singing) ♩ = 138
        Length: 40 measures
        Technique: melody and accompaniment in
            same hand, 5th finger melody, long melodic
            line, tonal control within a limited dynamic
            range (*p*)

XV. Bb Major F. and E.

The impetuous chordal opening requires great clarity, not an easy task at this tempo. In the subtle and evocative section in Eb Major the elegant arpeggio accompaniment supports the melodic line.

> Tempo: Frisch (Briskly) ♩ = 160
> Length: 56 measures
> Technique: large blocked chords in fast tempo, octaves, broken chord figurations, pedal control, balance between arpeggio accompaniment and long melodic line

XVI. G Major

This difficult scherzo has many light and rapid chords and octaves. Sensitively played at a fleeting tempo, it possesses a quick-silver elegance. The next movement follows without pause.

> Tempo: Mit gutem Humor (With good Humor)
> ♩ = 160
> Length: 41 measures
> Technique: fast changing staccato chords, leaps, octaves (some in intertwining hand positions), precise rhythm, sudden dynamic changes

XVII. B Major F. und E.

The richly poetic atmosphere of this fascinating piece is sustained through the use of long pedals. The second movement of the set is echoed in the B Minor section.

> Tempo: Wie aus der Ferne (As from afar)
> ♩ = 126
> Length: 99 measures
> Technique: wide stretches, hand independence, tonal control, accurate pedalling, inner voices, LH leaps, fast octaves and chord changes

XVIII. C Major

A serene epilogue, the concluding movement of Die Davidsbündler was originally prefaced by the following motto: "Quite superfluously Eusebius remarked as follows: but all the time quiet bliss spoke from his eyes." Although easy technically, this exquisite valediction exhibits the utmost sensitivity. Schumann suggested that the twelve low C's at the end might well represent the stroke of midnight. This extraordinary collection, a glittering repository of so much gaiety and enchantment, evaporates into an unforgettable hushed stillness.

> Tempo: Nicht schnell (Not fast) ♩ = 152
> Length: 59 measures
> Technique: LH leaps, careful pedal, tone control

TOCCATA, C Major, Opus 7 (1834)   Difficulty

Schumann's earliest sketches for the Toccata, Op. 7, date from 1829. The first version of the composition, intended for Clara, was entitled "Etude fantastique en doubles-sons." Throughout Schumann's early creative years, culminating in the Symphonic Etudes of 1834, the composer was profoundly interested in the piano etude, both as a technical and expressive vehicle. This fascination is apparent in the treacherous double-note figuration that permeates the Toccata. The didactic nature of the piece is revealed by Schumann's footnote, which allows the performer to make many of the choices regarding selection of dynamics. In 1833 Schumann completely revised the work, transcribing it from D to C Major. This final version was published by Hofmeister in 1834, and dedicated to the composer's colleague and companion, Ludwig Schunke (1810-1834). The Toccata is historically important as Schumann's first published work in sonata/allegro form.

Note: The following editions contain Opus 7 in its entirety.

BOETTICHER, Wolfgang: Schumann Klavierwerke, Band IV (Henle).
LIPSKY, Alexander: Robert Schumann Album II for Piano (Kalmus #3931/Belwin).
SAUER, Emil: Complete Works of Robert Schumann, Volume 3 (Peters #2300C).
SCHUMANN, Clara: Piano Music of Robert Schumann, Series I (Dover).
SCHUMANN, Clara: Robert Schumann--Complete Works, Volume 1 (Kalmus #3923/Belwin).
SHEALY, Alexander: Schumann--his Greatest Piano Solos (Ashley).

The Toccata, Op. 7, opens with a syncopated
chordal pronouncement, whose characteristic rhythmic
motive will provide the kinetic impetus of the work.
The first subject employs a constant sixteenth note
perpetual motion figuration.   This taxing section is
followed by a secondary theme, a brief legato melody in
dotted rhythm, that creates a welcome contrast in mood
and texture.   A lengthy closing passage based on
important melodic and thematic material leads to the
development. The development presents a reworking of
the important themes of the exposition, as well as
introducing new ideas based on repeated octaves and
octave scales. The recapitulation reviews and expands
the original material, and evolves into a flamboyant and
virtuosic coda.   Though the entire work makes severe
technical demands, the fiery coda particularly chal-
lenges the pianist's endurance and stamina.   After an
exciting accelerando, the piece subsides into a rich,
thickly textured conclusion. Four simple chords form a
quiet and subtle ending.

     Tempo: Allegro

     Length: 287 measures

     Technique: double note passages, fast chord
         changes, double 3rd scales, wide hand
         stretches, wide leaps, rapid octaves
         (repeated and in scales), sudden dynamic
         changes, widely spaced broken chords,
         endurance

ALLEGRO, B Minor, Opus 8 (1835)   <u>Difficult</u>

Like the <u>Toccata</u>, Op. 7, the <u>Allegro</u> testifies to Schumann's early struggle to achieve mastery of the longer, more expansive musical structures. Schumann, in common with so many composers of his generation, felt compelled by a high sense of aesthetic destiny to follow the formal example of the revered Beethoven. This created an enormous strain on the romantic imagination, as it labored to fill the symphonic mold. Schumann's numerous early attempts at the sonata form were usually abortive, yet the <u>Allegro</u> provides an intriguing glimpse of the composer attempting to synthesize romantic fervor with classical structural procedure.

The <u>Allegro</u> was originally intended as the first movement of a Sonata to be dedicated to Moscheles, but at the time of its initial publication by Friese in 1835, the work was inscribed to Ernestine von Fricken (1816-1844).

Note: The following editions contain Opus 8 in its
    entirety.

SAUER, Emil: Complete Works of Robert Schumann,
    Volume 3 (Peters #2300C).
SCHUMANN, Clara: Piano Music of Robert Schumann,
    Series I (Dover).
SCHUMANN, Clara: Robert Schumann--Complete
    Works, Volume 1 (Kalmus #3923/Belwin).
SHEALY, Alexander: Schumann--His Greatest Piano
    Solos (Ashley).

The <u>Allegro</u> opens with a brilliant and dramatic cadenza. Some of the material of this section derives from an early sketch for the <u>Papillons</u>, Op. 2. The cadenza is passionate and improvisatory, and leads directly into the exposition. Here, the principal theme employs constant broken chord figuration and rhythmic syncopation. The ornate character of this section obscures the important thematic motives it presents. The more lyrical secondary theme in the relative major possesses a stronger melodic definition. The development follows without pause and the closing measures of the second theme are so richly ornamented that a clear demarcation of the development is hardly audible. The modulatory development features many sequences and a profusion of pianistic devices. The development achieves a grandiose climax, which is followed by the return of the opening cadenza. The ensuing recapitulation delays the traditional tonic in yet another attempt to expand the scope of the sonata/allego argument. The secondary theme, complete with extended closing/developmental material, ushers in the coda. In the long-delayed B Major, the coda serves as a peroration of the central thematic material. The coda brings the Allegro to an effective conclusion.

Tempo: Prestissimo
Length: 197 measures
Technique: rapid broken chord figuration,
   octaves, 2-note slurs, inner voices, double
   3rds, syncopation, cross-rhythms, scales,
   unmetered sections, fast 16th note passage
   work

CARNAVAL, Opus 9 (1835)
Scènes mignonnes sur quartre notes

In 1834 Schumann became engaged to his most recent love, Ernestine von Fricken. Frederich Wieck, the girl's piano teacher, apparently cultivated and encouraged the relationship, due to grave concerns regarding the growing attachment between his prodigiously talented daughter, Clara, and the composer. Schumann's ardor towards Ernestine began to dissipate when vast differences in intelligence and character made the unsuitability of the match obvious. Finally, with the revelation of Ernestine's illegitimacy, Schumann quietly broke the engagement.

At the height of his passion for Ernestine, Schumann, always intrigued by musical ciphers and cryptic word-play, discovered that the name of his fiancee's birthplace, the Bohemian town of Asch, was readily translated into musical pitches. In German musical nomenclature this may be spelled in the following way: A. S. (Es - Eb C - H B - A). These pitches also correspond to S.C.H.A., the musical letters of the composer's own surname. Schumann at first tried to incorporate this material into a set of variations on Schubert's "Sehnsuchtwalzer" he had begun in 1833, but soon replaced the variation structure with short character pieces derived from the A.S.C.H. motive. As the work began to coalesce, Schumann considered entitling the composition, Fasching: Schwänke auf vier Noten fur Pianoforte von Florestan. However, the finished suite was published by Brietkopf und Hartel as Carnaval: Scènes mignonnes sur quartre notes, Op. 9.

To what functional extent Schumann's music is actually programmatic is unclear, and the composer provided seemingly contradictory evidence regarding this aspect of his work. While the suite is completely coherent in purely musical terms, the descriptive scenario is of vital importance because of a richer, more subtly varied texture of meaning that is created by the referential titles and allusions. Clearly the framework of the masquerade presented Schumann with ample opportunity to present a variety of fantastic imaginative vignettes. The masked countenance, reality hidden beneath artifice, was an important metaphor in romantic thought and art, and was particularly cherished by Schumann.

In Carnaval the composer delineates a number of highly stylized characters, each based on a clearly defined temperament or emotional state. These symbolic figures derive from two major sources. Many originate in the brilliantly improvisational, but curiously ritualized Commedia dell' Arte. These characters of the Italian popular theatre, hidden beneath stock situations and greasepaint, are like clowns, paradigms of the deceptive nature of appearance. The emblematic personages drawn from the ranks of the Davidsbündler are all distilled manifestations of the composer's own friends and musical acquaintances. The Davidsbündler were encased within fictitious names and identities. Similarly Schumann protected the wellsprings of his own creative imagination from the brutal and unthinking scrutiny of the Philistines through the creation of a fabric of artfully woven artifice and mystification. Perhaps it is this aura of mystery, of profound truth secreted just out of reach, that, combined with the extraordinary technical accomplishment of Carnaval, make it such an overwhelmingly compelling work.

Note: The following editions contain Opus 9 in its entirety. Other sources are listed with each piece.

BOETTICHER, Wolfgang: Schumann Klavierwerke, Band III (Henle).
KAIL, Robert: Easy Schumann Piano Pieces (Columbia #F1035PAX).
LIPSKY, Alexander: Robert Schumann--Album II for Piano (Kalmus #3931/Belwin-Mills).
SAUER, Emil: Complete Works of Robert Schumann, Volume 2 (Peters #2300B).
SCHUMANN, Clara: Piano Music of Robert Schumann, Series I (Dover).

SCHUMANN, Clara: Robert Schumann--Complete
Works, Volume 2 (Kalmus #3924/Belwin-Mills).

Préambule, Ab Major

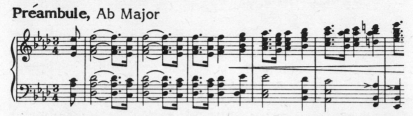

    <u>Carnaval</u> is ushered in by the majestic and sonorous
<u>Préambule.</u> The first 24 measures of this festive move-
ment derive from an earlier rejected set of variations
on a theme from Schubert's "Sehnsuchtwalzer," now
more generally recognized as the "Trauerwalzer," it is
the second of the "36 Originaltanze fur Klavier," Op. 9,
D.365. At the "Piu moto" the pace quickens and a
simple phrase, a germinal cell of great importance in
this and other works by Schumann, is subjected to a
vigorous and restless waltz treatment. From this point
the work becomes increasingly animated, and by the
"Presto" conclusion many themes and motives, which
will subsequently be developed throughout the suite,
have been introduced. The sophisticated metrical play
of the bass contributes to the technical demands, yet is
extremely effective. Imaginative scope will vivify the
many juxtapositions of articulation, tempo, and
atmosphere.

       Tempo: Quasi Maestoso
       Length: 141 measures
       Technique: large chords, legato octaves,
          fast broken-chord passage work, leaps

Pierrot, Eb Major

ALFRED (Publisher): Schumann--29 of His Most Popular
    Piano Selections.
SHEALY, Alexander: Robert Schumann--His Greatest
    Piano Solos (Ashley).

Pierrot is the first of the characters of the
Commedia dell' Arte to appear. This pale, often moon-
struck lover can also play the clown. Schumann
superbly delineates this eccentric personality through
sudden changes of articulation and dynamics which
clearly express Pierrot's antic flights of melancholy and
whimsy. Careful voicing of the portamento octaves will
avoid monotony, and Schumann's pedal indication will
strengthen the charming conclusion.
    Tempo: Moderato
    Length: 52 measures
    Technique: portamento touch, legato chords

Arlequin, Bb Major

Nimble and capricious Arlequin is portrayed in this
vivacious and acrobatic miniature. An extremely delicate touch will emphasize the effervescent qualities of
this work. The rhythmic flow should remain unimpeded
by the many leaps which are combined with sudden
dynamic accents.
    Tempo: Vivo
    Length: 44 measures
    Technique: sudden dynamic changes, leaps,
        syncopations, chords, octaves

Valse Noble, Bb Major

ALFRED (Publisher): Schumann--29 of His Most Popular
  Piano Selections.
SHEALY, Alexander: Robert Schumann--His Greatest
  Piano Solos (Ashley).
VOGRICH, Max: Schumann Album for the Piano,
  (G. Schirmer Vol. 100).

This expansive and elegant waltz features a soaring
melody, often in legato octaves. The tender and
sensitive middle section creates an effective contrast.
The bass accompaniment remains discretely subdued
throughout. A warm, well-focused tone and rhythmic
flexibility is essential.

  Tempo: Un poco maestoso
  Length: 40 measures
  Technique: legato octaves, sudden dynamic
     changes, widely spaced accompaniment
     figures

Eusebius, Eb Major

Langorous turns and ornaments characterize
Eusebius, the introverted dreamer. The many cross-
rhythms and unusual beat divisions create fascinating
sonic structures. Schumann's pedal indication will assist
the performer in achieving the appropriate mood of
graceful, slightly distracted melancholy.

Tempo: Adagio
Length: 32 measures
Technique: legato octaves, cross-rhythms,
    widely spaced chords

Florestan, G Minor

Mercurial shifts of tempo and effect dramatize the passionate and brilliant Florestan. Two brief quotations from the first section of Papillons, Op. 2 appear; here the original brisk tempo is slowed to "Adagio," and Schumann labelled the second, lengthier reference "Papillon." The final accelerando is difficult, and the work concludes on an unresolved diminished seventh chord.

Tempo: Passionato
Length: 58 measures
Technique: wide leaps, tempo changes,
    syncopation, scalar inner voices

Coquette, Bb Major

An air of effortless nonchalance pervades this deceptively difficult movement. The *fortissimo* interjections do not exceed the context of the generally quiet dynamic range. Sensitive rubato is especially effective in the more elaborately figured passages.

Tempo: Vivo
Length: 61 measures
Technique: fast 2-note slurs, leaps,
   sudden dynamic changes, arpeggiated
   figurations

Replique, G Minor (Reply)

Replique is an amusing epigrammatic appendix to
the previous movement. Careful pedalling and phrasing,
as well as clear definition of the voices, will emphasize
the sprightly grace of this miniature.
   Tempo: L'istesso tempo
   Length: 18 measures
   Technique: fast 2-note slurs, legato
      inner voices

Sphinxes

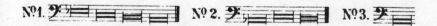

In the enigmatic Sphinxes, three tiny incipits present the basic A.S.C.H. material from which the entire
Carnaval is constructed. Sphinxes is not intended for
performance; it is a mystery, a riddle in which
Schumann exposes the secret interior of Carnaval.

Papillons, Bb Major (Butterflies)

ALFRED (Publisher): Schumann--29 of His Most Popular
    Piano Selections.
SHEALY, Alexander: Robert Schumann--His Greatest
    Piano Solos (Ashley).

The brilliant and ingratiating Papillons opens with a
left hand melody "quasi corni" (like hunting horns) and a
fleeting right hand sixteenth note countermelody. This
delightful movement possesses all the effervescent
charm of its cousins in Op. 2.
        Tempo: Prestissimo
        Length: 32 measures
        Technique: melody in inner voices, legato
            double note movement, difficult grace
            note leaps, sudden dynamic changes

A.S.C.H. – S.C.H.A. (Lettres Dansantes), Eb Major
    (Dancing Letters)

This whimsical little waltz features many grace
notes and sforzandi. Two-note slurs and displaced accents create impetuous rhythmic drive. At the "presto"
tempo staccato execution can be difficult, but precision
and lightness will reveal the aura of fantastic grace.
        Tempo: Presto
        Length: 32 measures
        Technique: syncopation, sudden *sf* in p
            range, pedal control

Chiarina, C Minor

It is in the guise of the beloved <u>Chiarina</u> that the youthful Clara Wieck makes her entrance. Though still little more than a child and temporarily supplanted in Schumann's affections, Clara is protrayed in extremely passionate terms. The descending countersubject (Ab, G, F, Eb, D) is derived from a phrase in Clara's own Opus 2, and appears as her "motto theme" in much of Schumann's music. Careful attention to dynamics and extended melodic phrases will intensify the romantic ardor of this work.

> Tempo: Passionato
> Length: 40 measures
> Technique: wide leaps, repeated notes, octaves

Chopin, Ab Major

BRIMHALL, John: Original Piano Masterworks, Recital
    Favorites, Levels 3 and 4 (Hansen).
DEXTER, Harry: Selected Piano Works--Schumann
    (Hansen).
DEXTER, Harry: The Young Pianist's Schumann
    (Hansen).
VOGRICH, Max: Schumann Album for the Piano
    (G. Schirmer Vol. 100).

The skill with which Schumann parodied his much admired contemporary should not obscure the depth of feeling found in this musical silhouette. Fluid left hand arpeggios provide a rich background on which the expressive melody is displayed. Tonal contrast is of the utmost importance, and the work may be played *pianissimo* on repetition.

> Tempo: Agitato
> Length: 14 measures
> Technique: dynamic control, arpeggiation
>   in LH

Estrella, F Minor

ALFRED (Publisher): Schumann--29 of His Most Popular
    Piano Selections.
SHEALY, Alexander: Robert Schumann--His Greatest
    Piano Solos (Ashley).

Schumann's current amour, Ernestine von Fricken, is depicted beneath the starry mask of Estrella. This tempestuous and extravagantly expressive waltz should never be harsh or bombastic, even in the face of the difficult left hand leaps in the middle section.

> Tempo: Con affetto
> Length: 36 measures
> Technique: legato octaves, leaps,
>   syncopation, inner voices

Reconnaissance, Ab Major

Like the opening <u>Préambule</u>, this piece is related to

the "Sehnsuchtwaltzer" of Schubert. One of the more difficult movements of the set, the right hand is particularly taxing. A unison octave melody is presented simultaneously in both legato and repeated note staccato forms. These repeated notes are played lightly and with great finesse by the thumb. In the B Major trio, graceful melodies alternating between the hands provide a refreshing lyrical dialogue.

> Tempo: Animato
> Length: 60 measures
> Technique: fast repeated notes in thumb,
>   legato melody and staccato accompaniment
>   in same hand, leaps, repeated chords, *pp*
>   texture

Pantalon et Colombine, F Minor

This sprightly movement introduces two more characters from the Italian comedy. Pantalon originated as a lampooning caricature of an elderly Venetian magnifico of the 17th century--a personage given to tiresome good advice and pompous tirade. In this work Pantalon is paired with the graceful "little dove" Colombine, the female counterpart of Arlequin. The juxtaposition of driving staccato and lyrical legato textures mimics the gay bantor of this charmingly mismatched couple. In ABA form, this miniature concludes with an engaging coda in the parallel major.

> Tempo: Presto
> Length: 39 measures
> Technique: legato double 6ths, staccato
>   chords, fast staccato touch

Valse Allemande, Ab Major

BRIMHALL, John: Original Piano Masterworks, Recital
   Favorites, Levels 3 and 4 (Hansen).
DEXTER, Harry: Selected Piano Works--Schumann
   (Hansen).
DEXTER, Harry: The Young Pianist's Schumann
   (Hansen).

The vigorous Valse Allemande is rhythmically
straightforward with ritardandos required only when
indicated. The first sixteenth note of the figure must
retain its identity as a downbeat. A decisive *forte*
ending brings this miniature to an unexpected close.
   Tempo: Molto vivace
   Length: 24 measures
   Technique: octaves, large blocked chords,
      sudden dynamic changes, sustained and
      moving notes in same hand

Paganini, F Minor

Paganini, like Chopin, was an honorary member of
the Davidsbündler. In this work Schumann brilliantly
evokes the spirit of the great violinist. The demonic
intensity and drive of the Italian vitruoso's style is
idiomatically translated to the piano with consummate
artistry. Large leaps for both hands, a "molto staccato"
texture, and constant syncopation mark Paganini as the
most flamboyantly virtuosic movement of Carnaval.

The final Eb7 chord (to be silently depressed, after which the damper pedal is changed) leads into a literal recapitulation of the Valse Allemande.

> Tempo: Presto
> Length: 61 measures
> Technique: fast leaps, syncopation, 2-note slurs, wide hand stretches

Aveu, Ab Major (Confession)

BRIMHALL, John: Original Piano Masterworks, Recital Favorites, Levels 3 and 4 (Hansen).
DEXTER, Harry: Selected Piano Works--Schumann (Hansen).
DEXTER, Harry: The Young Pianist's Schumann (Hansen).

The "passionato" qualities in this breathlessly whispered avowal should not exceed its painfully intimate scope. Within the limited dynamic range, a variety of tonal colors and shades will enhance the fragile beauty of this tiny surge of romantic passion.

> Tempo: Passionato
> Length: 12 measures
> Technique: octaves, limited dynamic range

Promenade, Db Major

The rhythmically flexible Promenade is one of the

most immediately engaging sections of Carnaval.   The
typical waltz accompaniment is difficult to subdue.
Though percussive accents are to be avoided, changes in
dynamic levels are immediate. Schumann quotes this
piece in the third movement of Davidsbündler, Op. 6.

> Tempo: Con moto
> Length: 95 measures
> Technique: legato octaves, sudden dynamic
>   changes, syncopation, careful pedal

Pause, Ab Major

Pause is an effusive outburst that leads directly into
the finale. The musical material is recapitulated from
Préambule.

> Tempo: Vivo
> Length: 27 measures
> Technique: rapid broken chord figuration,
>   leaps, octaves, syncopation

**Marche des Davidsbündler Contre les
Philistines,** Ab Major (March of the Davidsbundler
against the Philistines)

DEXTER, Harry: Selected Piano Works--Schumann
   (Hansen).
SHEALY, Alexander: Robert Schumann--His Greatest
   Piano Solos (Ashley).

The <u>Marche</u> provides a triumphant conclusion to <u>Carnaval</u>. This movement, in keeping with the dance character of the suite, is in triple meter, fittingly the Davidsbundler march against the reactionary Philistines in 3/4 time. Constant metric shifts and displacement of accents create a propulsive atmosphere of intense rhythmic vitality. The lengthy accelerando, beginning in measure 179 ("Animato molto") maintains a continual forward thrust. Two quotations of the <u>Grossvatertanz</u> occur in bass octaves, though the Davidsbündler soon rout both the Philistines and their anthem. The Davidsbündler, carefully disguised beneath carnival masks and antic postures, are swept along to the joyous apotheosis which concludes this great masterpiece of the romantic imagination.

Tempo: Non Allegro

Length: 286 measures

Technique: full *fortissimo* chords, repeated octaves, double dotted figures, wide leaps, syncopation, melody in thumb, broken chord figuration, legato and bravura passage work, endurance, immediate dynamic and tempo changes

SECHS CONCERT-ETUDEN NACH CAPRICEN VON PAGANINI, Opus 10 (Six Concert Etudes Based on Caprices of Paganini) (1835)

Composed one year after Schumann's Studien nach Capricen von Paganini, Op. 3, the second set of etudes based on "Caprices," Op. 1 of Paganini reveals a marked consolidation of the composer's technical powers. The Sechs Concert-Etuden nach Capricen von Paganini follow the Caprices with less literal fidelity than their predecessors, and Schumann freely altered the models through repetition, harmonic enrichment, and other compositional devices. These etudes reveal a more idiomatic pianism, and this collection employs some of the composer's most technically formidable figurative inventions. The entire set is brilliantly conceived, yet much of the writing is more difficult and imaginative than actually effective, and consequently, these works are seldom performed. Schumann originally intended to entitle these etudes Capricen fur das Pianoforte, auf dem Grund der Violinstimme von Paganini zu Studien frei bearbeitet, but the current title appeared on the first edition, published by Hofmeister in 1835. Schumann scrupulously avoided reviewing his own works, however, in 1836 he printed an enlightening article on these etudes in the Neue Zeitschrift fur Musik. With exemplary modesty Schumann merely detailed his intentions as a composer, rather than providing a critical evaluation of the etudes.

Note: The following editions contain Opus 10 in its entirety.

SAUER, Emil: Complete Works of Robert Schumann, Volume 4 (Peters #2300D).

SCHUMANN, Clara: Piano Music of Robert Schumann, Series I (Dover).

SCHUMANN, Clara: Robert Schumann—Complete Works, Volume 2 (Kalmus #3924/Belwin-Mills).

No. 1, Ab Major

This scintillating work is a transcription of Paganini's twelfth Caprice. Brilliant and demanding in a rounded binary form, it is an excellent study in finger tremolo and rotation technique.

      Tempo: Allegro molto
      Length: 73 measures
      Technique: wide leaps, thick texture, sudden
         dynamic changes, tremolo, endurance

No. 2, G Minor

Difficult

Derived from the sixth Caprice, Schumann has transformed the fiendishly difficult tremolo accompaniment of the original violin version into repeated sixteenth-note triplet intervals in this aria-like etude. The composer's own review of this piece suggests that a literal transcription would have proved unduly tiresome for both the pianist and the audience. In conjunction with these constantly repeated triplets, the right hand simultaneously provides a lyrical melody. The left hand is graced with arabesques and expressive syncopated interjections. The central section, "un poco piu moto," is dramatized through the use of quietly murmuring agitated accompanimental figuration.

      Tempo: Non troppo lento
      Length: 52 measures

Technique: melody accompanied by repeated
chords in same hand, wide hand stretches,
trills, 2 vs. 3, hand-crossings, voicing,
wide intervals, finger subsitiution

No. 3, G Minor   <u>Difficult</u>

The fiery third etude, based on Paganini's tenth
Caprice, is very demanding. Schumann was forced to
recognize that it was "not rewarding enough in relation
to its difficulty." The work opens with rapid staccato
octave scales. Perhaps the most challenging aspect of
this etude in ternary form is the voicing problems that
arise as a result of the density of the texture.

Tempo: Vivace
Length: 79 measures
Technique: fast staccato octaves, sudden
dynamic changes, melody with heavy
textured accompaniment, trills, awkward
figuration, quick hand shifts, double note
passages, broken octaves, mature technique

No. 4, C Minor   <u>Difficult</u>

Derived from the fourth Paganini Caprice, this
lengthy and dramatic work is the most musically
substantial of the Sechs Concert-Etuden nach Capricen
von Paganini. Schumann claimed that the Funeral
March of Beethoven's Symphony No. 3 "Eroica," Op. 55,

influenced the setting of this structurally interesting etude, and certainly this work is the most passionate and extensively developed of the set. Schumann provided copious indications of mood, tempo, and dynamics to enhance the range of the work's romantic intensity.

Tempo: Maestoso
Length: 119 measures
Technique: wide leaps, double 3rds and 6ths,
    sudden dynamic changes, thick texture,
    hand-crossings, quick hand shifts, full
    chords, rapid chords, finger independence

No. 5, E Minor   Advanced

A transcription of the second Caprice, the fifth etude is in ternary form. In contrast to its immediate predecessor, this work is completely devoid of expression markings. The dynamics and articulations are supplied by the performer, thus providing an etude for the intellect. The left hand has wide leaps and double notes, while the right hand is involved in perpetual motion figuration.

Tempo: none indicated
Length: 93 measures
Technique: wide leaps, 10ths, rotation, double
    3rd passages, rapid octaves, finger tremolo

No. 6, E Minor   Advanced

The final etude, based on Paganini's third Caprice, opens with a sonorous and dramatic "sostenuto" section featuring large rolled chords, over which the left hand crosses to present the solemn melody.   The ensuing "allegro" in a contrasting triple meter, is a demanding study in finger facility, with wide leaps and continual sixteenth-note figuration. Again, Schumann's dynamics are carefully considered, and will supply expressive variety and structural definition. The opening material makes a brief reappearance, and the etude concludes on the same note of melancholy grandeur with which it began.

Tempo: Sostenuto - Allegro

Length: 128 measures

Technique: melody in LH crossing over, rapid single note line in each hand containing awkward leaps, stretches, double note passages, sudden dynamic changes

INTRODUCTION TO THE SONATAS

With the exception of the Drei Clavier-Sonaten für die Jugend, Op. 118, Schumann's solo piano works in sonata form date from before 1840. The composer approached this form with caution and obvious trepidation. Several earlier sonata attempts remain in fragmentary states, while others, such as the Allegro, Op. 8, were published as independent movements. Schumann believed fervently in the unquestioned supremacy of the sonata as the means by which a composer's talents were assessed, and the example of Beethoven's unsurpassable accomplishments within the form weighed heavily on the younger generation of romantic composers. In the works of Beethoven, the sonata achieved a brilliant consummation in which structure and content were miraculously synthesized into a perfect paradigm of rational, if impassioned, thought. For Schumann and his contemporaries, this expressive mode, in which content and meaning were inherent in the dialectic of the form, could not support the volatile emotional crisis that was an essential factor in romantic art. Consequently Schumann, following the example of the greatly admired Schubert, attempted to expand the boundaries of the old sonata/allegro principle. In Schumann's hands, the solo sonata grew to embody a truly symphonic scope, in which sublimity of content replaced formal dialogue as the vivifying element. This tendency to burst the bonds of form through expressive effusions is typical of the composer's works. The sonatas of Schumann frequently contain such continual thematic transformation during the course of the exposition that the developments appear anticlimactic or even superfluous. Schumann relied heavily on sequential treatment of material, and the inevitable redundancy of such a tendency is only augmented by the sonata/allegro and rondo patterns. Many of Schumann's formal experiments, designed to achieve cyclic breadth and heightened expressivity, also create a certain excess and formal imbalance. When viewed from the traditional standpoint of function in classical sonata form, Schumann's compositions in this genre are flawed and inconsistent. However, it is essential to realize that in the context of romantic aesthetic theory these sonatas are completely viable works of art. If Schumann's sonatas are on occasion hindered by peculiar organizational methods, this does not detract from their sheer sensuous beauty and importance as epic landmarks of German romanticism. Schumann transcended the expressive possibilities of the strict sonata dialectic, and it is both the inherent fascination and tragedy of these works that he was unable to create an effective formal vehicle in which to express that passionate vision.

GROSSE SONATA, F# Minor, Opus 11   <u>Difficult</u>
(First Grand Sonata) (1835)

Schumann's earliest sketches for the <u>Sonata No. 1</u> date from around 1832, but like most of the composer's more complex extended works, this composition required a lengthy period of gestation and revision. This publication, described as "the collaborative effort of Florestan and Eusebius," was enigmatically dedicated to "Klara"--Clara Wieck. The second edition of 1840, entitled <u>Premiere Grande Sonate</u>, was printed under Schumann's own name. The <u>Sonata No. 1</u> is a highly esteemed work in this form, and it is germinal in the evolution of the later romantic sonata.

Note: The following editions contain Opus 11 in its entirety.

BOETTICHER, Wolfgang: Schumann Klavierwerke, Band IV (Henle).
SAUER, Emil: Complete Works of Robert Schumann, Volume 5 (Peters #2300E).
SCHUMANN, Clara: Piano Music of Robert Schumann, Series I (Dover).
SCHUMANN, Clara: Robert Schumann--Complete Works, Volume 2 (Kalmus #3924/Belwin-Mills).

Introduzione

The dark and disquieting <u>Introduzione</u> provides a dramatic prologue to the sonata. The scope of the <u>Introduzione</u>, in ternary form, is commensurate to the massive scale of the ensuing work. This movement serves an important purpose in the limited cyclic construction of the sonata by presenting a number of elements that reappear in the work. Aside from the exposition of certain prominent intervals and pitch groups, this ardent prelude contains a lengthy quotation from the opening melody of the second movement, the Aria.   Against a seething background of arpeggiated broken chord triplets, the intense melodic material is revealed. The Allegro Vivace follows without pause.

> Tempo: Un poco adagio
> Length: 52 measures
> Technique: tonal control, legato octaves,
>   widely spaced accompanimental figures

Allegro Vivace

This ambitious sonata/allegro originated as a "Fandango, Rhapsodie pour le piano" composed in 1831. Interestingly, the piece contains no traces of the 3/4 meter, or the formalized cadential progression that characterizes this Spanish dance. Schumann had originally prepared the "Fandango" for publication, but unfortunately lost the manuscript. When the score subsequently re-emerged, the composer expanded and remodelled the work into its current form. The first theme of the exposition is in itself a lengthy structure including a "passionato" episode in Eb Minor, and is based on two principal motives. The opening bass motive derives from Clara Wieck's "Le Ballet des revenants" from Soirees Musicales, Op. 5. The right hand presents a diatonic melody characterized by an invariable and inflexible rhythmic pattern. This material, with its obsessive rhythmic figuration, soon becomes the dominant force of the Allegro Vivace. The two motives are subjected to a variety of sequential and modulatory processes. A brief transition leads into the second key area. As is expected, this subject inhabits the relative major and forms an antithetical relationship with the opening material.   A lyrical legato phrase structure is featured, flowing into eighth note octaves. Though mercifully free of the ♫ ♪ rhythmic patterns that permeate the initial theme of the exposition, the second subject is so brief that it is overwhelmed by the vast proportions of the tonic material.   The entire exposition is repeated before a second ending introduces the development.

The development utilizes a three-part scheme. The first section exploits a difficult modulatory and sequential figure based on the two motives of the first subject of the exposition.   This material uses the relative major as an initial point of reference, but begins to modulate immediately. This turbulent passage soon extends into the equally agitated central area of the development.   In F Minor, this episode continues the brilliant sequential development, but interjects a note of subtle fantasy by concluding with a hushed reference to the opening theme of the "Introduzione." In a novel departure from the formal tradition, the opening section of the development is repeated in the key of B Major. A challenging and flamboyant extension firmly concludes the development in the tonic F♯ Major. The recapitulation is formally interesting as the first theme is drastically abbreviated, and the passionato episode is now shifted to C♯ Minor.   The opening bass motive closes the movement, but after the F♯ is sounded, the third degree of the scale remains depressed, providing a link to the Aria.

Tempo: Allegro vivace
Length: 349 measures
Technique: legato octaves, wide dynamic
    range, awkward and taxing passage work,
    wide leaps, fast repeated chords, sudden
    dynamic changes, syncopation

Aria

The Aria is a transcription of a song Schumann composed in 1828, entitled An Anna. To fit the sonata's key scheme, the composer transposed this work from F Major to A Major. Schumann also assured this movement of an integral position in the cyclic framework of the sonata, by quoting its principal melody in the Introduzione. The Aria retains the ternary form of the original. The outer sections employ simple melody and accompaniment textures, with the lyrical theme supported by steady repeated chords. Though subtle voicing is indicated, the rolled tenths and simple hand-crossings are not technically difficult. A mood of ethereal calm is maintained through the use of long pedals.

The central episode in F Major presents the melodic material in the bass, while the right hand spins a filagreed web of sixteenth note figuration. Schumann's unusual indication, "senza passione, ma expressivo" perfectly mirrors the melancholy introspection of the "Aria." In a review in the journal Revue et gazette musicale de Paris of 1837, signed by Franz Liszt, this composition was hailed as "one of the most beautiful pages we know."

Tempo: no indication

Length: 45 measures

Technique: singing tone in high register, wide stretches, legato octaves, careful pedal, subtle melodic voicing, simple hand-crossings, rolled 10ths

Scherzo e Intermezzo

   This brilliant and vivacious movement is cast in the
form of a scherzo with two trios. For the second trio
Schumann has substituted an intermezzo. The result is
an engaging ABACA structure. The scherzo itself is a
three part construction. The fleet opening features a
brisk martial left hand melody alternating with a
soaring ascending sequence, while the middle episode
continues to develop this spirited surging figure. A
literal repeat of the opening material terminates the
scherzo statement and leads directly into the trio.
   The trio, marked "piu Allegro," develops a particularly ingenious texture. Against a background of
sparse *pianissimo* left hand octaves, the right hand
presents a lyrical melody while simultaneously
accompanying itself with staccato eighth notes. The
clever and amusing trio is yet another ternary design,
and again the middle section elaborates the principal
motives rather than introducing new material. The
scherzo is repeated, and proceeds without interruption
into the intermezzo.
   The indication "Lento" prefaces the Intermezzo as
does the instruction "alla burla, ma pomposo," and this
spirit of hearty bumptious satire dominates the piece.
Heavy accented upbeats punctuate this section. The
polonaise binary design is a welcome contrast to the
three-part structures that pervade this movement. The
intermezzo concludes with an amusingly parodistic cadenza, which blithely indulges all of the most offensive
antics and mannerisms of the then popular Italian
opera. This cadenza serves as a transition to the final
recurrence of the scherzo material. Fully indicative of
Schumann's whimsical wit and musical inventiveness,
this delightful work provides an interlude of charm and
gaiety in the midst of a notably serious sonata.

Tempo: Allegrissimo
Length: 219 measures
Technique: octaves, large chords, awkward
     passagework, fast 2-note slurs, wide leaps,
     syncopation, careful pedal, sudden dynamic
     changes

Finale

The expansive Finale contains a variety of musical
ideas in a curious variation of traditional sonata form.
Its opening subject, an extremely taxing declamation in
F# Minor, achieves an overwhelming sonorous power
through the unswerving use of large chords. This section leads to the second subject, centered in Eb Major.
This material features a halting sixteenth-note pattern,
and surrounds a central episode of an expressively
lyrical legato nature. The first subject reappears,
though here in C Minor (the relative minor of the key of
the second subject), and is again succeeded by the
second theme, now in A Major. A lengthy and very
difficult transition leads to a shatteringly climactic
series of stark sequential chords. The following section
is developmental and episodic. After a poignant climax,
the music dwindles to a still and richly lyrical hush. At
this point the Finale clearly divides in half, and after a
brief rumbling transition, the opening material returns.
The second subject is recapitulated, now transposed to
C Major, and the principal and secondary themes make a
final appearance, this time in C Major and Eb Major
respectively. A literal repeat of the lengthy developmental episode occurs, and leads to the flamboyant and
virtuosic coda in F# Major. This coda combines the
opening theme with a broken octave figuration.

The formal arrangement of the work is obviously a complex and unusual one, and Schumann uses this carefully contrived structural ambiguity as a powerful source of dramatic impetus. Its modified sonata/allegro form may be summed up as follows: exposition (1st subject-2nd subject repeated) Development-repeated, and coda. Constant literal repetition makes it difficult to avoid structural monotony, yet the work contains many exciting musical ideas. Though the <u>Finale</u> is not a completely successful experiment, it is a compelling and admirable attempt to encompass the romantic spirit within a vigorous design of vast classical scope.

Tempo: Allegro un poco maestoso

Length: 462 measures

Technique: fast repeated chords, fast 2-note slurs, wide leaps, widely spaced chords, sudden dynamic changes, endurance, legato vs. staccato, awkward passage work, rapid legato octaves, hand-crossings, difficult broken-octave figuration, sustained and moving notes

PHANTASIESTÜCKE, Opus 12 (Fantasy Pieces) (1837)

In the Phantasiestücke Schumann's use of the format of the character piece attains new heights of structural and musical expressivity. Schumann's compositions in this genre are generally divided into two types: works such as Carnaval, Op. 9, in which brief miniatures are linked by consistent application of unifying devices such as thematic variation and programmatic content, and compositions like the Phantasiestücke. In the works of the latter type, the scope of each piece is expanded, and the individual movements become virtually autonomous compositions. Schumann has linked the movements of the Phantasiestücke through many subtle means. These pieces are all composed in flat keys. There are also a number of harmonic and motivic similarities derived from the descending and ascending scalar patterns that permeate and integrate the collection. Of course, the performance of any separate movement of Opus 12 can be an aesthetically satisfying experience, yet the work acquires added meaning when viewed as a whole.

Schumann possessed the rare ability to provide his works with evocative titles that stimulate the imagination. The Phantasiestücke, along with Carnaval are the first of the composer's works in which each movement is given a separate title. Schumann repeatedly stated that these titles were appended to the compositions after their completion rather than before it.

The Phantasiestucke were composed in 1837, and were dedicated to the Scottish pianist Anna Robena Laidlow. In the following year the pieces were published in two volumes of four works each by Breitkopf und Härtel. These works are notable for their brilliantly inventive handling of form and structure, ingratiating lyricism, and cogent expressivity. The Phantasiestücke are at the summit of Schumann's art, and perfectly embody the imaginative fantasy which is the paramount accomplishment of German romanticism.

Note: The following editions contain Opus 12 in its
   entirety. Other sources are listed with each piece.

BOETTICHER, Wolfgang: Schumann Klavierwerke,
   Band II (Henle).
LIPSKY, Alexander: Robert Schumann--Album II for
   Piano (Kalmus #3931/Belwin-Mills).
SAUER, Emil: Complete Works of Robert Schumann,
   Volume 2 (Peters #2300B).
SCHUMANN, Clara: Piano Music of Robert Schumann,
   Series I (Dover).
SCHUMANN, Clara: Robert Schumann--Complete
   Works, Volume 2 (Kalmus #3924/Belwin-Mills).

Des Abends, Db Major (Evening)   Early Advanced

SCHIRMER (Publisher): Selected Piano Solos by
   Romantic Composers, Book 3 (Vol. 1720).
SHEALY, Alexander: Robert Schumann--His Greatest
   Piano Solos (Ashley).
VOGRICH, Max: Schumann Album for the Piano
   (G. Schirmer Vol. 100).

An intense yet subdued lyricism is the dominant
characteristic of Des Abends.   Schumann employs a
favorite rhythmic device of a melody in triple meter
superimposed onto a duple beat division.   Long pedals
and subtle voicing will sustain this delicate work.   Des
Abends is in a modified binary form.   A brief coda
brings this enchanting composition to a fleeting
conclusion.

Tempo: Sehr innig zu spielen (Inwardly)
Length: 88 measures
Technique: quiet thumb, overlapping hand
positions, wide leaps, tonal control within
pianissimo dynamic range, legato melody,
melody and accompaniment in same hand

Aufschwung, F Minor (Soaring)　　　Early Advanced

AGAY, Denes: An Anthology of Piano Music--Romantic
Period, Vol. III (Yorktown).
BRADLEY, Richard: Bradley's Level Eight Classics
(Bradley).
BRIMHALL, John: Original Piano Masterworks, Recital
Favorites, Levels 3 and 4 (Hansen).
DEXTER, Harry: Selected Piano Works--Schumann
(Hansen).
HEINRICHSHOFEN (Publisher): Schumann--Easier
Favorites (Peters No.4052).
SHEALY, Alexander: Robert Schumann--His Greatest
Piano Solos (Ashley).
VOGRICH, Max: Schumann Album for the Piano
(G. Schirmer Vol. 100).

In the passionate sweep of this fiery work the pianist is provided ample opportunity to display impetuous
virtuosity. The difficult large stretches in the opening
may be mitigated by redistributing this material between the hands. Clarity of voicing will emphasize the
surging qualities of the second theme. Aufschwung is
based on a sonata/allegro form, as is In der Nacht.

Tempo: Sehr rasch (Very fast)
Length: 154 measures
Technique: wide leaps, 10ths, awkward
passage work, wide variety of touches,
melody and accompaniment in same hand

Warum?, Db Major (Why?)   Intermediate

BRIMHALL, John: Original Piano Masterworks, Recital
   Favorites, Levels 3 and 4 (Hansen).
DEXTER, Harry: Selected Piano Works—Schumann
   (Hansen).
DEXTER, Harry: The Young Pianist's Schumann
   (Hansen).
HEINRICHSHOFEN (Publisher): Schumann—Easier
   Favorites (Peters No.4052).
SHEALY, Alexander: Robert Schumann—His Greatest
   Piano Solos (Ashley).
VOGRICH, Max: Schumann Album for the Piano,
   (G. Schirmer Vol. 100).

A brief but compelling melodic fragment dominates
this tiny movement in binary form. The questioning
implications of this theme are left unresolved at the
close of the piece. The two grace note arpeggiated
figures will benefit from discreet pedalling. A carefully
voiced presentation of the upper voices will be
particularly effective if the left hand accompaniment is
subdued. Warum? is an exquisite example of Schumann's
penchant for combining the tender with the enigmatic.
           Tempo: Langsam und zart
              (Slowly and tenderly)
           Length: 42 measures
           Technique: melody in thumb, leaps, careful
                 pedal, inner voices, subdued accompaniment

Grillen, Db Major (Whims)   Early Advanced

DEXTER, Harry: Selected Piano Works—Schumann
   (Hansen).
HEINRICHSHOFEN (Publisher): Schumann—Easier
   Favorites (Peters No.4052).
SHEALY, Alexander: Robert Schumann—His Greatest
   Piano Solos (Ashley).

The vigorous and energetic Grillen makes use of the
sonata/rondo principle. Emphasis of the linear forward
motion will avoid the ponderous, bombastic quality that
often mars the work. The Gb Major episode features a
rhythmic syncopation typical of the composer, and
offers a welcome respite from the buoyant vitality of
the surrounding material.
      Tempo: Mit Humor (With humor)
      Length: 157 measures
      Technique: fast moving staccato chords, fluent
          chords, syncopation, fast register changes,
          sudden dynamic changes

In der Nacht, F Minor (In the Night)   Advanced

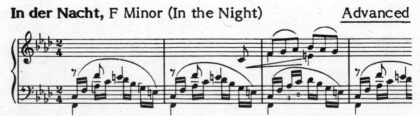

Unceasing agitated sixteenth notes form a turbulent
backdrop to the violent melodic outbursts that punctuate this work. The perpetual motion figuration and the
many cross-rhythms make this movement one of the
most difficult of the Phantasiestücke. In der Nacht
contains a lyrical central section in F Major, in which
the melodic material soars above the welter of accompanimental textures. A lengthy and challenging transition proceeds the return to the tumultuous opening.
Schumann considered "In der Nacht" one of his finest
and most characteristic works, and came to associate
this evocative masterpiece with the myth of Hero and
Leander.

Tempo: Mit Leidenschaft (With Passion)
Length: 223 measures
Technique: cross-rhythms, rapid *p* figuration
in lower register, wide stretches, broken
chord accompaniment distributed between
the hands, leaps, fast double note passages,
endurance

Fabel, C Major (Fable)   <u>Early Advanced</u>

SHEALY, Alexander: Robert Schumann--His Greatest
Piano Solos (Ashley).

<u>Fabel</u> begins with a slow introductory phrase which
serves a ritornello function in this engaging movement.
The sectional nature of this composition with its many
fermatas will be best served by a constant forward
momentum.   The ensuing fast sections involve an agile
staccato touch, as well as finger dexterity.
Tempo: Langsam (Slowly) - Schnell (Fast)
Length: 89 measures
Technique: fast *pp* staccato, melody and
accompaniment in same hand, legato and
staccato in same hand, syncopation, sudden
character changes, many fermatas

Traumes Wirren, F Major   <u>Advanced</u>
  (Disturbing Dreams)

A fully developed technique is a prerequisite for this difficult movement. Against a taxing bass line, the right hand is engaged in a rapid stream of constant sixteenth note figurations, all making conspicuous use of the fourth and fifth fingers. In ternary form, Traumes Wirren contains a tranquil legatissimo central episode in Db Major, which leads directly into a false recapitulation in Gb Major. In this section the left hand figures, as well as the sudden shifts of register, can be quite difficult. Through clever and circuitous routes the work returns to F Major, and the expected recapitulation occurs. The whimsical and fantastic aura of Traumes Wirren is heightened by an approach of the utmost delicacy and finesse.

> Tempo: Aeusserst lebhaft (Extremely lively)
> Length: 177 measures
> Technique: fast leaps, constant RH 4th and 5th
> finger figuration, wide stretches,
> hand-crossing

Ende Vom Lied, F Major   Early Advanced
(The End of the Story)

SHEALY, Alexander: Robert Schumann—His Greatest
Piano Solos (Ashley).

Ende vom Leid provides a stirring conclusion to the Phantasiestücke. The ascending octave motive that introduces this work lends a poignant, yearning quality to the otherwise triumphant opening. Like many of its companions, this epilogue is in ABA form. Here the vivid central section in Bb Major employs a motive familiar from the opening and closing movements of Carnaval, Op. 9. The rhythmic vitality of this section creates considerable momentum, as do the many modulation sequences. Treatment of the repeated chords is firm, but not bombastic. The spirited opening material returns, and Schumann introduces a quiet, reflective coda based on the principal theme, ending the Phantasiestücke on a note of blissful calm.

Tempo: Mit guten Humor (With good Humor)

Length: 117 measures

Technique: full chordal passages, 2-note slurs, character contrast within small frame, tonal control within limited dynamic range (p-ppp)

Supplement to Fantasiestücke, Op. 12

No. 9, A Major * * *

WERNER, Joseph: Autograph Series of Unknown
    Classics--Fantasiestuck, Op. 12, No. 9--Schumann
    (J. Curwen/G. Schirmer).

Schumann headed the manuscript of this piece with
the title <u>Phantasiestücke</u>, Op. 12, No. 9, and prefaced
the work with the three asterisks with which he also
labeled several untitled pieces in the <u>Album für die
Jugend</u>, Op. 68. That Schumann originally intended the
work for publication is clear from the care with which
the dynamics and articulations are notated. Formally
the work is closely related to a rondo, and an opening
introductory phrase serves a quasi-ritornello function.
The piece is charming and relatively simple, but lacks
the   acute   mastery   and   inspiration   of   the
<u>Phantasiestücke</u>.   Schumann probably suppressed this
composition when it became obvious that it was missing
those qualities that make the rest of Opus 12 such
fascinating fragments of the romantic spirit.
    Tempo: Fuerigst (con fuoco) (Fiery)
    Length: 68 measures
    Technique: arpeggiated figuration, grace
        notes, una corda pedal

ETÜDEN IN FORM VON VARIATIONEN   <u>Difficult</u>
(Symphonische Etüden), C# Minor, Opus 13
(Etudes in the Form of Variations (Symphonic
Etudes)) (1834, revised in 1852)

Like so many of Schumann's more extended works,
the <u>Etüden in Form von Variationen</u> are the product of a
lengthy and complicated process of evolution. The
theme is from a set of variations composed by the Baron
von Fricken. He had sent it to Schumann for criticism
in 1834. Schumann soon began work on variations of his
own. Later he projected a set of twelve etudes, probably inspired by the daringly expanded virtuosity and
expressive sophistication of the enormously influential
etudes Chopin published the previous year. This version
was to have borne the title <u>Zwolf Davidsbündler
Etüden</u>. Throughout the next three years the etude
character of this composition was gradually consumed
by the variation format. A manuscript entitled <u>Tema
quasi marcia funebre</u> survives from this period, and
contains some of the musical material of the present
work. Finally in 1837 Schumann prepared the work for
publication as <u>Etüden im Orchester Character, von
Florestan und Eusebius.</u> However, out of deference to
the publisher Hasling, the work was issued under
Schumann's own name, and as <u>Etüden in Form von
Variationen</u> the variations were dedicated to the young
composer William Sterndale Bennet (1816-1875), whose
work Schumann championed. In 1852 Schumann again
reworked the composition, eliminating the third and
ninth variations, revising the finale, and conferring the
work's final title. However the <u>Etüden in Form von
Variationen</u> has always been more familiarly known by
the subtitle <u>Simfonische Etüden</u> (Symphonic Etudes), and
is commonly heard in the posthumous version of 1862,
which includes the third and ninth variations and retains
the revised finale.

The <u>Etüden in Form von Variationen</u> consists of a
theme, nine variations, two etudes, and a lengthy finale.
Each is based on a two-reprise binary form, but the
potentially monotonous regularity of such a procedure is

deftly circumvented. The first of the etudes also uses binary structure, though the second etude is considerably more episodic in form. Schumann manipulates the variation form with a mastery and originality that remains unsurpassed, and the composer synthesizes his genius for the characteristic romantic miniature with an extended, potentially dramatic structure.

The Etüden in Form von Variationen are significant as Schumann's interest in both the etude and variation genres achieves an astonishing consummation in this work. The etude character of the piece is revealed in the challenging but marvelously inventive pianism with which the work abounds, while Schumann's use of the variation form is a miracle of structural clarity. The Etüden in Form von Variationen are possibly the greatest set of variations of the romantic era, and certainly such familiar works as the variations of Schumann's protege Brahms are unimaginable without the example of this monumental work. Schumann brings a seriousness and sense of high purpose to this form, so often a mere vehicle for virtuoso display, and even the most brilliant bravura sections bear an unmistakenly somber atmosphere.

Note: The following editions contain Opus 13 in its entirety.

BOETTICHER, Wolfgang: Schumann Klavierwerke, Band III (Henle).

LIPSKY, Alexander: Robert Schumann--Album II for Piano (Kalmus #3931/Belwin-Mills).

SAUER, Emil: Complete Works of Robert Schumann, Volume 3 (Peters #2300C).

SCHUMANN, Clara: Piano Music of Robert Schumann, Series III (Dover).

SCHUMANN, Clara: Robert Schumann--Complete Works, Volume 2 (Kalmus #3924/Belwin-Mills).

Thema

The grave and tragic Thema possesses an aura of tarnished grandeur and reserved melancholy that is both immediately compelling, and indicative of the general character of the ensuing variations. It has a simple strophic structure of four regular phrases, yet it is melodically and harmonically resourceful. Although not technically difficult, this work benefits from a sensitive approach. The sustained trill with melody in the same hand conveys the effect of a gentle murmur.

Tempo: Andante ♩ = 52
Length: 16 measures
Technique: widely spaced rolled chords, tonal control, 5th finger melody in chordal structure

Variation I

From the depths a spectral march emerges, and inexorably winds its way through ascending registers. The theme now appears, and forces the opening motive down again into the lowest reaches of the keyboard, from whence it renews its upward struggle. This martial figure with the rather furtive cast creates an eerie, macabre mood. This atmosphere will be emphasized by the clear differentiation of the notated articulation. The second reprise achieves a somewhat brighter climax, yet never completely dispels the air of lacrymose disquiet. Though not particularly difficult, this variation involves a skillful application of voicing techniques, and a focused, well-controlled tone, especially in the context of the limited dynamic range.

Tempo: Un poco più vivo ♩ = 72

Length: 16 measures

Technique: legato melody with staccato accompaniment, legato chordal passages, wide stretches, tonal control in lower register

Variation II

In this noble but melancholy nocturne the first phrase of the theme appears in augmentation in the bass. The second phrase is replaced by new material, though the original harmonic structure is generally preserved. The second reprise is similarly organized, though in this case the third strain of the theme appears in the tenor voice. Throughout this haunting variation a passionately lyrical melody is displayed against a brooding repeated chord background. With careful voicing, both right hand melody and left hand theme may be disentangled from the relentless accompaniment figures.

Tempo: espressivo ♪ = 72

Length: 18 measures

Technique: thick texture with repeated chords as inner voices, fast register changes, melody in thumb, sudden dynamic changes, legato octaves

Etude III

    This fey etude bears only the most tenuous relationship to the theme. Rather than detracting from the cohesive unity of the set, the insertion of the unrelated material adds immeasurably to the fantastic character of the Etüden in Form von Variationen. The formidable pianistic difficulties encountered in this work include a brilliant and fleeting right hand staccato figuration, with the left hand weaving an independent contrapuntal web that can be easily obscured by the accompaniment. The second reprise begins with a new, sweeping figuration that is less difficult than the rest of the etude, yet still requires much dexterity. Perhaps the supreme challenge of this work is that it must convey the impression, in the face of such overwhelming demands, of effortless ease and studied nonchalance.

        Tempo: Vivace ♩ = 63
        Length: 20 measures
        Technique: rapid staccato and legato
            figuration with sudden register shifts, leaps,
            wide stretches, hand independence

Variation III

    The third variation is an ingenious canon at the octave in which the rhythmically simplified theme is presented in blocked chord form. An arresting quality is achieved through the use of sudden sforzando accents. Though not as difficult as some of the other variations, this work contains taxing chords, and the occasional octave grace notes of the second reprise may be disconcerting. The fourth variation follows without pause.

Tempo: ♩ = 132
Length: 20 measures
Technique: widely spaced blocked chords, hand independence, LH octave grace notes

Variation IV

This sprightly variation contains canonic imitation, and is pervaded by a single rhythmic figure. Interestingly this work opens in C♯ Minor but concludes in the relative major. The prevailing air of elfin grace is heightened by light staccato octaves in a consistently quiet dynamic range punctuated by occasional sforzando outbursts. The technical demands are considerable, and the entanglement of the hands in close proximity at the beginning is especially troublesome.

Tempo: ♩. = 108
Length: 16 measures
Technique: rapid staccato octaves, leaps, close hand positions, hand independence

Variation V

Constant syncopated displacement of the theme, a device frequently favored by Schumann, creates a mood of intense agitation. There is a distinct temptation to allow the accented left hand upbeat to sound like a downbeat. By avoiding this, the performer heightens the rhythmic drive and interplay of the work. The breathtaking leaps in the left hand are the most formidable technical obstacle. The figuration of this fiery variation is closely related to the fifth of the posthumously published <u>Exercises: Etüden in form freier variationen über ein Thema von Beethoven.</u>

Tempo: Agitato ♩ = 60
Length: 18 measures
Technique: wide leaps, 2-note slurs, legato
    melody in 5th finger, syncopation, chordal
    texture against staccato accompaniment

Variation VI

Marked "sempre brillante," this engaging variation will test the pianist's repeated chord technique as well as endurance. A certain amount of subtlety regarding the dynamics will avoid the monotony that a strictly *forte* presentation of this variation can produce. By using this kind of restraint the performer can shape a stunning explosion of sound through the final crescendo. Like the fourth variation, this glittering work cadences in the clarity of the relative major.

Tempo: Allegro molto ♩ = 96
Length: 30 measures
Technique: rapid repeated chords, 3-note slurs,
    dynamic control, wide leaps, legato octaves

Variation VII

The somber and dramatic quality of this piece, as well as the nature of its extraordinarily wrought onramentation, evoke the bizarre mood of the first variation. The fantastic tracery of this magical work is generally graceful to play, but a sense of rhythmic propulsion is essential. Schumann's indication "tenuto per il pedale" in measure 15 refers to the dotted half notes in the bass, and the pedal is released with the change of harmony on the fourth beat.

> Tempo: ♩ = 80
> Length: 18 measures
> Technique: hand independence, wide leaps,
>   trills, complex rhythms

Etude IX

An effervescent scherzo, this vivacious movement is extremely challenging. The "Presto possible" tempo, "senze pedale" staccato figuration, and generally quiet dynamic level, combine to create a work of transcendental difficulty. The rapid *fortissimo* chordal passage in measures 33-40 is one of the most notorious in the repertoire. In the face of these technical difficulties, the necessary mood of Mendelssohnian wit and clarity is not easily projected. Like the third etude, this movement bears no resemblance to the theme, and is formally inventive. This brilliant bravura exercise concludes with an ethereal ascending and descending diminished seventh arpeggio, a fleeting vision dissolving into crystalline air.

> Tempo: Presto possibile ♪ = 116
> Length: 82 measures
> Technique: rapid staccato chords in
>   texture, leaps, dynamic control

Variation VIII

   Though this impetuous variation is labeled "sempre con energia," the tempo should not exceed the range in which the staccato left hand figuration can maintain the requisite beauty.   Throughout the eighth variation articulation is of prime importance, and the brief but subtly inventive legato passage at measure 11 is a particularly effective example of Schumann's use of varied touch.

> Tempo: sempre con energia ♩ = 92
> Length: 16 measures
> Technique: fast staccato scalar passages,
>   sudden dynamic changes, staccato chordal
>   passages, legato octaves

Variation IX (G♯ Minor)

   The infinitely dark and brooding tonality of G♯ Minor casts a pall of intense melancholy over this exquisite nocturne. The left hand with faultless control produces a gossamer murmur over which the right hand's poignant melody hovers. At measure 7 the melody takes on a two-voiced contrapuntal texture which presents the pianist with grave technical and interpretative dilemmas. Obviously the extremely wide right hand intervals must be broken, yet the distinct melodic lines should never sound fragmented. The complexity of the cross-rhythms are notable, but inevitably serve expressive ends. The profound emotional qualities of this variation are revealed only through the most sensitive and imaginative nuance. Pedalling, in particular, should be discreet. Long, shallow pedals will avoid heavy unsubtle textures. This final variation, possessing an atmosphere of poignant sadness and dejection, sounds the most profound depths of the romantic spirit.

> Tempo: Con espressione $\downarrow$ = 66
> Length: 20 measures
> Technique: cross-rhythms, rapid chordal
>   accompanimental figuration, long melodic
>   lines, wide stretches, two independent
>   voices in same hand

Finale (Db Major)

The Finale blazes forth with an explosion of glorious Db Major sonority. The striking opening phrase was intended as an elaborate complement to the work's dedicatee, Schumann's young friend, the English composer Sterndale Bennet. It quotes a passage in praise of England from Heinrich Marschner's (1795-1861) opera "Der Templer und die Judin," based on Sir Walter Scott's "Ivanhoe." Juxtaposed against this music is material derived from the original variation theme. The Finale utilizes an extended modified sonata/rondo form of considerable scope and dramatic impact. A single rhythmic figure permeates the work, and though the dotted rhythms may verge on the obsessive, with skillful presentation they create enormous impetus and serve as a vital unifying force. The technical demands are great, and a passage involving scalar double tenths is extremely taxing, if not impossible, for smaller hands. Due to the large amount of literal repetition found in this work, the Finale will benefit from scrupulous observation of the dynamic markings. Equally important are the composer's pedal indications, without which it is impossible to achieve the necessary range of color and sonority. Though the Finale contains many harmonic felicities, the brief and dashingly violent shift to Bb Major in the coda is particularly effective. This spectacular movement, so bright and exuberant, provides an immensely satisfying ending to the Etüden in Form von Variationen -- a work that opened in tragic despair, yet concludes with a cry of victorious triumph.

    Tempo: Allegro brillante ♩ = 66
    Length: 197 measures
    Technique: widely spaced blocked chords with skips, sudden dynamic changes, repeated notes, long melodic lines, wide dynamic range, textural changes

SYMPHONISCHE ETÜDEN, C♯ Minor, Opus 13
(Anhang zu Opus 13)
(Supplement to Symphonic Etudes)

Of great historical and musicological interest, these works are variations Schumann discarded from the initial publication of the Symphonische Etüden. Though completed by 1837, these compositions were not made available until 1893, when Brahms included them in the edition of Robert Schumann's Werk issued by Brietkopf und Härtel. Six unpublished variations were found among Schumann's sketches, but Brahms chose to release only five. As the original manuscript lacks virtually all tempo, dynamic, and expression indications, Brahms supplied the variations with appropriate and effective editorial suggestions. With the exception of the fourth supplemental variation, which was intended to precede the Finale, Schumann's projected ordering of these movements is unknown. Because of the great beauty of these bravura miniatures, it has become common to interpolate them into performances of Symphonische Etüden. However, such a practice is completely contrary to Schumann's intentions, and in a work as meticulously honed as this, the resultant disruption of the structural and expressive unity is disastrous.

Note: The following edition contains the Supplement to Opus 13 in its entirety.

SCHUMANN, Clara: Piano Music of Robert Schumann, Series III (Dover).

Variation I

In this variation the theme is generally presented by the left hand while the right hand is engaged in a flurry of increasingly difficult thirty-second notes. At the opening of the second reprise the theme appears in the right hand as the upper voice in a series of three part chords. Here, the left hand provides the swirling accompaniment pattern, but soon the original distribution of function is restored. This attractive and elegant work with its brisk tempo more closely resembles an actual technical exercise than many of its companions.

>Tempo: none indicated
>Length: 16 measures
>Technique: rapid accompanimental figuration
>   with wide stretches, octaves, finger facility

Variation II

The opening measures of this unusual episodic variation contain two pairs of emotionally ambiguous phrases based on antecedent/consequent relationships. In both cases the interrogative phrase exploits the upper registers, while the reply utilizes the bass range via a lengthy hand-cross passage. The left hand is faced with widely spaced chords that may challenge the pianist who has small hands. The musical material of this section is not related to the theme, though the theme is prominent in the tempestuous tremolo study that immediately follows. This new section has a marked virtuoso character, yet a shimmering veil of sound is more desirable than clarity of individual notes. This interpretively and technically demanding variation is frought with awkward hand-crosses and chordal grace notes.

Tempo: none indicated
Length: 17 measures
Technique: hand tremolos, rapid arpeggiation
  of broken chords, long melodic line in legato
  octaves, scales, hand-crosses, chordal
  grace notes

Variation III

An unusual ABB form adds variety to this imposing
variation.   The double-stemmed notes in the bass
demarcate the theme and central melodies, and respond
well to a penetrating, carefully voiced approach.   This
variation   builds   considerable   rhythmic   momentum
through a constant triplet flow.   The atmosphere of
solidity and grandeur should not degenerate into mere
bombast.

Tempo: none indicated
Length: 24 measures
Technique: wide leaps, cross-rhythms, heavy
  textured accompaniment to LH melody,
  wide dynamic range

Variation IV

Schumann   originally   conceived   this   evocative
variation in binary form as a prelude to the Finale. A
wistful and elegantly melancholy waltz, it is the only
movement among those intended for the Etüdes en Form

de Variations in a triple dance meter. A simple melody and accompaniment format prevails throughout this exquisite piece, but grace notes and sixteenth-note arabesques enliven the texture. A wide range of expressive nuance and touch is beneficial, and the use of long pedals will strengthen the climactic moments.

     Tempo: none indicated
     Length: 57 measures
     Technique: syncopation, leaps, long melodic
        line (some in high register) in single notes

Variation V (Db Major)

     This extraordinary variation exhibits many of Schumann's most salient mannerisms. The continuous syncopation by means of accent displacement is typical of the composer, as is the perpetual motion figuration. Again in binary form, this variation exploits the upper registers to an extent that is common in Schumann's works, and the high tessitura is responsible for the fleeting and ephemeral charm of the piece. The final plagal cadence is particularly effective, and may be made more emphatic through the use of a warm, richly sonorous tone. Schumann obviously rejected this gracious and virtuosic variation because the Db Major tonality and vivacious spirit of the work would have lessened the impact of the Finale.

     Tempo: none indicated
     Length: 16 measures
     Technique: broken chordal figuration spanning
        large intervals, syncopated melodic line,
        melody within chordal figuration, wide
        stretches

DRITTE GROSS SONATE. Concert ohne   Advanced
Orchester, F Minor, Opus 14 (Third Great Sonata.
Concerto without Orchestra) or "Sonata No. 3,"
"Konzert ohne Orchestre" (1836)

Schumann began the Sonata in F Minor in 1835, and
completed it one year later in June of 1836. At this
time the work was in five movements, with two scher-
zos surrounding the central set of variations. The composer offered the work to the publisher Haslinger, who
issued it in 1836. However, Haslinger intended to titil-
late the curiosity of the public by titling the sonata
Concert sans Orchestre, Op. 14, and in keeping with this
fanciful appellation, deleted the scherzi. Rather than
stimulating interest in the composition, the title
confused the bulk of Schumann's contemporaries, and
even the work's dedicatee, Moscheles, found the designation unwarranted. This sonata remains the least
familiar and most misunderstood of Schumann's large
scaled works, and it did not receive its public premier
until Brahms performed it in Vienna in 1862. Interestingly, Brahms' Sonata Op. 5, No. 3, also in F Minor, was
composed in the same year, 1853, that the Schumann
work was reissued. There are several striking similarities between the two works. In the revised edition
Schumann reinstated what was originally the second
scherzo, and changed the name to Troisieme grande
Sonate, Op. 14. This explains the curious circumstance
by which the second sonata is designated Op. 22, while
the Third Sonata bears an earlier opus number.
    The Sonata, Op. 14, is the most tautly organized of
Schumann's sonatas from the motivic standpoint, and
reveals a masterly exploitation of the possibilities
inherent in a single germinal idea. This motivic core
derives from the descending scalar theme of the
"Andantino" by Clara Weick. Schumann obviously
intended this motivic feature as the unifying factor
within each movement, and as the catalyst of the cyclic
form of the sonata. Though undeniably a masterwork,
this sonata is noticeably hampered by a dearth of lyrical
elements, and a number of critics have suggested that

the extensive cyclic format of the composition creates a lack of variety. Schumann's particular innate genius and aesthetic sensibilities led him to solve problems of formal structure and scope by way of musical frameworks better suited to smaller, self-contained forms than to the dynamic functional structures of Beethoven. However, a strictly modified conception of "sonata form" was not yet generally accepted in Schumann's era, and the occasionally disconcerting aspects of these sonatas should not obscure their inherent musical worth.

Note: The following editions contain Opus 14 in its entirety.

BOETTICHER, Wolfgang: Schumann Klavierwerke, Band IV (Henle).
SAUER, Emil: Complete Works of Robert Schumann, Volume 5 (Peters #2300E).
SCHUMANN, Clara: Piano Music of Robert Schumann, Series I (Dover).
SCHUMANN, Clara: Robert Schumann--Complete Works, Volume 3 (Kalmus #3925/Belwin-Mills).

Allegro

The <u>Allegro</u> opens with a forceful introductory outburst whose most prominent feature is a descending left hand scalar melody. This particular scalar descent is the principal material from which the entire sonata is constructed. Derived from the theme of the "Andantino" by Clara Wieck which is the basis for the third movement, this figure pervades and unifies the entire sonata. After this essential material is revealed, a cadence on the dominant leads into a passionate right hand melody featuring a constant syncopation. This section is based on the central descending scalar motive gaining in this version a compelling sweep and rhythmic drive. The left hand provides a restless accompaniment of broken chord sixteenth note arpeggiations. A brief modulating passage introduces the second subject.

Schumann presents the second theme, an inversion of the original motive, in the unusual tonality of C Minor. A rhythmically contrasting theme in Eb Major follows. The exposition ends with great verve as the first theme is repeated in the relative Major of Ab. This soaring cantabile passage is constructed on the principle of the ascending scale, the inversion of the descending scalar motto that generates the sonata.

After this dramatic exposition, the development seems all too brief and relies heavily on sequental material. Schumann revised this section extensively when reworking the sonata in 1853. Originally the passage in dotted rhythm contained broken chords divided between the hands. The rest of the development is primarily occupied with transformations of the first theme, leading to a tempestuous and dramatically charged climax. This expressive apogee is announced by four shattering minor chords that are repeated to telling effect. The opening arpeggiated chordal accompaniment of the first theme is resumed, and the entire section elaborates on the G7 chord (V of V), creating an overwhelming aura of tension and anticipation. The dominant is finally achieved, and the development subsides into a second inversion tonic harmony.

The imposing descending octaves of the opening herald the recapitulation. This first section is curiously extended before the arrival of the anticipated right hand melody. Otherwise, the recapitulation proceeds in the expected fashion. An unusual feature is now introduced. The entire development is reiterated, though with the appropriate key changes. The development rushes to an intensely passionate climax and immediately expands into the exciting coda. The coda is based on the opening theme, and roars to an imposing finish.

Tempo: Allegro ♩ = 76
Length: 250 measures
Technique: rapid broken chord figuration,
 syncopation, sudden dynamic changes,
 independent voices within a four voice
 texture, leaps, arpeggios, sustained and
 moving notes, wide legato LH skips

Scherzo (Db Major)

The Scherzo in Db Major, originally the second of
the two intended for the sonata, was deleted from the
first edition, but was assigned its current position in
Schumann's revision of 1853. It employs the familiar
ternary design typical of the form, and is based on the
alternation of two principal motives. The first of the
motives consists of a rhythmically buoyant melodic
pattern derived from the descending scalar pattern that
forms so much of the sonata. This first section, and
indeed the entire movement, relies heavily on parallel
and conjunct motion, with displaced accents heightening
the rhythmic vitality. The second eight bars exposes an
ascending scale as the other central motive. Schumann
clearly is accenting the cyclic rhetoric of the work
through the presentation of two prominent themes in
the Scherzo whose melodic shapes are analogous to the
first and second themes of the opening movement. As
in the first section, displaced accents create an aura of
a fantastic caprice. The third section is more
developmental in character, and employs such devices
as limited canonic imitation, sustained and moving
notes, and sequential and modulatory passages. This
very lengthy and difficult passage takes up both the
major themes of the movement, and having arrived at a
climax, concludes with a recapitulation of the opening

material, transposed a fourth higher to Gb Major.

A dramatic change to a key signature of first three, then two, sharps announces the trio. The first part features a rich four-part texture, enlivened by ascending arpeggiated and scalar figurations of the inner voices. The construction of the second important theme is most ingenious. The right hand proffers a simple diatonic melody in octaves while the left hand weaves a shimmering fabric of diminished seventh arpeggios that cross both over and under the melody. This passage is extended by episodic and developmental material, and soon the first theme of the trio returns. This theme is now developed primarily through the interjection of material based on the opening gesture of the Scherzo. The ensuing second section of the trio mirrors the first half, though here the music is transposed to Bb Major. A further modulation occurs, and the concluding developmental passage of the first half of the piece is recapitulated in the key of Db Major. An intensely chromatic bridge passage expands the principal motive of both scherzo and trio, and leads subtly but inevitably into a literal recapitulation of the Scherzo.

Tempo: Molto commodo ♩ = 116
Length: 238 measures
Technique: octaves, leaps, staccato chords,
    independent voices in thick texture,
    character changes, hands in close proximity

Quasi Variazioni

This extraordinary movement, the spiritual epicenter and motivating force of the sonata, is based on an earnest choral-like "Andantino" by Clara Wieck. The poignant scalar descent found in this theme is the central generating motive of both this sonata and several other important compositions. Cast in a free variation form, the Quasi Variazioni combine romantic vision with a simple yet expressive formal structure. Schumann's profound mastery of the variation structure is revealed in this powerful little work. The Andantino theme consists of three four-bar phrases, each of which is repeated after its initial statement.

Variation I utilizes an elegant four-part texture in which a lyrical right hand melody is counterpointed against billowing left hand sixteenth note passage work. This variation concludes with a hymn-like section, reminiscent of the opening. The second variation is pervaded by the continual gentle flow of triplets. Against this background the graceful melody is displayed. Although following the basic ABC structure of the theme, this variation expands both the range and scope of the composition. The third variation creates a more virtuosic 'effect through the use of a steady staccato eighth-note left hand, against which an accented offbeat syncopated melody is juxtaposed. This pattern prevails thoughout the variation, though another voice is briefly added. The agitated etude-like qualities of this section form an effective foil to the lyrical variations that it follows. The fourth and final variation is the most passionate of the set, and in a short period it achieves that type of noble yet fantastically imagined grandeur which is a notable feature of many much larger and technically demanding romantic masterpieces. Octaves and chord passages abound, though the work is less difficult than its effect would imply. A second ending introduces a dramatic coda, in which sensitive voicing creates the essential atmosphere of vivid enchantment. Three groups of F Minor chords conclude the work, and recall the mood of wistful melancholy that characterizes the opening. The touching beauty of this movement has occasionally led to its separate performance, and though this is not inconsistent with the performance practice of the romantic era, Schumann obviously intended that the Quasi Variazione be performed in the context of the sonata.

Tempo: Andantino ♩ = 84
Length: 145 measures
Technique: octaves, legato playing, wide hand
    stretches, careful pedal, cross-rhythms,
    sudden character changes, lyrical legato,
    sensitive voicing, 2 vs. 3, sustained and
    moving notes, wide rolled chords

Prestissimo possibile

Among the most technically formidable and emotionally challenging of Schumann's works, the
Prestissimo possibile is a wildly passionate movement.
To some extent defying formal designation, it is best
described as a sonata form with three subjects. This
seething triplet figure actually outlines ascending and
descending scalar motions in a manner consistent with
the unified motivic organization of the sonata.   The
triplet rhythm occurs constantly throughout the piece,
and is an important amalgamating force throughout the
work.   The opening subject reaches its apex with an
ornamented fermata, and procedes into a transitional
section of eight measures. Though this material plays a
conspicuous role later in the movement, it serves a less
individual purpose, and functions primarily as a bridge.
In this brief passage both hands alternate in presenting
the sixteenth-note rhythmic pattern, and the displaced
accents emphasize the ascending and descending scalar
nature of this material. Having modulated to Gb Major,
this tumultuous passage introduces the second subject.
This lyrical effusion presents the sixteenth-note triplet
figuration as a middle voice while a yearning melody is
produced through alternating hand-crossing and sonorous
bass octaves. The next section elaborates on the short
transition that linked the principal and second theme.
This material, though returning to the F Minor tonal

center, is developmental and modulatory, and employs the sixteenth-note perpetual motion figuration sequentially. This section is linked to a lyrical third subject marked "con anima," generally centered in Eb Major. Here a graceful melody pirouettes around the rushing onslaught of sixteenth-note figuration leading to the reappearance of the transitional and developmental material, now firmly centered in Bb Major. The next section is an extension and musically important developmental passage. It is pervaded by ascending scalar sixteenth-notes and the triplet rhythmic pattern leads to a restatement of the second subject, again in Gb Major.

The final "Piu presto" section employs a sequence based on the ascending scalar impulse, as well as the rhythmic motive introduced in the earlier extended bridge passages. Wide leaps and very difficult sixteenth-note triplet figurations will test even the most seasoned professional's technical prowess, and the difficulties are further increased. This grandiose section concludes on a diminished seventh chord, and rushes immediately onward.

The recapitulation opens with the first reappearance of the rondo theme, which is followed by an altered version of the eight-measure transitional material. The second subject is presented in Db Major. The transitional material eventually modulates to Bb Major and the third subject appears transposed to this key. Schumann now recapitulates the closing section. The climactic measures of this passage dissolve into a scintillating alternating hands trill (senze misura). This trill prepares the final statement of the principal theme which is followed by a brilliant coda marked "Piu presto." An abrupt transformation from minor to the parallel major concludes this expansive movement with a sweeping onrush of sonorous power.

The Prestissimo possibile is among the noblest and most stirring of Schumann's sonata movements, and forms a fitting conclusion to this powerful, if little-known masterwork.

Tempo: Prestissimo possibile $\quad \downarrow = 96$

Length: 358 measures

Technique: rapid figuration, long legato line, leaps, sudden dynamic changes, voicing, articulation, coherent structural organization, difficult 16th-note triplet figuration, endurance

ANHANG ZU OPUS 14,
(Supplement to Sonata No. 3) (1836-1866)

Schumann originally created two Scherzi for the F minor Sonata, both of which were deleted in the initial publication. The second edition reinstated what had been intended as the second of the Scherzi, but the first Scherzo, composed in 1836, was not issued until 1866 when it was posthumously published by C.F. Peters in conjuncture with the discarded Finale of Op. 22, as Scherzo und Presto passionata. The musical value of the F Minor Scherzi is possibly greater than that of its companion, and Schumann apparently excluded it from the Sonata only because of its lack of tonal contrast and extremely tenuous connection to the descending scalar "Clara" motive. Though seldom performed, this brilliant composition is of more than mere musicological interest, and remains a compelling exposition of Schumann's most extreme and fantastic romantic vein.

Note: The following edition contains the Supplement to Opus 14 in its entirety.

SCHUMANN, Clara: Piano Music of Robert Schumann, Series III (Dover).

Scherzo, F Minor

The wild and mercurial Scherzo employs the traditional ternary design with great imagination and aplomb. Extreme beat displacement, syncopation, and ambiguity of meter characterize the opening material. The metric complexity is augmented by such ternary dilemmas as double sixths, staccato broken triad figuration, and particularly by the fleeting and delicate nature of much of the music. An exciting "stringendo" transition leads to a reappearance of the principal theme, now transposed to C♯ Minor. At the indication "piu vivo," a new lyrical melody is introduced as an inner voice in the metrically displaced sustained and moving note figuration. A modulatory passage, bearing the key signature of C Major, leads to the recurrence of the Scherzo's initial theme. This agitated material reaches a powerful apogee, and the Trio begins immediately.

The Trio, in F Major, features a warm and expansive left hand melody in a sustained and moving note texture, accompanied by right hand triplets. The triplets are an important unifying force in both the Trio and the Scherzo, though in the Scherzo consistent beat displacement creates greater rhythmic complexity. Eventually the right hand takes up this melody, in a displaced, syncopated form, while the left hand presents staccato eighth notes in a sustained and moving note figuration. Another expressive melody is also recapitulated, though in an abbreviated and harmonically altered form. Schumann deftly increases the drive and density of the work in such a manner as to insure the searing intensity of climactic and dramatically abrupt ending. Among the most rhythmically inventive, and technically and interpretatively demanding of Schumann's works, this Scherzo is an inspired example of masterly compositional craft at the service of an impassioned and fervent imagination.

Tempo: Vivacissimo
Length: 171 measures
Technique: rhythmic and metric complexities,
    sustained and moving notes, 2 vs. 3,
    bravura figuration

KINDERSCENEN, Opus 15 (Scenes from Childhood) (1838)

In a March of 1838 letter to Clara, Schumann described "about 30 quaint little things from which I have selected 12 (sic) and called 'Kinderscenen'". Schumann intended these scenes to be reflections by adults, for adults. The titles were "merely hints as to treatment and interpretation" (Schumann). Conception and craftsmanship are kept extremely simple throughout the entire set. The melodic outlines of almost all the movements bear a resemblance to each other, and the key scheme is well integrated.

Note: The following editions contain Opus 15 in its entirety. Other sources are listed with each piece.

BANOWETZ, Joseph: Robert Schumann--An Introduction to the Composer and his Music--Album for the Young, Scenes from Childhood (GWM/Kjos).

IRMER, Otto von: Schumann Klavierwerke, Band I (Henle).

LIPSKY, Alexander: Robert Schumann Album I for Piano (Kalmus #3930/Belwin).

SAUER, Emil: Complete Works of Robert Schumann, Volume 4 (Peters #2300D).

SCHUMANN, Clara: Piano Music of Robert Schumann, Series I (Dover).

SCHUMANN, Clara: Robert Schumann--Complete Works, Volume 3 (Kalmus #3925/Belwin).

SHEALY, Alexander: Schumann--His Greatest Piano Solos (Ashley).

No. 1 **Von Fremden Ländern und**   Intermediate
Menschen, G Major (Of Strange Lands and People)
or "From Foreign Lands and People"

AGAY, Denes: Classics to Moderns, Intermediate,
    Vol. 37 (Consolidated).
BRADLEY, Richard: Bradley's Classics for Piano--
    The Third Level (Bradley).
BRADLEY, Richard: Bradley's Level Five Classics
    (Bradley).
DEXTER, Harry: Selected Piano Works--Schumann
    (Hansen).
HERRMANN, Kurt: Easy Schubert, Schumann, and
    Weber (Kalmus 9541/Belwin-Mills).
HUGHES, Edwin: Schumann--Master Series for the
    Young (G. Schirmer).
LANNING, Russell: Music by the Masters
    (Musicord/Belwin-Mills).
LYKE, ELLISTON, HARTLINE: Keyboard Musicianship,
    Book Two (Stipes).
NOONA, Walter and Carol: The Classical Pianist C
    (Heritage).
PALMER, Willard: Schumann--An Introduction to His
    Piano Works (Alfred).
VOGRICH, Max: Schumann Album for the Piano
    (G. Schirmer Vol. 100).
WEYBRIGHT, June: Course for Pianists, Book Six
    (Mills).

A mature musical sense, tonal control, and dynamic
sensitivity will heighten the effectiveness of this
"technically easy" work. The beauty and simplicity is
evident in the long line of the melody. The subdued
inner accompaniment is divided between the hands. The
bass sequences create countermelodic interest when the
performer observes the ritard indications and the

fermata sings. This first motive is the "germ" of nearly all the other pieces.

> Tempo: none indicated (Henle ♩ = 108)
> Length: 22 measures
> Technique: single note melodic line, broken
>   chord accompaniment divided between the
>   hands, tonal and dynamic control within a
>   limited range, melodic repetition,
>   double 3rds

No. 2 **Curiose Geschichte**, D Major   Intermediate
  (Curious Story) or "Kuriose Geschichte"

HUGHES, Edwin: Schumann—Master Series for the
  Young (G. Schirmer).

This straightforward and rhythmic piece in triple meter employs a very steady tempo. Two-note appoggiaturas are played quicky on the beat. The martial theme is contrasted by unison legato lines between the hands that rely more on finger legato than on the pedal for smoothness.

> Tempo: none indicated (Henle ♩ = 112)
>   (Kalmus ♩ = 132)
> Length: 40 measures
> Technique: chordal technique, strong rhythm,
>   wide hand stretches, inner voices, tonal
>   control

No. 3 **Hasche-Mann,** B Minor   <u>Advancing Intermediate</u>
(Catch Me)

BASTIEN, James: Piano Literature, Vol. 4 (GWM/Kjos).
NOONA, Walter and Carol: The Classical Pianist C
    (Heritage).

Light touches and flexible rhythms give an air of a
slavic dance.   Legato and staccato touches are
intricately combined and all are kept light and clear.
The entire work is played as fast as can be controlled.
Although overall dynamics are subdued, occasional *sf*
and *sfp* accents occur.
    Tempo: none indicated (Henle ♩ = 138)
                (Kalmus ♩ = 120)
    Length: 21 measures
    Technique: rapid staccato running 16th notes,
        leaps, 2-note slurs, arpeggios broken
        between the hands, legato and staccato
        combinations

No. 4 **Bittendes Kind,** D Major   <u>Intermediate</u>
(Entreating Child)

This plaintive, wistful piece has a limpid sound. It
is composed of four measure phrases, each containing a
piano theme and its exaggerated *pianissimo* echo.
Coordination between the hands is needed as accompanimental figures are in two-note groups, taken first by
the right hand and then by the left hand. The final A

chord provides an evocative conclusion to the piece.
>Tempo: none indicated (Henle ♪= 138)
>>(Kalmus ♪= 88)
>Length: 17 measures
>Technique: tonal control, accompaniment
>>divided between the hands, melody and
>>accompaniment in same hand, legato
>>playing, limited dynamic range

No. 5 Glückes Genug, D Major   Advancing Intermediate
(Perfect Happiness) or "Contentedness"

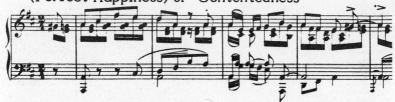

FERGUSON, Howard: A Keyboard Anthology, Second
>Series, Book III (Assoc. Board/Belwin-Mills).
LANNING, Russell: Music by the Masters
>(Musicord/Belwin-Mills).
VOGRICH, Max: Schumann Album for the Piano,
>(G. Schirmer Vol. 100).

A naive sort of happiness is expressed by this fast-
paced piece. Hands shift quickly, with the right hand
taking sustained and moving notes with the melody on
top, and the agile left hand moving between eighth and
sixteenth notes. Altered notes throughout help to
create a bouncy, circus-like character. An important
dialogue occurs between the hands (contrapuntal nature
of the piece), capturing the "Perfect Happiness."
>Tempo: none indicated (Henle ♪= 132)
>>(Kalmus ♩= 72)
>Length: 24 measures
>Technique: melody and accompaniment in
>>same hand, imitation, hand independence,
>>legato octaves, wide hand stretches

No. 6 **Wichtige Begebenheit,** Advancing Intermediate
A Major, (Important Event)

AGAY, Denes: An Anthology of Piano Music, Romantic
  Period, Vol. III (Yorktown).
ALFRED (Publisher): Schumann—18 of His Easiest Piano
  Selections.
ALFRED (Publisher): Schumann—29 of His Most Popular
  Piano Selections.
BASTIEN, James: Piano Literature, Vol. 4 (GWM/Kjos).
NOVIK, Ylda: Young Pianist's Guide to Schumann
  (Studio P/R).
PALMER, Willard: Schumann—An Introduction to His
  Piano Works (Alfred).
PALMER and HALFORD: The Romantic Era—An
  Introduction to the Piano Music (Alfred).

This martial piece in 3/4 is a good technical study
for *fortissimo* right hand chords and left hand octaves.
Heavy accents are performed with vitality throughout
the various *forte* dynamic levels.
           Tempo: none indicated (Henle ♩ = 138)
                        (Kalmus ♩ = 120)
           Length: 24 measures
           Technique: strong rhythm, chordal and octave
                  sequences and technique, careful pedal,
                  dotted rhythms, *fortissimo* playing

No. 7 **Träumerei,** F Major (Dreaming) Intermediate
or "Reverie"

ALFRED (Publisher): Schumann--18 of His Easiest Piano
Selections.

ALFRED (Publisher): Schumann--29 of His Most Popular
Piano Selections.

BRADLEY, Richard: Bradley's Level Seven Classics
(Bradley).

BRIMHALL, John: My First Book of Classics--Schumann
(Hansen).

COLUMBIA (Publisher): Claire de Lune and Moonlight
Sonata + 24 Popular Classics.

DANA, Walter: My Favorite Classics--Level Four
(Hansen).

DEXTER, Harry: Selected Piano Works--Schumann
(Hansen).

DEXTER, Harry: The Young Pianist's Schumann
(Hansen).

FROST, Bernice: Popular Classics for Piano
(J. Fischer/Belwin-Mills).

HEINRICHSHOFEN (Publisher): Schumann--Easier
Favorites (Peters No.4052).

HUGHES, Edwin: Schumann--Master Series for the
Young (G. Schirmer).

KAIL, Robert: Easy Schumann Piano Pieces
(Columbia #F1035PAX).

NOONA, Walter and Carol: Classical Patterns C
(Heritage).

NOVIK, Ylda: Young Pianist's Guide to Schumann
(Studio P/R).

PALMER, Willard: Schumann--The First Book for Young
Pianists (Alfred).

PALMER, Willard: Schumann--An Introduction to His
Piano Works (Alfred).

PALMER and HALFORD: The Romantic Era--An
Introduction to the Piano Music (Alfred).

SCHIRMER (Publisher): 59 Piano Solos You Like to Play.

THOMPSON, John: Modern Course for Piano, The
Fourth Grade Book (Willis).

VOGRICH, Max: Schumann Album for the Piano
(G. Schirmer Vol. 100).

WARNER (Publisher): Super Classics for Piano--59 of
the World's Most Famous Solos (#PF0164).

WEISMANN, Wilhelm: Romantic Masters
(Peters No.5033).
WEYBRIGHT, June: Course for Pianists, Book Six
(Mills).

To achieve the expressive phrasing of this popular sentimental piece, the melodic lines and harmonies should not be blurred by the damper pedal. Large hands may be a help in mastering sustained and moving notes and spans of a tenth. The counterpoint of the occasional secondary melody is of interest and can compliment the top melody.

> Tempo: none indicated (Henle ♩ = 100)
> (Kalmus ♩ = 80)
> Length: 24 measures
> Technique: melody in high register with
> thickly scored accompaniment, clear inner
> voicing, tonal control, pedal control, long
> melodic line, expressive playing

No. 8 **Am Camin,** F Major,   Intermediate
(By the Fireside) or "Am Kamin"

PALMER, Willard: Schumann—An Introduction to His
Piano Works (Alfred).
VOGRICH, Max: Schumann Album for the Piano
(G. Schirmer Vol. 100).

The figuration and overlapping hands tend to make the dynamics of this intimate fireside scene a challenge to the performer. The overall sound is delicate and interpreted within the *p-mf* range. Accent marks occur on various strong and weak beats and help indicate musical emphasis and direction. The coda uses double notes and a legato melody to bring the piece to a slow, ritardando ending.

Tempo: none indicated (Henle ♩ = 138)
(Kalmus ♩ = 108)
Length: 33 measures
Technique: wide hand stretches, inner voices,
single note melody in high register,
syncopation, pedal control

No. 9 **Ritter vom Steckenpferd,** C Major   Intermediate
(Knight of the Rocking Horse)

The vitality of this work is structured around a
syncopated pattern on the third beat.   A contrast of
rhythmic drive and stasis is brought about through the
use of harmonic tension and pedal points. The left hand
emphasizes the melodic lines. The damper pedal recommended by Clara Schumann for the last eight measures
adds to the excitement and conclusion of this highly
patterned piece.

Tempo: none indicated (Henle ♩ = 80)
(Kalmus ♩ = 76)
Length: 24 measures
Technique: pedal points, accurate rhythm,
hand independence, leaps, wide LH hand
stretches, careful pedal

No. 10 **Fast zu Ernst,** G# Minor   Early Advanced
"Almost Too Serious"

120 **Kinderscenen**

This lovely work is characterized by one mood within a similar texture throughout. The upper melodic voice is conceived horizontally with phrases terminating at the seven fermata points. Proper hand coordination will facilitate the constant overlapping positions. The accompanying figures are dynamically reserved within a legato p to pp level throughout.

Tempo: none indicated (Henle ♩ = 69)
        (Kalmus ♪ = 104)

Length: 57 measures
Technique: overlapping hand positions, wide LH leaps, syncopation, pedal control, expressive and legato playing

No. 11 **Fürchtenmachen,**   Advancing Intermediate
      G Major (Frightening)

This sectional work makes use of intellectual and musical contrasts in its execution. Thematic and tempo changes between sections are coordinated effectively. This dramatic selection contains many similarities to "Fabel," Opus 12, No. 6. Both have introductory material that functions as an interlude: legato melodies with off-beat staccato accompaniment, and sectional forms that integrate fine tonal control of mood and tempo.

Tempo: none indicated (Henle ♩ = 96)
        (Kalmus ♩ = 108)

Length: 48 measures
Technique: syncopation, sudden dyamic, mood, and tempo changes, inner voices, leaps in LH accompaniment, legato vs. staccato

No. 12 **Kind im**   Advancing Intermediate
Einschlummern, E Minor (Child Falling Asleep)

AGAY, Denes: An Anthology of Piano Music--
   Romantic Period, Vol. III (Yorktown).
ALFRED (Publisher): Schumann--29 of His Most Popular
   Piano Selections.

    This lovely lullaby in 2/4 creates a sustained mood
with minimal melodic movement supported by beautiful
harmonies. A rhythmic motive is found in dialogue
using cross-phrasing between hands. Sensitive nuances
within the *p* to *pp* dynamic levels are important. The
key scheme is E Minor - E Major - E Minor. The *ppp*
harmonic chord of A Minor is befitting the final long
decrescendo.
           Tempo: none indicated (Henle ♪ = 92)
                 (Kalmus ♪ = 80)
        Length: 32 measures
        Technique: independent voices, melody in
           inner LH, full chords in *pp* dynamic range,
           careful pedal, tonal control

No. 13 **Der Dichter Spricht,**   Advancing Intermediate
   G Major, (The Poet Speaks)

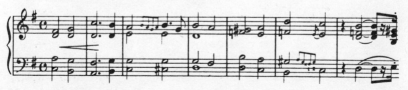

ALFRED (Publisher): Schumann--18 of His Easiest Piano
   Selections.

ALFRED (Publisher): Schumann—29 of His Most Popular
    Piano Selections.
PALMER, Willard: Schumann—An Introduction to his
    Piano Works (Alfred).

Der Dichter Spricht has an improvisatory sound that
incorporates chorale-like homophony and recitative
sections.   Measure 12 is an extended cadenza with no
bar lines.   All musical elements are at a premium.
Sensitivity to phrase, shape, ritard, tone, and dynamics
contribute to a successful performance.   Schumann's
penchant for epilogues finds a beautiful and typical
expression here.

> Tempo: none indicated (Henle ♩ = 112)
>   (Kalmus ♩ = 92)
> Length: 26 measures
> Technique: 4-voice choral texture in   and
>   dynamic range, rubato, single note
>   recitative passage, tonal control

KREISLERIANA, Opus 16 (1838)   <u>Early Advanced</u>

Subtitled "Phantasien," <u>Kreisleriana</u> was composed in four days in April of 1838. It was published by Haslinger the same year, and was dedicated to Chopin although it was originally intended for Clara. The eight pieces are intended to be played as a set. In explaining the name Schumann stated that "the title means nothing to any but Germans. Kreisler is one of E. T. A. Hoffman's creations, an eccentric, wild and witty conductor." The model of this character was Ludwig Bohner (1787-1860). "He was like a lion with a thorn in his foot...but the old fire flashed out now and again." In his letters to Clara, Schumann stated, "Play my Kreisleriana often, a positively wild love is in some of the movements, and your life and mine, and the way you look."

While the pieces are not as technically difficult as some of Schumann's earlier works, they are "wonderfully intricate" and have a high degree of personal musicianship. They are basically in ternary form or simple rondo with contrasting sections. The B E D A motive (or "Clara's theme") prevails throughout.

Note: The following editions contain Opus 16 in its entirety.

BOETTICHER, Wolfgang: Schumann Klavierwerke, Band III (Henle).
SAUER, Emil: Complete Works of Robert Schumann, Volume 2 (Peters #2300B).
SCHUMANN, Clara: Piano Music of Robert Schumann, Series I (Dover).
SCHUMANN, Clara: Robert Schumann--Complete Works, Volume 3 (Kalmus #3925/Belwin-Mills).

No. 1, D Minor

The incessant sixteenth note triplet figures throughout this piece provide a tempestuous opening to the
set. The unusual phrasing joining the third note of each
triplet with the first note of the next with the accents
on the beat provides the driving force of this wonderfully brilliant movement. The soft middle section with
its even accompaniment figures that move between the
hands provides a lovely contrast to the perpetual motion
A sections. The movement ends with a powerful
crescendo.

> Tempo: Äusserst bewegt (Extremely agitated)
> Length: 74 measures
> Technique: complex melodic slurs, rapid
>   figuration, sudden dynamic changes, octaves

No. 2, Bb Major

The lovely octave theme keeps coming back in this
rondo-like movement. The initial section is gentle and
reflective in nature with good tonal control and a
smooth legato touch. Using a different tone color, the
Intermezzo I is busy and cheerful with a staccato bass
part taking the melody in many different directions.
The A section reappears in the original tempo.
Intermezzo II has an octave bass accompaniment with

the right hand rhythmic figure ⌐⌐ throughout. The
thick and intricate Langsamer (erstes Tempo) section

has important voicing and is a lovely bridge to the original A section, which ends the movement with a simple Adagio ending.

>Tempo: Sehr innig und nicht zu rasch (Very sincerely and not too fast)
>Intermezzo I--Sehr lebhaft (Very vivacious)
>Intermezzo II--Etwas bewegter (Somewhat more agitatedly)
>Langsamer (erstes Tempo) (Slower--original tempo)
>Erstes tempo (Original tempo)
>Length: 174 measures
>Technique: legato octaves, legato double notes careful pedal, simultaneous legato and staccato, arpeggios with quick register shifts

No. 3, G Minor

The initial rhythmic figure of the sixteenth note triplets ending with a staccato eight note propels this movement in a clear, light manner. The Etwas langsamer section has many large stretches and a very legato feel. The A section comes back to the driving, energetic rhythmic figure. The coda, characterized by clear accented octaves in quarter notes, ends this lively movement.

>Tempo: Sehr aufgeregt (Very agitatedly)
>Length: 166 measures
>Technique: rapid 3-note slurs, cross-rhythms, wide stretches, legato

No. 4, Bb Major

The improvisatory nature of this movement enhances the slow sad mood. The chordal section, with smooth voicing of the melody lines of the top and bottom notes, contains many sustained and moving notes and has almost a dissonant sound. The middle section is a lovely flowing movement with quarter note parallel melodies in both the left and right hands. An accompaniment of sixteenth notes is divided between the hands. The beautiful adagio ending on a D Major chord acts as a bridge to the next movement.

Tempo: Sehr langsam (Very slow) ♪ = 66
   Bewegter (Agitatedly)
Length: 27 measures
Technique: tonal control, figuration
   distributed between the hands, legato

No. 5, G Minor

This movement begins very softly and lightly with phrases of sixteenth notes ending in an eighth note and a sixteenth rest. The section beginning at bar 19 after the second ending, is bright and improvisatory. The middle section after the double bar and the fermata is distant and reflective using quarter note chords and eighth note passages in the unison. The *fortissimo* climax fades to a *pianissimo* before this section is repeated. It then settles back into the first section with a bright and propulsive sound. The second edition ends the piece in G Minor, while the first edition ends in the dominant.

> Tempo: Sehr lebhaft (Very lively)
> Length: 161 measures
> Technique: 2-note slurs, rhythmic repetition,
>   independent voices in imitation

No. 6, Bb Major

A mellow, beautiful melody with a singing tone exemplifies this slow movement. The dynamic level is mostly *pianissimo* with a few sf chords to add spice. This is a lovely contrast to the other movements with its moments of repose and reflection. There are many immediate and decisive changes of tempo. The lovely adagio ending is fitting for this serene movement.

> Tempo: Sehr langsam (Very slow) ♪ = 84
> Length: 39 measures
> Technique: tonal control, double notes,
>   independent voices, pedal control

No. 7, C Minor

The clear passagework, decisive rhythm, and sharp accents in this movement provide a lively contrast to No. 6. The first section has rolled accompaniment chords in the bass with many diminished seventh passages. The fast and furious pace will be fun to play and to listen to. The middle section has traditional, classical sound passagework in a predominantly *forte* and *fortissimo* setting. The Etwas langsamer ending is like a hymn bringing this flashy movement to an unusual ending with a release of tension. The portamento indications give this passage a breathless quality.

Tempo: Sehr rasch (Very fast)

Length: 118 measures

Technique: finger independence, perpetual
motion figuration, wide leaps, widely spaced
rolled chords

No. 8, G Minor

This movement is the least captivating of the Kreisleriana. It starts with a *pianissimo*, quick dotted rhythm which can become very monotonous. The middle section is a hand-cross part that starts in the bass of the keyboard. With many repeated chords and some disso-nant sounds, it ends with a return to the rhythmically pervasive sound with a decrescendo to *ppp* played in a light legato manner.

Tempo: Schnell und spielend (Fast and playful)

Length: 146 measures

Technique: *pp* staccato touch, rhythmic
repetition, leaps, syncopation, repeated
chords, wide dynamic range

PHANTASIE, C Major, Opus 17   <u>Very Difficult</u>
  (Fantasy) or "Fantasie" (1839)

During the decade of the 1830's a group of admirers and townspeople formed a committee to erect a monument in Bonn to that city's most distinguished native son, Ludwig van Beethoven. Appeals for contributions were issued throughout Europe, and Schumann, always devoted to Beethoven's art, felt obliged to comply with this request. In 1836 the composer decided that the most appropriate means of aiding in the fund raising process would be to donate the proceeds of a specially composed work to the memorial committee. Consequently, Schumann began composing a large three movement work for piano to be ceremoniously entitled <u>Obolon auf Beethovens Monument: Ruinen, Trophaen, Palmen: grosse Sonata fur das Pianoforte, fur Beethovens Monument, von Florestan und Eusebius.</u> Schumann immediately presented an elaborate scheme for the publication of the work, even detailing suggestions for the cover design, to the publisher Kistner. However, the work awaited publication until 1839, when bearing the title <u>Phantasie</u>, Op. 17, it was issued under the imprint of Brietkopf and Härtel.

Unfortunately, by 1839 the original impetus behind the drive to erect the Beethoven monument had dwindled. At this juncture, Franz Liszt, like Schumann an ardent admirer of Beethoven, stepped in, and through the expenditure of intense personal energy as well as financial reserves, the brilliant Hungarian was able to rescue the project from certain oblivion. Out of gratitude to Liszt's unstinting efforts, and to reciprocate the virtuoso for a generous article praising Schumann's music, the composer dedicated the <u>Phantasie</u> to Liszt. Though the friendship between the two men was later to deteriorate, Schumann was electrified by a private performance of the work that Liszt gave while visiting Leipzig in 1839. Overzealous admirers of Schumann have regularly criticized Liszt's failure to publicly program the <u>Phantasie</u>, though the virtuoso was an early and fervant champion of

Schumann's work. Many of Liszt's pupils testified to the aging master's high opinion of the Phantasie and its creator, and he in turn dedicated the monumental Sonata in B Minor S. 178 to Schumann. Both Sonata and Phantasie remain a compelling testament to this deep if unfortunately truncated friendship.

The influence of Beethoven naturally marks the Phantasie. Aside from the motivically important song quotation from An die ferne Geliebte found in the opening, Schumann had originally included a fragment of the "Allegretto" of Beethoven's Symphony No. 7, Op. 92 in the final movement. The composer's choice of sonata form, as well as the cyclic symphonic scope and expressive depth of the work, pay tribute to the great master of the structural design. The composition is prefaced by an enigmatic motto from Schlegel:

> "Durch alle Tone tonet
> Im bunten Erdentraum
> Ein leiser Ton gezogen
> Fur den der heimlich lauschet."

> "Through all the tones that sound
> In Earth's unquiet dream
> There is one gentle note
> For the secret listener."

This mysterious "note" appears to be a veiled reference to the beloved Clara, and so called "Clara" motives, descending scalar phrases, are prevalent in the work. It is appropriate that the Phantasie should combine the structural unity and formal inventiveness of Beethoven with the emotional warmth and tender passion with which Clara inspired Schumann. When not forced to comply with the structures and conventions of strict sonata form, Schumann's imaginative fantasy bursts forth, and this great masterpiece is one of the composer's most sublime creations.

Note: The following editions contain Opus 17 in its
   entirety.

BOETTICHER, Wolfgang: Schumann Klavierwerke,
   Band IV (Henle).
SAUER, Emil: Complete Works of Robert Schumann,
   Volume 3 (Peters #2300C).
SCHUMANN, Clara: Piano Music of Robert Schumann,
   Series III (Dover).
SCHUMANN, Clara: Robert Schumann--Complete
   Works, Volume 3 (Kalmus #3925/Belwin-Mills).

I. **Durchaus phantastisch und leidenschaftlich
   vorzutragen**

   The <u>Phantasie</u> opens in a world of veiled sensuous
beauty.   Schumann considered entitling the work,
"Ruinen" (ruins), an epithet entirely appropriate to the
movement's melancholy grandeur. Against a difficult
background of perpetual motion left hand sixteenth
notes, a poignant octave melody is projected.   This
melody, like the principal themes of the sonatas,
features a descending scalar motion. Schumann appears
to have associated this motive with Clara, and indeed a
similar melody, utilizing the same pitches, is found in
the "Nocturne" from her <u>Soirees Musicales</u>, Op. 6. This
material unfolds in broad expansive paragraphs of
enormous expressive potential.   A stirring transition
leads from this theme to the second major melodic
area.   The second subject is a lyrical melody
accompanied by a sixteenth note figuration in the left
hand. It is derived from both the "Clara" descending
motive and the quotation from Beethoven's song "An die
ferne geliebte" which haunts this movement. A triplet
rhythm now emerges, and the second thematic group

concludes with a sweeping octave unison passage. A brilliantly inventive passage ensues, in which material derived from the two principal themes is interrupted by episodic interjections.   Numerous tempo changes, startling modulations, and syncopated rhythms heighten the atmosphere of extreme romantic fantasy.   A glittering climax is achieved and the work subsides into a tranquil bridge passage.

The central episode, bearing the indication "Im legendenton" (in the style of a legend), is a seemingly self-contained interlude. However, the expansive theme of this section actually derives from an inner voice that begins in the 33rd measure of the opening section. When this factor is realized, the section clearly corresponds to the development section of the sonata/allegro. The Beethoven quotation appears again, though more agitated.

An abbreviated recapitulation begins in mid-stream, and the second theme appears immediately, transposed to G Minor. The magical fantasia section also recurs. At the conclusion of this extraordinary movement the Beethoven quotation heard earlier is elaborated upon. A fragment of the sixth song of Beethoven's cycle An die Ferne Geliebte, Op. 98, it appears at an adagio tempo. The text of this melodic quotation reads: "Accept, then, these melodies that I sang for you, my love," and must surely be regarded as Schumann's cry of longing to the "distant beloved" Clara, whom he was not permitted to see, as well as a tribute to the memory of the revered Beethoven. The movement closes in hushed tranquility, with a lovely coda of perennial freshness.

Tempo: Durchaus phantastisch und leidenschaftlich vorzutragen (To be played throughout with fantasy and passion) ♩ = 80

Length: 309 measures

Technique: rapid accompanying figures, octaves, trills and melody in one hand, large leaps, sudden dynamic changes, long legato lines, sudden tempo changes, difficult pedal requirements, 5 vs. 2, sustained and moving notes, voicing problems

II. Mässig, Durchaus energisch (Eb Major)

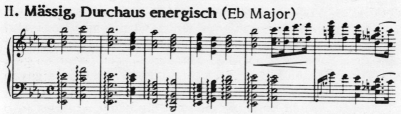

At one point Schumann considered entitling the imposing and monumental second movement of the Phantasie "Trophaen" (trophies) or Triumphal Arch. This work, featuring a grand, march-like theme is in sonato-rondo form. The boisterous gaiety of the piece, as well as structural considerations, mark its spiritual affinities to the Scherzi of Beethoven. The broadly expansive march tune, utilizing wide and rather taxing rolled chords, opens the movement. It is soon followed by a theme pervaded by an insistent dotted rhythm which is expanded and developed in a lengthy exploratory episode that precedes the reappearance of the opening theme. Though the writing contains some formidable technical difficulties, the exacting synthesis of chordal and contrapuntal textures is handled with consummate imagination and skill.

The central section of the movement, bearing the indication "Etwas langsamer" (a little slower) is in the key of Ab Major. This rather whimsical material is an effective and timely foil to the martial pomp of the surrounding march. This episode employs a three part structure, in which the opening section is marked by unusual and fleeting syncopated beat displacements. This material is further enlivened by the introduction of a vivacious dotted rhythm, and the "development" concludes with material derived from the central section of the opening march. The first two strains of the march are now recapitulated, but Schumann replaces the expected final appearance of the broad principle theme with a fiery and impetuous coda, marked "Viel bewegter" (faster or Piu animato) tempo.

Perhaps the most technically unmitigating passage of Schumann's piano works, the difficulties are at least proportional to the profound and expansive emotional warmth of this stirring composition.

> Tempo: Massig. Durchaus energisch
> (Moderately, with energy throughout) $\downarrow$ = 66
> Length: 260 measures
> Technique: large rolled chords, sustained and
> moving notes, melody and accompaniment in
> same hand, octaves, difficult pedallings,
> syncopations, wide leaps

III. Langsam getragen

   The final movement of the Phantasie is a poignantly
lyrical work. An extensive introductory episode exposes
the arpeggiated eighth note triplets that pervade the
piece. Many germinal phrases and relationships are
presented in this section, though none of this material is
literally restated in the course of the work. After this
passage of sublime mood setting, the first of the two
principal melodic outpourings is introduced.   This
material consists of a descending right hand melody in
duplets, which is juxtaposed against the pervasive left
hand triplet accompaniment. A brief interlude in Ab
Major, whose arpeggiated harmonies recall the opening
measures, leads to a new theme, marked "Etwas
Bewegter" (somewhat faster). This new melody appears
as a titillating fragment, but soon dissolves into the
arpeggiated texture. This process is repeated, and the
soaring melody, implied but never previously stated, is
revealed in a series of expansive paragraphs of tender,
yet rhapsodic beauty. The music, having modulated to F
Major, grows more intense, and the work is propelled to
a powerful and sonorous climax.

   Although avoiding repetition of the opening passage,
the remainder of the material is now recapitulated,
though here it passes through the remote key of Db

Major before returning to the opening tonic of C. An inspired and noble climax is achieved once again, followed by a final impassioned surge in the arpeggiated harmonies of the coda. This aura of transfigured radiance is illustrative of the composer's projected title, "Wreath of Stars," and the movement, which originally contained yet another quote from Beethoven (the Allegretto of the Seventh Symphony, Op. 92), is a glowing testament to the emotional and intellectual lodestars that guided Schumann's artistic destiny.

> Tempo: Langsam getragen. Durchweg leise zu
>   halten (Slow and sustained. Keep it soft
>   throughout) $\downarrow$. = 66
> Length: 142 measures
> Technique: smooth broken chords, melody and
>   accompaniment in same hand, cross-
>   rhythms, dotted rhythms, voicing, 2 vs. 3

ARABESKE, C Major, Opus 18 (1839)   <u>Early Advanced</u>
    (Arabesque)

Note: The following editions contain Opus 18 in its
    entirety.

ALFRED (Publisher): Schumann--29 of his Most Popular
    Piano Selections.
BOETTICHER, Wolfgang: Schumann Klavierwerke,
    Band II (Henle).
DEXTER, Harry: Selected Piano Works--Schumann
    (Hansen).
LIPSKY, Alexander: Robert Schumann--Album I for
    Piano (Kalmus #3930/Belwin-Mills).
SAUER, Emil: Complete Works of Robert Schumann,
    Volume 1 (Peters #2300A).
SCHUMANN, Clara: Piano Music of Robert Schumann,
    Series I (Dover).
SCHUMANN, Clara: Robert Schumann--Complete
    Works, Volume 3 (Kalmus #3925/Belwin-Mills).
SHEALY, Alexander: Schumann--His Greatest Piano
    Solos (Ashley).
VOGRICH, Max: Schumann Album for the Piano
    (G. Schirmer Vol. 100).

        The <u>Arabeske</u> is rare among Schumann's composi-
tions of this time in that it is not part of a cycle.
Written in simple rondo form (ABACA), this piece is a
favorite of both performers and audiences.   The A
section consists of a charming legato melody in C Major
with a broken chord accompaniment, one note of which
is taken by the right hand.   The B section, in E Minor,
presents a four voice texture with a simple melody in
the soprano, generally doubled by the tenor, and
accompanied by simple harmonies in the alto and bass

voices. An expressive bridge back to the A section presents excursions through remote key areas. Unfortunately the <u>Arabeske</u> is exceptionally long for the amount of thematic materal presented. The brief second section provides rhythmic contrast in the dotted accompaniment to a scalar melody. The A section returns in its entirety and the piece closes with a quiet reflective coda.

Tempo: Leicht und zart (Lightly and tenderly)
♩ = 152
Length: 224 measures
Technique: smooth broken chords against
legato melody, some widely spaced chords,
singing tone, difficult pedalling, flexible
line, appoggiaturas

BLUMENSTÜCK,Db Major, Opus 19   <u>Early Advanced</u>
(Flower Piece) (1839)

Note: The following editions contain Opus 19 in its
entirety.

BOETTICHER, Wolfgang: Schumann Klavierwerke,
Band II (Henle).
LIPSKY, Alexander: Robert Schumann--Album I for
Piano (Kalmus #3930/Belwin-Mills).
SAUER, Emil: Complete Works of Robert Schumann,
Volume 1 (Peters #2300A).
SCHUMANN, Clara: Piano Music of Robert Schumann,
Series I (Dover).
SCHUMANN, Clara: Robert Schumann--Complete
Works, Volume 3 (Kalmus #3925/Belwin-Mills).
SHEALY, Alexander: Schumann--His Greatest Piano
Solos (Ashley).
VOGRICH, Max: Schumann Album for the Piano,
(G. Schirmer Vol. 100).

Originally entitled "Guirlande," Schumann described
this piece as "Variations but not upon any theme." The
sections are clearly marked in the score as I, II, III, II,
IV, V, Minore II and IV, being slightly varied upon each
appearance.   The <u>Blumenstück</u> is characterized by a
rhythmic figuration (alternating melody and accompaniment notes in a continuous flow of eighth notes) that is
constant throughout the composition. In each variation
the "falling" motive associated with Clara is woven into
the music. This is not surprising when one considers
that the <u>Blumenstück</u> was written the year before
Schumann's marriage.

Tempo: Leise bewegt (Moving Softly) ♩ = 69
Length: 157 measures
Technique: melody and accompaniment in
  same hand, opposing touches, rhythmic
  flexibility

HUMORESKE, Bb Major, Opus 20 (1839)   <u>Very Difficult</u>
(Humoresque)

Note: The following editions contain Opus 20 in its
  entirety.

SAUER, Emil: Complete Works of Robert Schumann,
  Volume 3 (Peters #2300C).
SCHUMANN, Clara: Piano Music of Robert Schumann,
  Series II (Dover).
SCHUMANN, Clara: Robert Schumann--Complete
  Works, Volume 4 (Kalmus #3926/Belwin-Mills).

"I have been all week at the piano, composing,
writing, laughing, and crying, all at once. You will find
this state of things nicely described in my opus 20, the
Grosse Humoreske--twelve sheets composed in a week."
So wrote Schumann to Simonin de Sire, his Belgian
acquaintance. <u>Humoreske</u> is a sprawling and personal
work that covers a broad spectrum of moods and pianistic devices. The title seems applicable not to any
humorous aspects of the piece, but to the older sense of
"humors" as quirks or caprices. A tremendous, innate
musicianship will project the rapid character changes
and hold the many varied sections together. In some
ways the piece is a compendium of the musical and
technical devices characteristic of Schumann. The
"hastig" section has a notated "innere Stimme" (inner
voice) which is not meant to be played. The "Intermezzo" contains difficult octave passages, while many
double sixths are found in the "Einfach un zart" section. The listener may find <u>Humoreske</u> difficult to
follow, and there has been much speculation as to a
secret master theme which might provide the key to the
organization of the piece. Yet the individual sections
do cohere, never straying far from the central Bb

tonality. The ending is a marvelous and fitting finish to this major work.

Tempo: Einfach (Simply) ♩ = 80
Etwas lebhafter (Somewhat livelier)
Sehr rasch und leicht (Very fast and light)
♩ = 138
Noch rascher (Even faster)
Erstes tempo (First tempo)
Wie im Anfang (As at the beginning)
Hastig (Hastily) ♩ = 126
Wie ausser Tempo
Nach und nach immer lebhafter und
stärker
(Gradually livelier and stronger)
Wie vorher (As before)
Adagio
Einfach und zart (Simply and tenderly)
♩ = 100
Intermezzo ♩ = 126
Innig (Inwardly) ♩ = 116
Sehr lebhaft (Very lively) ♩ = 76
Stretto
Mit einigem Pomp (With some pomp) ♩ = 92
Zum Beschluss (In conclusion) ♩ = 112
Adagio
Allegro

Length: 965 measures

Technique: fast chordal figuration, arpeggios,
rapid octaves and scales, double notes,
endurance, pedal, opposing touches, full
chords, double 6ths, awkward hand stretches

NOVELLETTEN, Opus 21 (Novelettes)

"I have composed a shocking amount for you, jests, Egmont stories, family scenes with fathers, a wedding-- and called the whole Novelletten." So Schumann wrote to Clara in February of 1838, and on other occasions he was able to speak of the Novelletten as almost entirely inspired by her. Opus 21 is the largest collection of the period, with each piece well able to stand on its own. They are untitled, and the dedication is to Adolph Henselt. Schumann admitted to a friend that the content of Novelletten was more melancholy than humorous.

Note: The following editions contain Opus 21 in its
    entirety. Other sources are listed with each piece.

BOETTICHER, Wolfgang: Schumann Klavierwerke,
    Band II (Henle).
SAUER, Emil: Complete Works of Robert Schumann,
    Volume 2 (Peters #2300B).
SCHUMANN, Clara: Piano Music of Robert Schumann,
    Series II (Dover).
SCHUMANN, Clara: Robert Schumann--Complete
    Works, Volume 4 (Kalmus #3926/Belwin-Mills).

No. 1, F Major   Early Advanced

VOGRICH, Max: Schumann Album for the Piano
    (G. Schirmer Vol. 100).

This novellette is a more easily grasped study in contrasts than many of Schumann's other works. The robust opening with its detached, square chords is alternated with a smooth, lyrical trio in an accessible sonata/rondo form. Chord and octave technique and long melodic lines are not excessively difficult, making this an excellent teaching and performing piece. It has long been the popular favorite of the set.

> Tempo: Markirt und kräftig (Marcato and
>   powerful) ♩= 108
> Length: 137 measures
> Technique: large blocked chords, octaves,
>   legato melody with broken chord
>   accompaniment, large dynamic range

No. 2, D Major   Advanced

The second novellette first appeared in a sketch headed "Sarazene und Suleika" (perhaps a reference to Byron's "Bride of Abydos"). This well balanced piece combines bravura and intermezzo sections in an ABA form, and can be satisfying to both performer and audience. The A section is based on broken chord figures with the harmonic elements having more importance than the melodic or rhythmic aspects. The thumb is given the melody, with the top notes taking a parallel line. The beautiful intermezzo (B section) involves a mood change to "tender" and long lines and phrases which create a sweeping effect. There is some use of two against three in this section. Large hands are an asset in performing this successful piece, which is one of the most effective of the set.

> Tempo: Äusserst rasch und mit Bravour
>   (Very fast and with bravura) ♩ = 92
> Length: 343 measures
> Technique: fast staccato, octaves, smooth
>   arpeggiated chords, cross-rhythms, legato
>   scales, repetitive thumb notes, endurance

No. 3, D Major   Advanced

This light and humorous piece can be a bit trite unless played with a great deal of character. The long introduction depends on chromatic inner lines for interest as harmonic and melodic elements are minimal. This introduction gives way to a B Minor intermezzo marked "Rasch und Wild," in ABA form. This intermezzo was published in the Neue Zietschrift fur Musik with the following quotation from MacBeth, "When shall we three meet again,/In thunder, lightning, or in rain?" The coda is based on material from the introduction.

> Tempo: Lèicht und mit Humor
>   (Lightly, and with Humor) ♩ = 138
> Length: 246 measures
> Technique: light staccato octaves, double 6ths, intertwining hands, stretches of a 10th, fast staccato chords, LH leaps, legato and staccato execution

No. 4, D Major   Early Advanced

DEXTER, Harry: Selected Piano Works—Schumann (Hansen).

This gently flowing waltz rarely employs a typical waltz bass. It has a graceful sound that can be negotiated by a smaller hand. Opposing touches are prevalent and make this an interesting study in hand independence. Clever rhythmic aspects involve hemiolas and cross-rhythms.   This novellette seems to evoke the dance mood of two of Schumann's earlier works, the masked balls of Carnaval and Papillons.

Tempo: Ballmässig. Sehr munter ♩. = 66
    (In the spirit of a ball. Very lively)
Length: 208 measures
Technique: cross rhythms, octaves, melody in
    thumb, staccato chords, staccato vs. legato

No. 5, D Major

Advanced

    This long, spirited novellette is one of the most interesting of the set, a polonaise in contrast to the previous waltz.   The form is quite extended, but cohesion is created through the frequent return of the first theme.   The bridge section is presented in orchestral textures. The ending is perhaps anticlimactic after the demanding technical work found throughout, but otherwise this is an appealing performance piece.

Tempo: Rauschend und festlich
    (Quickly and festively) ♩ = 116
Length: 259 measures
Technique: large hand stretches, leaps in both
    hands, chordal passages, polonaise rhythms,
    staccato octaves, double 3rds and 6ths,
    lively repeated chords

No. 6, A Major

Advanced

This light-hearted peasant dance has a rich slavic sound and programs well, though tapering to a *pianissimo* ending. The tempo gets increasingly fast throughout the work, as indicated by the composer, but the original speed is recovered at the end. Keys and moods change instantly, and sudden dynamic contrasts abound. The lovely melody in measures 107-130 is divided between the hands. Long phrasing and line is important for structuring unity.

> Tempo: Sehr lebhaft, mit vielem Humor
> (Very vivacious, with much Humor) ♩ = 72
> Length: 338 measures
> Technique: large hand stretches, light
> execution of staccato figuration, extreme
> legato in chordal passages, double 3rds,
> opposing touches in one hand and between
> hands, long lines, phrasing

No. 7, E Major   Early Advanced

Not quite as long or as difficult as others in the set, this robust scherzo is more accessible. The A Major "etwas langsamer" section charms with its lovely and sentimental song melody. The piece has fine contrast in its ABA form.

> Tempo: Äusserst rasch (Extremely fast) ♩ = 116
> Length: 194 measures
> Technique: octaves, large hand stretches
> (some 10ths), arpeggiated chordal passages,
> sudden dynamic changes

No. 8, F♯ Minor

    This long and structurally complex work requires enormous musicianship to hold together and make sense of the many sections. The form has been best described as a pair of scherzos, each with its own two trios. From the second trio emerges the mysterious "Stimme aus der Ferne," (Voice from afar) with its tender descending motives. This last novellette could well be the wedding Schumann described in his letter to Clara (Kathleen Dale and Gerald Abraham, <u>Schumann: a Symposium</u> London 1952 p. 57).

> Tempo: Sehr lebhaft (Very lively) ♩ = 100
> > Trio I: Noch Lebhafter ♩ = 144
> > Trio II: Hell und Lustig ♩ = 132
> > Fortsetzurg und Schluss Munter,
> > > nicht zu rasch ♩ = 120
>
> Length: 561 measures
> Technique: variety of touches, hand-crosses, quick staccato chords, dotted rhythms, quick leaps, sustained and moving notes in same hand

ZWEITE SONATE, G Minor, Opus 22   Advanced
(Second Sonata) (1839)

The gestation period of Schumann's G Minor Sonata was the most protracted for any of the composer's works; the earliest material employed in this composition dates from 1828, while the Rondo was not completed until 1838.   Bearing the title Deuxieme Grande Sonata, published by Brietkopf und Härtel in 1839, the dedication was to Henriette Voight, an intimate friend of Schumann who had acted as both confidante and liaison during the composer's abortive romance with Ernestine von Fricken.   Clara gave the premier performance of the Sonata in Berlin during 1840, at which time the work was received with some enthusiasm.

The most accessible of Schumann's three sonatas, this work is an elegant and finely honed masterpiece, in which traditional structural and formal implications are combined with romantic breadth and passion.

Note: The following editions contain Opus 22 in its entirety.

BOETTICHER, Wolfgang: Schumann Klavierwerke, Band IV (Henle).
BOETTICHER, Wolgang: Schumann Klaviersonate, Opus 22 (Henle #3931).
SAUER, Emil: Complete Works of Robert Schumann, Volume 5 (Peters #2300E).
SCHUMANN, Clara: Piano Music of Robert Schumann, Series II (Dover).
SCHUMANN, Clara: Robert Schumann—Complete Works, Volume 4 (Kalmus #3926/Belwin-Mills).

So Rasch Wie Möglich (As fast as possible)

A startling sforzando chord prefaces this impetuous and volatile sonata/allegro. Steady streams of sixteenth note broken chord left hand figurations provide an opaque wash of sound, against which the dark impassioned melody of the first theme is declaimed. This melody features a descending scalar motion, a characteristic common to all three of Schumann's sonatas. The composer originally projected this material at a slower, more lyrical tempo. The first theme, and indeed the entire movement, is kept in a constant state of flux by the sixteenth note figuration. After a fiery and extended sequential passage, the first theme reaches its apogee, and a triumphal march employing octaves is proclaimed.

An abrupt dominant seventh chord, rooted on F, dispels this stirring material, and the secondary theme is presented. Appropriately centered in Bb, the relative major, this theme is less tempestuous than the opening material, but is notable for its continual syncopations which maintain an unsettling atmosphere. The characteristic brevity of Schumann's second theme is apparent, though the proportional balance with the shorter opening theme is more in keeping with the traditional sonata dialectic. Avoiding the sixteenth note accompanimental scheme at the onset, this figuration soon engulfs the second theme, which becomes agitated and fragmented. A stormy descending sequence leads to the closing material in which the left hand presents a contrapuntal inversion of the opening material. After a repetition of the exposition, a second ending leads immediately to the development.

The compact development opens with a left hand staccato broken interval pattern, which is soon joined by the right hand in octaves. The next brief episode features a mildly contrapuntal sequential elaboration of the first theme of the exposition. These two sections are alternated once again, and a further broken interval ornamentation of the opening material of the development leads to a bridge passage. Here the left hand descending scale is punctuated by off-beat chordal right hand interjections. The ensuing episode is a lyrical foil to the turbulent material that surrounds it, and features left hand sustained and moving notes within a murmuring sixteenth note figuration.   Above this graceful accompaniment, a passionate melody, related both rhythmically and structurally to the second theme of the exposition, hovers.   A lengthy modulatory passage exploits the upper registers of the instrument, and achieves a compelling climax derived from the descending scalar theme.   The concluding measures of this section are firmly rooted in D Minor which is in turn altered to become the dominant seventh of G Minor, the tonic key.   The opening measures of the sonata reappear, but immediatley begin to modulate.   This stroke of imaginative genius, a false recapitulation, heightens the dramatic impact of the development.   A stirring broken chord passage leads into the actual recapitulation.

The recapitulation deviates from the traditional precedure in that the second theme appears not in the expected tonic G Minor, but in the parallel major.   The tonality shifts back to G Minor, and the glittering bravura coda begins.   An amusing feature of the sonata is the two tempo markings of the coda: "Schneller" (Faster), and "Noch schneller" (Even faster), all in the context of the initial "as fast as possible" indication. Though requiring a fleet and extremely energetic pace, it is notable that Schumann cautioned Clara against too frantic a tempo, enjoining her "not to take the Sonata too wildly, think of him who made it."   Broken chord figuration in unison octaves marks this brilliant passage, which concludes with a dazzling flourish based on the principal thematic material.

Tempo: So rasch wie möglich
(As fast as possible) $\quad\downarrow$ = 144
Length: 319 measures

Technique: broken chord figuration with wide
extensions, octaves, double note passages,
broken interval figuration with wide
extensions, heavy texture with independent
inner voices, endurance and stamina,
sustained and moving notes

Andantino (C Major)

The exquisite Andantino, notable for its aura of
ineffable lyric grace, is an expanded and altered
transcription of a youthful song composed in 1828, "Im
Herbste." The earliest movement of the sonata, the
Andantino had appeared as part of a piano piece entitled
"Papillote" in June of 1830. The structure of this lovely
movement enlarges a basic strophic pattern with a small
developmental section before a reprise of the theme and
a coda. From a state of chaste and innocent simplicity,
the work develops consistently more elaborate textural
accompaniments. The florid central section,
ornamented by ingenious harmonic contortions, leads to
a recapitulation of the opening material. A lovely coda,
graced by the wistful repeated thirds that permeate the
work, subsides into an atmosphere of haunting
tranquility. The technical difficulties of the Andantino
are moderate, though a full control of such pianistic
nuances as voicing and tonal shading will heighten the
enchanting individuality of this glowing aria.

Tempo: Andantino ♪ = 104
Length: 61 measures
Technique: tonal control, melody and
accompaniment in one hand, double note
passages, dynamic control, voicing,
tonal shading

Scherzo

The brief and fleeting Scherzo is as terse as it is impetuous and fiery.   Structurally this movement follows the standard three part sectional format with a central trio episode providing a certain amount of contrast.   The Scherzo itself presents three basic ideas.   The first of these is a technically demanding dotted sixteenth note rhythmic figuration.   This is followed by a right hand octave melody, prominently displaying the all-important descending scalar motif against a left hand broken interval accompaniment. The ensuing eight-bar episode is based on characteristically Schumannesque syncopation and unison chordal passages.   A repetition of the first and second ideas ends the scherzo.

This richly imaginative material is developmental in character, involving large leaps, thick chords. and rhythmic syncopation.   An abbreviated recapitulation of the scherzo brings this vital and driving movement to an abrupt, breathless conclusion.

Tempo: Sehr rasch und markirt
(Very fast and marked) ♩ = 138
Length: 64 measures
Technique: clean articulation, legato octaves,
wide extensions, syncopation, wide leaps,
finger facility, sustained and moving notes,
LH stretches of a 10th

Rondo

The <u>Rondo</u> was composed in 1838 as a replacement for the original finale, the Presto of 1835, with which Schumann had become dissatisfied. This ingratiating rondo, the most economically constructed of Schumann's sonata finales, is completely in keeping with the spirit, technical demands, and motivic precepts of the earlier movements of the work. Though a more compact design than the closing movements of the two other sonatas, this work also exhibits features characteristic of both rondo and binary sonata forms. Like the first movement, the rondo is pervaded and integrated by an abundance of sixteenth note perpetual motion figuration. The rondo opens with a right hand broken octave passage while the left is engaged in sustained and moving notes. The atmosphere is unsettled and dramatically charged as the rondo theme builds to an exhilarating zenith and suddenly ceases. After an eighth rest held by a fermata, the second theme commences. This lyrical and engaging episode displays a fluid, almost ingenuous style, and is essentially based on the repetition and evolution of a single phrase. Schumann further heightens the motivic connections by basing the theme on the descending scalar pattern. Marked "Etwas Langsamer," this compelling interlude provides an effective contrast to the stormy histrionics of the surrounding sections. The purity of this simple song, set in the relative Bb Major, is soon shattered by the appearance of the third principal section. This agitated passage resumes the sixteenth note figuration, and, though centered in G Minor, is intensely modulatory. An element of steady left hand rhythmic syncopation is introduced which contributes to the restless impetus of the material, as does the unceasing murmuring quality of the *piano* and *pianissimo* dynamic levels. The third section subsides, serving as a bridge to the lengthy development.

Dealing almost exclusively with the material of the rondo theme, this development features sequential and modulatory passages of considerable power. Though the development opens in the remote tonality of Bb Minor, it concludes firmly on the dominant of the tonic G

Minor. The rondo theme is recapitulated, as is the second theme, now transposed to Eb Major. As before, this lyrical effusion is interrupted by the brusque, if mysterious third section, which now begins to unfold. In a fashion characteristic of Schumann, the development is repeated, though here the initial tonal area is Eb Minor. The harmonic complications are soon resolved, and the rondo theme is presented for the third and final time. This fiery material reaches its climax in a diminished chord, ornamented by a fermata, and the coda begins. The difficult Prestissimo coda, marked "quasi cadenza" is a glittering shower of sequential melodic fragments that gradually increase in speed and dynamic intensity. Finally, the opening phrases of the rondo theme burst forth, and the sonata conludes in a dazzling sweep of searing pyrotechnical splendor.

Tempo: Presto ♩ = 160

Length: 337 measures

Technique: rapid broken octaves, syncopation,
  perpetual motion 16th note figuration,
  wide leaps, wide dynamic range, endurance,
  clear voicing, broken intervals, sustained
  and moving notes, rolled 10ths

ANHANG ZU OPUS 22, G Minor   Difficult
(Supplement to Op. 22) (1866)

Initially intended as the concluding supplement of
the Sonata, Op. 22, the Presto was completed in 1835.
Schumann became dissatisfied with this work and
replaced it with the present Finale of 1838, probably at
the urging of Clara, who found the work unnecessarily
difficult. It is also clear that by 1839 the composer had
realized the structural imbalances inherent in the hybrid
sonata/allegro with repeated development which he had
previously favored. The Presto was posthumously published by C.F. Peters in 1866, in conjunction with a
scherzo intended for the Sonata, Op. 14. It has since
been established that this publication is based on the
manuscript of a truncated version of the work that does
not represent Schumann's final intentions. In recent
years a definitive version of the Presto has emerged,
and was published in 1981 by Henle. This final version is
considerably more extensive than the earlier, more
familiar publication. Though the Finale of 1839
provides a more appropriate conclusion to the sonata,
the Presto remains an inspired example of Schumann's
genius at its most volatile.

Note: The following editions contain the supplement to
      Opus 22 in its entirety.

BOETTICHER, Wolfgang: Schumann Klaviersonate,
      Opus 22 (Henle #331).
SAUER, Emil: Complete Works of Robert Schumann,
      Volume 5 (Peters #2300E).
SCHUMANN, Clara: Piano Music of Robert Schumann,
      Series III (Dover).
SCHUMANN, Clara: Robert Schumann—Complete
      Works, Volume 4 (Kalmus #3926/Belwin-Mills).

Presto, G Minor

The wild and technically difficult <u>Presto</u> utilizes the curious hybrid Sonata allegro/rondo structure of which Schumann was fond, perhaps excessively. It is characteristic of the composer to espouse a form in which a traditional convention is extravagantly expanded in an attempt to fully explore expressive potential. The opening theme of the exposition features a perpetual flow of sixteenth notes that are interestingly divided into metrical groups of both duple and triple inclinations. This continual rhythmic interplay adds vigor to the material. Traces of the descending "Clara theme" are imbedded in this theme and elsewhere in the movement, and the entire passage bespeaks the most passionate urgency. The second theme of the exposition employs the traditional relative Bb Major. Though pervaded by the flowing sixteenth triplets, the principal material is a warmly lyrical melody in dotted notes based on ascending motives featuring movement by thirds. The second subject builds in intensity through a long sequential and modulatory passage. The second theme flows uninterruptedly into the development.

The development is based on the alternation of the two basic groups of thematic materials. The opening section features a lyrical melody in eighth note triplets which creates a fascinating rhythmic counterpoint to the sixteenth note triplets that accompany it. Though obviously related to the exposition's second theme, this material has a distinct and separate identity. The next theme group utilizes the exposition's "feminine" theme in an effective crossed-hands texture. The final germinal idea of the developmental section is based on the opening bars of the exposition. These elemental cells follow each other in an ABCABC pattern. The development is intensely modulatory, but the second theme group oddly prefigures the recapitulation due to its G Minor tonality. At this point the stunning climax of the development occurs where a lengthy (95 measures) and magnificent episode in ternary form is introduced.

The episode opens with a four bar section featuring four spasmodic fragments revealing an ascending chromatic line. A staccato octave passage, marked *ppp*, stealthily enters. This material is immediately repeated, and again the left hand octaves proclaim a familiar thematic fragment. The central section of the episode, in 2/4 meter follows, and it becomes clear that the mysterious left hand theme, now presented in a magnificent chordal form in the right hand, is actually a quotation of the principal theme of the concluding rondo of Beethoven's celebrated Kreutzer Sonata, Op. 47 for Violin and Piano. After a stunning climax, the opening materal of the episode reappears. It is an interesting manifestation of Schumann's worshipful devotion of Beethoven's achievement in the sonata genre, that he crowned the latest of his own sonatas with a tribute to his great forebearer. An exact repeat of the opening section of the episode leads to the recapitulation.

The recapitulation begins by following the standard pattern, and the second theme occurs in the tonic key of G Minor. Schumann next indulges in one of his favorite expansive devices: a repeat of the entire development, now bearing the signature of G Major. The development builds to its zenith, and rather than restating the Beethoven episode, rushes impetuously to a brilliant and demanding coda. The vibrant coda concludes on an imaginative plagel cadence.

Among the most exacting of Schumann's sonata movements, a clear understanding of phrase structure and formal design will allow the pianist to articulate the occasionally ungainly structure of the work. Though the technial demands are legion, the single greatest challenge of the work is the execution of such virtuoso pyrotechnics at the often quiet dynamic levels. However, in spite of the technical hazards and structural inconsistencies of the work, it possesses the boundless energy and expressive sweep of high romanticism.

Tempo: Passionato
Length: 468 measures
Technique: rapid figuration in perpetual
motion, sudden extreme dynamic contrasts,
rapid staccato octaves and chords, wide
leaps, cross-rhythms, syncopation, repeated
ppp rapid octaves, endurance, musical and
technical maturity, virtuoso pyrotechnics

NACHTSTÜCKE, Opus 23 (Night Pieces) (1839)

"While I was composing, I kept seeing funerals, coffins, and unhappy despairing faces, and when I had finished, and was trying to think of a title, the only one that occured to me was 'Funeral Fantasy.'"--Schumann

Written in Vienna in 1839 and dedicated to F.A. Becker, these funeral pieces were originally assigned individual titles: 1. Traurzug (Funeral Procession), 2. Kuriose Gesellschaft (Strange Company), 3. Nachtliches Gelanges (Nocturnal Carouse or Feast), and 4. Rundgesang mit Solostimmen (Round with Solo Voices). The collection was to be called Leichenfantasie (corpse fantasy), and Schumann wrote to Clara of the strange presentiments of death that haunted him while composing it. On hearing of his brother Edward's demise soon afterward, he immediately changed the name to Nachtstücke. Besides the melodic and harmonic elements that tie the four pieces together, the night pieces are unified in tonality, form (ABACA is the most common), and their use of fluctuation between the major and minor modes.

Note: The following editions contain Opus 23 in its entirety. Other sources are listed with each piece.

BOETTICHER, Wolfgang: Robert Schumann
   Klavierwerke, Band III (Henle).
SAUER, Emil: Complete Works of Robert Schumann,
   Volume 4 (Peters #2300D).
SCHUMANN, Clara: Piano Music of Robert Schumann,
   Series II (Dover).
SCHUMANN, Clara: Robert Schumann—Complete
   Works, Volume 4 (Kalmus #3926/Belwin).

No. 1, C Major   Advanced

In his original conception, Schumann entitled this first piece "Trauerzug" or funeral procession, in reference to the march-like detached chords of the opening section of this ternary form. The melodic material of the middle section is related to the opening theme, but provides contrast in its use of legato in imitiation between the hands. In its return, the march-like theme is slightly altered by the substitution of different melodic material in one brief section, and towards the end by widely spaced chords followed by a clever fade-away ending.

> Tempo: Mehr langsam, oft zurückhaltend
>   (More slowly, often holding back) ♩ = 100
> Length: 112 measures
> Technique: LH octaves, chords (some
>   widely spaced), dynamic range

No. 2, F Major   Advanced

The second piece of the opus is in an enlarged ternary form (two contrasting middle sections), all of which is held together by improvisatory bridges. Thus:

A ** B ** a C B ** a   **--indicates bridges
                                a--represents an
                                abbreviation of A
                                The material of the
                                bracketed areas is
                                identical.

The energetic main theme is built on a series of descending diminished seventh chords and their resolutions. The B section in Ab uses similar descending scale melodic material in a legato treatment. The march-like C section is in steady staccato eighth note rhythm and is followed immediately by a return of the first contrasting section and a brief return of the main theme. The final three measures are marked "Presto" and provide an appropriate close.

Tempo: Markirt und lebhaft
    (Marcato and vivacious)
Length: 142 measures
Technique: fast chord changes, scales, finger
    legato, inner voices, staccato chords

No. 3, Db Major   Early Advanced

This smooth scherzo moves at a quick tempo felt in one pulse per measure. Arpeggiated and blocked chords form the thematic base of both the main subject and the two "trios" (the B and C sections) of this ABACA form. The lengthy B section features sweeping arpeggiated figures which envelop the melody, placed in the right hand thumb. The C section is an abrupt contrast with staccato chords in quarter note rhythm in F# Minor, an increase in tempo, and shifting rhythmic pulses.

Tempo: Mit grosser Lebhaftigkeit
    (With great vivacity)
    Noch lebhafter (Even more vivacious)
Length: 249 measures
Technique: arpeggios, large blocked chords,
    octaves, staccato chords, melody in thumb,
    smooth hand coordination, rhythmic drive

No. 4, F Major   Early Advanced

LEWENTHAL, Raymond: Encores of Great Pianists
    (G. Schirmer).

Effective interpretation of this short final piece
depends on the character indication, "Simply." The
piece opens with a two measure "ad libitum" introduction of two chords (the first chord, a diminished
seventh, recalls the harmonic material that opens both
numbers 1 and 2 of this opus). The main theme consists
of large rolled chords, most of which span a tenth, under
a simple melody. Notation indicates a detached sound,
but the damper pedal is also marked. The brief middle
section is an expansion of thematic and harmonic
material of the main theme presented in imitative
fashion.

Schumann's original title, "Round with Solo Voices,"
refers to the two sections. The A section is the round,
and the B section is the solo voices. The melody of the
round was later arranged as the hymn tune "Canonbury"
(Lord Speak to Me That I May Speak).

Tempo: Einfach (Simply) ♩ = 96
Length: 46 measures
Technique: large rolled chords (10ths, 11ths,
    13ths), 5th finger melody, inner voices,
    tonal control

FASCHINGSSCHWANK AUS WIEN, Opus 26   Advanced
(Carnival Jest from Vienna) (1841)

All of the movements of Faschingsschwank aus Wien, with the exception of the Finale which was written after the composer's return to Leipzig, were conceived during Schumann's protracted stay in Vienna. The festive and convivial charms of the Austrian capital inspired one of Schumann's most festive and accessible works, and indeed the dancing vitality of the Viennese waltz and landler, only occasionally touched by tender melancholy, prevail throughout the work. The Faschingsschwank aus Wien was eventually published by Mechetti and bears a dedication to Schumann's cultivated correspondent, the Belgian amateur, Simonin de Sire.

In a letter to the dedicatee, Schumann described the work as a "great romantic sonata." Though this is an overly ambitious program for the work, it is clear that the structural, and especially the functional, patterns of the sonata form were never far from the composer's thoughts. The presence of an extra movement and the inversion of rondo and sonata/allegro movements bar the Faschingsschwank aus Wien from classification as a true sonata design, but the composition does exhibit cohesive harmonic and motivic unity. On another occasion Schumann referred to the work as "ein romantisches Schaustruck," and this categorization as a "romantic showpiece" perfectly conveys the lighthearted spirit of this delightful divertimento.

The title Faschingsschwank aus Wien is reminiscent of the early projected appellation of Carnaval, Op. 9, and alludes to several rhythmic ambiguities and musical quotations in the first movement. Of course, sustained wit and humor pervade much of the suite. The subtitle, "Fantasiebilder" (Fantasy Pictures) link the work to Schumann's many collections of character pieces. Lacking the profound emotional urgency of much of Schumann's oeuvre, the Faschingsschwank until recently received little attention. However, its careful and masterly construction, limited technical and interpretive demands, and sprightly charm make it a compelling example of Schumann's imagination at its most genial and ingratiating.

Note: The following editions contain Opus 26 in its entirety. Other sources are listed with each piece.

BOETTICHER, Wolfgang: Schumann Klavierwerke, Band III (Henle).
LIPSKY, Alexander: Robert Schumann--Album II for Piano (Kalmus #3931/Belwin-Mills).
SAUER, Emil: Complete Works of Robert Schumann, Volume 1 (Peters #2300A).
SCHUMANN, Clara: Piano Music of Robert Schumann, Series II (Dover).
SCHUMANN, Clara: Robert Schumann--Complete Works, Volume 4 (Kalmus #3926/Belwin-Mills).

No. 1 **Allegro,** Bb Major

The Allegro of the Faschingsschwank aus Wien is a jovial but elaborately balanced free rondo, a form that preoccupied Schumann during his stay in Vienna. The festive opening theme, employing a basic two-reprise form, serves as the ritornello element of the movement, and features a propulsive rhythmic pattern consisting of a quarter note and four eighth notes. The first episode, in the relative minor, utilizes a simple but elegant melody and arpeggiated accompaniment texture. It is skillfully integrated to the rondo by a quarter note and four eighth note rhythmic ostinati in the accompanying left hand voice. Careful voicing will heighten the textural clarity of this brief ternary episode, as well as emphasize the graceful lyricism of the melody. The rondo theme, with a harmonically altered reprise recurs, and leads immediately to the second episode. In Eb Major, this section is notable for the consistently imaginative use of syncopated beat displacement to create an effect of vital rhythmic instability. The texture is uniformly chordal, and the incessant two note slurs outline a suspension/resolution pattern. A rather extended binary structure characterizes this typically Schumannesque material. After another appearance of the rondo theme the elegant and imaginative third episode appears. Closely related to the first episode, this section is also in F Minor and features the ♩♫♫ rhythmic figure in the fetching inner voice that threads through the texture. It is, however, much longer and more expansive than the initial episode, and is a tiny rondo-like structure. The writing is grateful and quite idiomatic, and the many sustained and moving notes are not difficult. The rondo theme is resumed and after the conclusion of this boisterous material, there is a short pause.

The brilliant central core of the Allegro, marked "Tempo wie rocher," (original tempo) blazes forth in the totally unexpected key of F♯ Major, an amusing and effective prank. Constructed out of four short sections, this great central episode employs an ABCB formula. The brief initial paragraph provides a fetching chordal presentation of a new rhythmic pattern. This material is immediately supplanted by a magnificent modulatory stanza, whose martial strains make obvious references to the concluding Marche des Davidsbündler contre les Philistines, Op. 9, as well as the famous Grossvatertanz. The allusion to Carnaval is entirely appropriate to this composition, and the earlier, projected title for Op. 9, Fasching: Schwanke auf vier Noten, is clearly related to the current work. The following section contains the principal "jest" of the work: a clever, but not particularly cryptic quotation of Rouget de Lisle's stirring revolutionary hymn, La Marseillaise. This was an anthem officially proscribed in Austria under the repressive anti-republican regime of Prince Metternich. A return to the brilliantly modulatory material concludes this section. Though this

166 Faschingsschwank aus Wien

dramatic interlude does not expand on the principal
motivic ideal of the Faschingsschwank, its modulatory
character and contextual position in the movement
imply a "developmental" function.

The return to Bb and the instruction, "Hochst
leghaft" (Extremely lively) marks the beginning of a
"quasi-recapitulation." This material combines the
rondo theme's characteristic rhythm with new octave
unison material which neatly suggests a restatement,
without forcing a return to the by now familiar
ritornello. Episode four follows, and exhibits many
characteristics, such as tonality, chordal textures, and
two note slurs that organically link it to the second
episode. The rhythmic emphasis is altered, and the
length is expanded, but the parallels between episodes I
and III, and II and IV are obviously responsible for much
of the Allegro's cohesive unity. An expanded bridge
passage combining elements of the second and third
episodes excitingly delays the final appearance of the
rondo theme. After the triumphal statement of the
ritornello, the coda begins. The coda juxtaposes
fragments of the "quasi recapitulation" theme and the
second episode, as well as introducing new closing
material. The entire movement is pervaded by lilting
Viennese dance rhythms, and the brilliant coda is no
exception. The dance swirls upward through sweeping
scalar passages, and climaxes in a buoyant outburst.
This Allegro, characterized by extroverted gaiety, may
lack the charged emotional depth of some of the
composer's other works, but for a work that claims to be
a mere "Carnaval Joke" it reveals an astonishingly
complex and unified formal design.

Tempo: Sehr lebhaft (Very lively) ♩. = 76
   Erstes Tempo (Original tempo)
   Tempo wie vorher (Original tempo)
   Höchst lebhaft (Extremely lively)
   Tempo wie im Anfang (Tempo as in the
      beginning)
Length: 553 measures
Technique: large chords, chordal figuration
   between the hands, displaced rhythms, large
   chordal leaps, staccato octaves, sustained
   and moving notes

No. 2 **Romanze,** G Minor (Romance)

AGAY, Denes: Early Advanced Classics to Moderns,
   Vol. 47 (Consolidated).

The brief <u>Romanze</u> reveals Schumann's penchant for creating an exquisitely refined miniature with the greatest economy of means. The opening section of this ternary form is based on the strophic repetition of a single melodic phrase. This lyrical fragment is subtly varied, and many suspensions color this poignant song. The thick chordal textures of this warmly lyrical episode form an enchanting contrast to the sparser textures of the surrounding sections. The opening material returns, and the work closes on a picardy third which is achieved through the magical use of a familiar Neopolitan harmony. The technical requirements are minimal, though a command of voicing techniques and sensitivity to rhythmic and phrase structures will heighten the impact of this touching epigram.

Tempo: Ziemlich langsam (Rather slowly)
♪= 92
Length: 25 measures
Technique: long melodic phrases, tonal
control, expressive playing

No. 3 **Scherzino,** Bb Major

The sprightly and vivacious <u>Scherzino</u> is the pivotal
movement in the arch-shaped span of the <u>Faschings-</u>
<u>schwank aus Wien.</u> Though quite short, this fleeting
movement is formally unusual. The simple ABA
structure usually associated with the scherzo is
abandoned in favor of an episodic, rondo-like format.
The mood of the piece is consistently jovial, and precise
martial rhythms propel the work forward. Careful
dynamic control will heighten the wit and charm of this
genial composition.

Tempo: ♩ = 112
Length: 128 measures
Technique: sensitive pedal, imitative
passages requiring tonal control in fast
tempo, large broken *ff* chords, unpianistic
imitation, general facility, staccato 3rds,
rolled chords, careful dynamic control

No. 4 **Intermezzo,** Eb Minor

AGAY, Denes: An Anthology of Piano Music--Romantic
Period, Vol. III (Yorktown).

The impassioned Intermezzo is charged with greater
expressive potential and more complex keys than the
other movements of the Faschingsschwank aus Wien,
inspiring Schumann to create particularly poignant
music.   Ceaselessly agitated sixteenth note triplets
provide a seamless textural background against which
the soaring lyricism of the melody unfolds. Schumann's
tempo indication insures an atmosphere of fiery aria-
like intensity, so effective that Schumann reworked this
material in the song "Schone Fremde" from the cycle
Leiderkries, Op. 39.   Schumann published this surging
movement separately in December of 1839 as a part of
the supplement to the Neue Zeitschrift fur Musik.   In
this printing the work was described as a "fragment
from the Nachtstücke to be published shortly."   The
Intermezzo is a haunting and completly typical example
of Schumann's romantic inventiveness at its zenith.
  Tempo: Mit grösster Energie (With great
      energy) ♩ = 116
  Length: 45 measures
  Technique: rapid arpeggiated chordal passages,
      long melodic line, heavy texture, voicing of
      the sustained and moving notes

No. 5 **Finale**

Written after Schumann's return to Leipzig from
Vienna in 1839, the Finale is Schumann's most concise
and regular approach to the sonata/allegro principle.
The first theme opens with a glittering fall of sixteenth
notes that provide the initial impetus for the work.
New material is immediately introduced that features

ascending and descending four and five note scalar patterns, interrupted by punctuating chords. This vital section is closely followed by a thematic group that now eschews the constant sixteenth note motion in favor of an eighth note flow. Utilizing a consistent four part texture, the material is imaginatively phrased so as to create considerable rhythmic interplay. This passage serves as a bridge to the second theme. In the expected dominant key, F Minor, the second theme is also divisible into three component parts. The opening melody is warm and lyrical, and is accompanied by an attracive left hand triplet figuration. The second section of "feminine" material is also pervaded by triplets, but consists of a richly chromatic series of sequential passages featuring elaborate and very effective hand-crossing. A brief passage brings the second theme full circle by echoing its opening measures.

The development begins with a brilliant restatement of the opening material, transposed to the startling key of Db Major. A lengthy sequential passage featuring murmuring triplets and engaging hand-crossing brings the neat and compact development to a conclusion. An abbreviated recapitulation follows, and as is expected, the second thematic group has now modulated to the tonic. An exciting coda crowns the movement with bravura figuration and scales, all in triplet rhythm. A short passage of left hand tenths may challenge the pianist with small hands. The second half of the coda, bearing the indication "Presto" provides a scintillating shower of brilliant and sweeping two against three figuration, and a flamboyant chordal passage brings this vivacious and spirited work to a joyous culmination.

Tempo: Höchst Lebhaft (Extremely vivacious)
♩ = 138
Length: 321 measures
Technique: wide leaps, sudden dynamic
    changes, fast staccato chords, sudden
    staccato to legato touch changes, cross-
    rhythms, hand crossings, scales, endurance

DREI ROMANZEN, Opus 28 (Three Romances) (1839)

These lovely romances were written in October of 1839 while Schumann was in the midst of turmoils, trying to arrange a marriage between himself and Clara Wieck. Clara wanted these dedicated to herself, but the published dedication went to Count Heinrich II Reuss-Kostritz. Schumann wrote in a letter of 1839 that he considered these Romanzen among his best works.

Note: The following editions contain Opus 28 in its entirety. Other sources are listed with each piece.

BOETTICHER, Wolfgang: Schumann Klavierwerke, Band II (Henle).
SAUER, Emil: Complete Works of Robert Schumann, Volume 1 (Peters #2300A).
SCHUMANN, Clara: Piano Music of Robert Schumann, Series III (Dover).

No. I, Bb Minor   Early Advanced

This work uses similar chordal figuration in perpetual motion throughout to create a very passionate sound. The 2/4 meter is divided into triplet sixteenth notes which contain chords broken between the hands. These figures are placed dynamically under the melody and bass lines, providing the major impetus and drive. The inner accompaniment is soft and unobtrusive. The melody is produced almost entirely by the right hand fifth finger and contains wide intervallic leaps in the second section. Various melodic accents are quite frequent, and help project the marked character intended by the composer. The key scheme of the four sections is Bb Minor - F# Major - Eb Minor - Bb Minor, and with the exception of the F# Major section, each uses the same melodic theme. This driving work would stand quite well by itself, and is a fine study for developing melody with the outer right hand.

Tempo: Sehr markirt (Strongly marcato) ♩ = 88
Length: 111 measures
Technique: melody in outer RH, wide leaps,
      even accompaniment, rapid broken chord
      figuration divided between the hands,
      sudden dynamic changes, long melodic line

No. II, F# Major   Early Advanced

AGAY, Denes: An Anthology of Piano Music, Romantic
      Period, Volume 3 (Yorktown).
DEXTER, Harry: Selected Piano Works—Schumann
      (Hansen).
FERGUSON, Howard: Style and Interpretation, Vol. 4:
      Romantic Piano Music (Oxford).
HEINRICHSHOFN (Publisher): Schumann—Easier
      Favorites (Peters No.4052).
KAIL, Robert: Easy Schumann Piano Pieces
      (Columbia #F1035PAX).
LEWENTHAL, Raymond: Encores of Great Pianists
      (G. Schirmer).
LIPSKY, Alexander: Robert Schumann, Album I for
      Piano (Kalmus #3930/Belwin-Mills).
SCHIRMER (Publisher): 59 Piano Solos You Like
      to Play.
THOMPSON, John: John Thompson's Modern Piano
      Course, The Fifth Grade Book (Willis).
VOGRICH, Max: Schumann Album for the Piano
      (G. Schirmer Vol. 100).

This familiar work deserves its popularity. It is concise and highly effective, with an accessible and clear sound. It begins with an inner melody in thirds, produced by the thumbs of both hands, accompanied on both sides by broken chords. A three stave score is used. The melody employs the utmost legato even in the dotted rhythms. Proper voicing will give the textures clarity. In a second section (measures 9-17), the melody moves to the top voice and is imitated by the bass line in a canon effect. Hemiola is implied by the use of ties. An improvisatory, recitative-like section is followed by a lovely, sustained ending employing the opening theme. In the final measure, the pedal is released slowly to reveal the opening melodic third that began the piece. Apart from the complete editions, the Agay and Ferguson editions present clear uncrowded engravings. The Lewenthal edition rewrites the main theme to appear on two staves.

Tempo: Einfach (Simply) ♪ = 100

Length: 34 measures

Technique: voicing, legato melody in thumb, sustained and moving notes in same hand, limited dynamics

No. III, B Major   Advanced

The concluding romance is in an entirely different vein than the previous two. It offers great contrasts in character, length, form, and material in a dramatic expanded rondo form. The main, march-like theme is found throughout, interspersed with two intermezzi and various transitional material of a free and improvisatory nature. The sectional nature of this piece makes a coherent reading difficult, as many ideas are packed into a relatively short space. Technical demands, the

sectionalized nature employing sudden contrasts of
mood, and a demanding use of the full keyboard sets this
work apart from the first two romances.

Tempo: Sehr markiert (strongly marcato)
$\quad \quad \quad$ ♩ = 138
$\quad \quad$ Etwas bewegter
$\quad \quad \quad$ (Somewhat more agitatedly)
$\quad \quad$ Presto
$\quad \quad$ Erstes Tempo (Original tempo)
$\quad \quad$ Etwas langsamer (Somewhat more slowly)
$\quad \quad$ Wie vorhor (As before)

Length: 379 measures

Technique: large chords, legato double 3rds,
$\quad$ sustained and moving notes in same hand,
$\quad$ octaves, endurance, maturity, solid rhythm,
$\quad$ fast register shifts

SCHERZO, GIGUE, ROMANZE UND FUGHETTE,
Opus 32 (1838-1839) or "Vier Clavierstücke"

Opus 32 was written in Vienna in 1838, though the Fughetta was added later in Leipzig in 1839. It was dedicated to Amalie Rieffel. The pieces were not originally intended as a group, as the Gigue and Fughetta were actually first published by themselves. However, the key scheme, centered around G Minor, is an effective unifying factor.

Note: The following editions contain Opus 32 in its entirety. Other sources are listed with each piece.

SAUER, Emil: Complete Works of Robert Schumann, Volume 4 (Peters #2300D).
SCHUMANN, Clara: Piano Music of Robert Schumann, Series III (Dover).
SCHUMANN, Clara: Robert Schumann—Complete Works, Volume 4 (Kalmus #3926/Belwin-Mills).

No. 1 **Scherzo,** Bb Major   Early Advanced

This spirited Scherzo is basically a ternary form using a dotted rhythmic figure as a unifying factor throughout. The first two phrases of its main theme rise in a crescendo to a fermata on the last chord. A brief contrasting section uses imitation in a three voice texture. The theme of the D Minor B section is a brief cantabile phrase which is answered by a single note descending passage in the dotted rhythmic motive. An abbreviation of the A section provides a delightful close to the piece.

Tempo: Sehr markirt (Very marcato) ♩ = 160
Length: 117 measures
Technique: fast staccato chords, syncopation,
constant repetition of dotted rhythmic
pattern, awkward inner voices

No. 2 **Gigue,** G Minor   Advancing Intermediate

KAIL, Robert, Easy Schumann Piano Pieces
(Columbia #F1035PAX).

This charming gigue is treated in fugal style. The
theme is presented as a solo voice in the left hand, then
is taken up by two voices and developed in closely
related keys by the use of simple melodic motives and
fragments. With the exception of two 4-voice chords, a
three-voice texture is maintained.

Tempo: Sehr schnell (Very fast) ♩. = 116
Length: 115 measures
Technique: hand independence, syncopation,
2-note slurs, careful rhythm

No. 3 **Romanze,** D Minor   Early Advanced
(Romance)

The Romanze, also in ternary form with a coda,
features an ardent staccato melody against stormy
double note figuration in triplets. Constrast is provided
in the slower F Major B section with a cantabile *piano*

melody and an accompaniment resembling that in the A
section. The coda is similar to the A section in both
melodic material and rhythmical accompaniment.

> Tempo: Sehr rasch und mit Bravour
> (Very quick and with Bravura) ♪ = 144
> Length: 97 measures
> Technique: leaps, rapid staccato touch,
> double-note accompanimental figuration
> distributed between the hands,
> cross-rhythms

No. 4 **Fughette,** G Minor   Advancing Intermediate

Schumann was experimenting with a new form, the
harmonic fugue, in this <u>Fughette</u>. The quiet fugal
subject (which never appears in stretto), is presented in
the left hand with a simple chordal accompaniment, to
be similarly taken up in the upper voices. The piece
continues in this manner, with the subject, or fragments
of it, jumping from one voice to the other, always with
the light staccato chordal accompaniment. The
<u>Fughette</u> is brought to a quiet close in the major by
three Adagio chords.

> Tempo: Leise (softly, quietly) ♩. = 84
> Length: 46 measures
> Technique: quiet staccato touch, hand
> independence, wide hand stretches, good
> tonal control

STUDIEN FUR DEN PEDAL-FLÜGEL, Opus 56
(Six etudes in canon) (1845)

Dedicated to J.G. Kuntsch, these accompanied canons show quite a diversity of style. The use of the pedal is generally restricted to simple harmonic support. Both strict, imitative elements and free episodic aspects are combined. Although Schumann does not seem at ease in this form, these are interesting studies. Homage to Bach and the baroque masters is evident. The instrument they were written for was a piano equipped with a set of organ pedals. Another version is for pianoforte requiring 3 or 4 hands.

Note: The following editions contain Opus 56 in its entirety.

DUPRÉ, Marcel: Oeuvres de Robert Schumann—Six Études en Forme de Canon et Quatre Esquisses—Six Fugues sur B.A.C.H. (Bornemann).
SCHUMANN, Clara: Robert Schumann—Complete Works, Volume 5 (Kalmus #3927/Belwin).

No. I, C Major   Early Advanced

The most traditional sounding of the six studies, this canon uses baroque figuration. The two-voice canon is basically unaccompanied except for long and simple pedals. The canon, at the octave, is uninterrupted throughout. In measure 17 the tonal center shifts to the subdominant, and in measures 21-24 transitional material moves to a return of the initial subject and the tonic center. The quick sixteenth note movement begins to slow in measure 37, and more romantic harmonies are used to approach the final quarter note cadence.

Tempo: Nicht zu schnell (Not too fast) ♩ = 88
Length: 40 measures
Technique: finger independence, trills, running
16ths (some in scales) in both hands
simultaneously, fast finger work,
difficult fingering

No. II, A Minor   Early Advanced

This lyrical work is a very romantic contrast to the first study. The 12/8 meter gives the legato a smooth lilt. The two voice canon appears in the upper two voices at the unison. Because of this placement and the canonic repetition at a distance of one measure, the piece is consistently and continuously divided into two bar groupings, the second measure sounding almost as an echo of the first. The imitation finally ends at measure 52 to prepare for the major ending. The left hand staff contains accompaniment material, but the left hand often must help take notes on the treble staff. Suspensions and nonharmonic tones aid the beautiful harmonic progressions. A lovely sequence occurs in measures 48-49. Measure 22 is shortened and only contains two beats (6/8).

Tempo: Mit innigem Ausdruck
(With heartfelt expression) ♩. = 60
Length: 56 measures
Technique: independent voices in same
hand, legato double note passages, touch
contrasts (legato, staccato, portamento)

No. III, E Major   <u>Early Advanced</u>

This andantino uses simple melody and accompaniment with a romantic sensibility reminiscent of Mendelssohn. Of the opus, this study is the easiest to transfer to the piano because the pedal line and the left hand staff can generally be incorporated and taken by the left hand. The canon at the fifth follows at a distance of two beats. When performed on the piano, the second entrance sounds like an echo of the first. This delicate piece will benefit from the melodic shading of each note that the piano can offer.

Tempo: Andantino - Etwas schneller
(Somewhat faster) ♩ = 80
Length: 34 measures
Technique: independent voices in same hand,
LH double note arpeggiated figuration,
heavy accompaniment against thin melodic line

No. IV, Ab Major   <u>Advanced</u>

The quick note values found in this pretty etude are taken at a moderate tempo and create a lyrical effect.

The canon begins at the fifth, and appears at distances of 3, 2, 1, and ½ measures. The ABA form contrasts the initial Ab Major with F Minor in the middle section, though the opening and closing sections rarely use the subject in counterpoint. With sixteenth notes prevalent, the top two voices carry the canon with repeated chords and a simple pedal line accompaniment. In the more agitated B sections, the thirty-second note is the basic note value, while the coda (measures 58-66) contains figurations from both sections. The overall sound is perhaps the most passionate and driving of the opus.

> Tempo: Innig (Sincerely) ♪ = 68
> Length: 66 measures
> Technique: rapid running 16ths, repeated
>   chordal accompaniment, cross-rhythms in
>   same hand

No. V, B Minor   Advanced

According to Clara's diary, this is the etude that Mendelssohn liked the best. This particular work seems more like a character piece than a canon. The polyphonic movement is well hidden within the very animated, detached chords. The light, lively sound almost belies the minor mode. The pedal goes beyond its usual harmonic function and provides an occasional embellishment of the motion. The B section provides a slight change of material, but not of the character or mode. The accompanimental figures that are introduced in the coda are taken from the thirty-second note figures of the previous study (Opus 56, No. 4).

Tempo: Nicht zu schnell (Not too fast) ♩ = 96
Length: 111 measures
Technique: melody within staccato chord
texture, hand independence, sustained and
staccato notes in same hand

No. VI , B Major

The final canon of this opus is the most organ-like
in sound and technique. Again in ABA form, the opening
and closing sections have a very homophonic sound. The
two voice canon found in these sections is at the octave
at a distance of one measure. The middle section
(measures 17-32) uses imitation in all four voices. The
subject appears in each line at a distance of four
measures. The imitation is not strict in this middle
part. Throughout both sections, the opening notes of
the subjects are found in the pedal. The pedal's
important role contrasts its use in the rest of this opus.
A strange chromatic cadence ends this last canon.

Tempo: Adagio ♩ = 62
Length: 65 measures
Technique: legato playing in chordal texture,
voicing, finger independence, tonal control

VIER SKIZZEN FUR DEN PEDAL-FLÜGEL, Opus 58
(Four Sketches for Pedal Piano) (1845)

Consistency is the mark of this opus for pedal piano, an instrument Schumann became briefly enamored with. Similar elements found throughout this include simple ternary ABA form, homophonic texture and sound, martial thematic material, and 3/4 meter. Key schemes of individual movements and of the set as a whole show a fluctuation between major and minor modes. They may be played on the pianoforte by three or four hands.

Note: The following editions contain Opus 58 in its entirety.

DUPRÉ, Marcel: Oeuvres de Robert Schumann--Six Études en Forme de Canon et Quatre Esquisses--Six Fugues sur B.A.C.H. (Bornemann).
SCHUMANN, Clara: Robert Schumann--Complete Works, Volume 5 (Kalmus #3927/Belwin).

No. 1 **Sketch,** C Minor

This march in 3/4 meter presents a forceful sound. The strong beat emphasis is not clear. The strong march in the A sections uses detached chords in the minor mode. Dynamics are terraced, employing *piano* and *forte* levels, with the pedal offering harmonic support. In the B section, the right hand continues the large chords while the left hand switches to running eighth notes. This homophonic sound does not seem to call for a piano with pedals.

Tempo: Nicht schnell und sehr markirt
(Not fast and well marked)
Length: 68 measures
Technique: large chords, LH figuration,
chordal voicing, syncopation, sudden
dynamic changes, strong rhythm, staccato
LH vs. legato RH

No. 2 **Sketch**, C Major

The main thematic material of this second sketch is similar to that of the first. The mode is changed, but the 3/4 march-like chords present a very strong sound that is marked by ambiguous strong beat emphasis. Phrasing is somewhat asymmetrical also. The middle section of this ABA form obscures the 3/4 meter even more by implying a 2/4 time signature. The B section uses accompanimental figures in both hands underneath the melody. These patterns often include strange nonharmonic tones.

Tempo: Nicht schnell und sehr markirt
(Not fast and well marked)
Length: 82 measures
Technique: RH broken octaves, voicing, large
chords, sustained and moving notes

No. 3 **Sketch**, F Minor

Drama and passion are given free expression in this third sketch. It is definitely the largest in terms of form, sound, scope, and size. Even the middle section of the ABA form is enlarged to include more contrasting material. Within this B section some elements of dialogue between parts offer contrast to the almost strictly homophonic nature of this Opus. The opening thematic material bears strong resemblance to the third Nachtstucke, Op. 23, No. 3. Another similarity appears when key schemes are compared. The main subject fluctuates between major and minor keys.

> Tempo: Lebhaft (Fast)
> Length: 157 measures
> Technique: sustained and moving notes, large
>   chords, voicing, octaves, hand independence

No. 4 **Sketch,** Db Major

Again in ternary form, the A section repeats note for note upon its repetition. The main thematic material utilizes a tympani-like motive (♩ 𝄾 ♪♩) that is in character with the subjects of the first three sketches. The pedal makes great use of this rhythmic figure. In the middle section, the right hand has running eighth notes over left hand quarter note chords of which the down beat is rolled. There are some points of imitation in measures 43-50. Dynamics are generally quiet throughout.

> Tempo: Allegretto
> Length: 86 measures
> Technique: sustained and moving notes in same
>   hand, large rolled chords, octaves, voicing,
>   light staccato touch in chordal texture,
>   independence of hands and pedals

SIX FUGUES ON BACH, Opus 60 (1845)

Written when Schumann's interest in contrapuntal music was at its apex, these six fugues are certainly the most complete and competent compositions in that style. Their sound is not romantic in the least. As opposed to the other canonic and fugal forms, he uses subject and episodic material in a more traditional manner. Schumann indicates that these six pieces are for organ or pedal piano, and they seem more suited to the organ than either Opus 56 or 58. The role of the pedal is much more developed here than in any other piece for this medium.

Note: The following edition contains Opus 60 in its
     entirety.

DUPRÉ, Marcel: Oeuvres de Robert Schumann—Six
     Études en Forme de Canon et Quatre Esquisses—Six
     Fugues sur B.A.C.H. (Bornemann).

No. 1 **Fugue,** Bb Major

The first fugue on Bach presents the motive in its simplest form. In the 4/2 meter, the half note occurs in five voices. Subject entrances are at a distance of two measures with the exception of the pedal's statement. The tonal center moves around quite a bit and includes both major and minor modes. The subject appears in parallel motion between voices in several places (ie. measures 20 and 27). The subject and episode sections are clearly delineated. Diminution is used beginning in measure 37. The sound begins to open up in measure 41 and builds gradually to a large more homophonic ending.

Tempo: Lento ♩ = 56
Length: 64 measures
Technique: finger independence, sustained and
moving notes in same hand

No. 2 **Fugue**, Bb Major

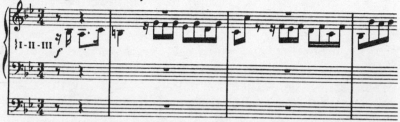

This four-voice form is really a double fugue. The initial subject is a light vivace theme using dotted notes and quick sixteenths. Both parts of this subject are employed in many thematic and accompanimental functions throughout. The second subject, BA.C.H. presented simply in quarter notes, appears in measure 74. It is usually presented in stretto. The pedal is an integral part of the subject presentation and accompanimental support. The form sounds more sectional than it does in other movements of Opus 60 because of the variety of material used. After the entrance of the second subject, the fugue begins to take on a fantasia-like air. The sound becomes more improvisatory and new episodical material is introduced. One of the most interesting and varied fugue of Opus 60, this work is quite a technical workout.

Tempo: Vivace ♩ = 76
Length: 174 measures
Technique: finger facility, sustained and
moving notes, chordal section, voicing

No. 3 **Fugue,** G Minor/G Major

The shortest and simplest fugue of the set, this work also contains some of the least interesting material.   The subject employs simple rhythms and appears in 5 voices. Entrances follow at a distance of four measures except for the pedal which is delayed. The B.A.C.H. intervals often appear in altered form.

> Tempo: Andante ♩ = 80
> Length: 59 measures
> Technique: sustained and moving notes, trill in
>   inner voice

No. 4 **Fugue,** Bb Major

This fourth fugue may be the most successful in terms of variety, accessibility, dramatic scope, and harmonic and melodic interest. The subject uses octave displacement to appear in a form that lends itself to chromaticism and sequential patterns. This subject also generates accompanimental material.   A retrograde form of B.A.C.H. appears first in measure 30 and is treated as a second fugal subject throughout the rest of the piece.   The pedal is used sparingly, but in important roles.   This well balanced, dramatic fugue has a quiet ending.

Tempo: Moderato, mo non troppo lento ♩ = 72
Length: 116 measures
Technique: hand independence, sustained and
moving notes, double 3rds, RH and LH take
each other's notes, legato chords

No. 5 **Fugue,** F Major

Detached, triple beat divisions dominate this
lengthy fugue. There is little variety to either the
rhythms or the subjects and the effect is eventually
monotonous. Elements that may help add interest are a
lively tempo, a variety of detached touches, and the
organ registration indicated by Marcel Dupré
(Bornemann-1949). The subject, which appears in four
voices in a very fast tempo, is later used in
augmentation beginning in measure 37. This lengthened
subject uses legato touch to contrast the detached
triplet material. The ending uses the compacted feeling
of a stretto combined with the augmented subject to
bring this lengthy fugue to a close.

Tempo: ♩. = 88
Length: 124 measures
Technique: variety of touches, hand-crosses,
intertwining hands

No. 6 **Fugue,** Bb Major

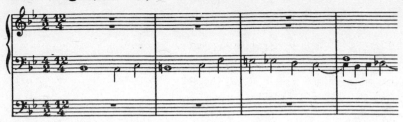

Although well crafted, this very, very long double fugue does not contain enough variety to justify its length. The meters marked in the Marcel Dupré edition (12/4 and 4/2) indicate the duple and triple beat divisions and their occasional combination. The first subject presents the B.A.C.H. motive in half and whole notes. The second subject, beginning in measure 58, is the only theme in the opus that does not use Bach. It is simply a descending line in half notes which later appears in its inversion.   Chromaticism is used extensively in some sections. The ending builds through rising dynamics (to *fff*) and slowing rhythms (half and whole notes).

Tempo: Moderato, poco a poco piu vivace
♩ = 72
Length: 155 measures
Technique: sustained and moving notes, legato chords, *mf-fff* dynamics, finger facility

Note: The M.M. markings are taken from the Dupré edition.

CLAVIERSTÜCKE FÜR DIE JUGEND, Opus 68
(Album for the Young) (1848)
or "Album for die Jugend"

Unlike the Kinderscenen (Scenes from Childhood), the Album für die Jugend was composed for children, from a childish point of view. Schumann writes that "it contains more ideas, imaginations, and imminent experiences for younger people." The first pieces were composed as a birthday present for his daughter Marie (born September 1, 1841), but the project soon grew to encompass 43 short pieces. Schumann completed these within sixteen days in September of 1848, but it is evident that he put considerable thought and effort into them. His sketchbooks show much revision, including several pieces that were rejected altogether. Some of these have been published posthumously. At one time the album was to have featured pieces in the style of prominent composers (No. 28, Erinnerung, in memory of Mendelssohn remains), as well as Schumann's "Rules and Maxims for Young Musicians." Originally entitled Weinnachtsalbum (Christmas Album) the work was rechristened when published in December.

Opus 68 is divided into two parts: numbers 1 through 18 for the younger player (with the exception of No. 13), and 19 on for the older student. The first pieces are fittingly very simple, as Marie was only seven at the time, but they grow progressively more difficult. From number eight onward the left hand is given the melody as often as the right. Nowhere does Schumann stray beyond four sharps or three flats in his key signatures.

This collection demonstrates again and again Schumann's delight in fantasy, and sympathy with the childish imagination. He had the album published with a cover by the illustrator Ludwig Richter, a specialist in children's books.

The metronome markings listed are taken from the Dover edition, Series II.

Note: The following editions contain Opus 68 in its
   entirety. Other sources are listed with each piece.

IRMER, Otto von: Schumann Klavierwerke, Band I
   (G. Henle).
LIPSKY, Alexander: Robert Schumann--Album I
   (Kalmus #3930/Belwin-Mills).
SAUER, Emil: Complete Works of Robert Schumann,
   Volume 1 (Peters #2300A).
SCHUMANN, Clara: Piano Music of Robert Schumann,
   Series II (Dover).
SCHUMANN, Clara: Robert Schumann--Complete
   Works, Volume 5 (Kalmus #3927/Belwin-Mills).

No. 1 **Melodie,** C Major   Advancing Elementary
   (Melody) or "Humming Song"

AGAY, Denes: An Anthology of Piano Music, Romantic
   Period, Vol. III (Yorktown).
AGAY, Denes: Easy Classics to Moderns, Vol. 17
   (Consolidated).
AGAY, Denes: The Joy of Classics (Yorktown).
ALFRED (Publisher): Schumann--18 of His Easiest Piano
   Selections.
AMSCO (Publisher): It's Easy to Play Classics.
ANSON, George: Anson Introduces Schumann, Book One
   (Willis).
ANTHONY, George W.: Beethoven to Shostakovich,
   Easy, Vol. 2 (Presser).
BANOWETZ, Joseph: Robert Schumann--An Introduction
   to the Composer and His Music (GWM/Kjos).
BARRATT, Carol: Chester's Piano Book, No. Four
   (Chester).
BIG 3 (Publisher): 79 Renowned Classics,
   Home Library Series, Vol. 10

BRADLEY, Richard: Bradley's Level Three Classics
   (Bradley).

BRADLEY, Richard: Easy Teaching Pieces for Piano,
   Vol. 2 (Bradley).

BRIMHALL, John: My Favorite Classics, Level One
   (Hansen).

BRIMHALL, John: The John Brimhall Piano Method,
   Book 4 (Hansen).

BRIMHALL, John: My First Book of Classics—Schumann
   (Hansen).

CURTIS, Helen: Fundamental Piano Series, Book Two
   (Lyon-Healy).

DEXTER, Harry: Selected Piano Works—Schumann
   (Hansen).

DEXTER, Harry: The Young Pianist's Schumann
   (Hansen).

ETTS, May L.: Beginning to Play Schumann
   (Schroeder & Gunther).

FERGUSON, Howard: A Keyboard Anthology, Second
   Series, Book One (Assoc. Board/Belwin-Mills).

FLETCHER, Leila: The Leila Fletcher Piano Course,
   Book Four (Montgomery).

FROST, Bernice: First Classic Collection
   (J. Fischer/Belwin-Mills).

GLOVER, David Carr: Adult Piano Student, Level Three
   (Belwin-Mills).

GLOVER and GARROW: Piano Repertoire, Level 4
   (Belwin-Mills).

HUGHES, Edwin: Schumann—Master Series for the
   Young (G. Schirmer).

KAIL, Robert: Easy Schumann Piano Pieces
   (Columbia #F1035PAX).

KOVATS, Gabor: 300 Years of Piano Music—German
   Romanticism (Musica Budapest/Boosey & Hawkes).

McGRAW, Cameron: Four Centuries of Keyboard Music,
   Book 2 (Boston).

MOTCHANE, Marthe Morhange: An Introduction to
   Pianistic Styles, Book 3—Romantic (Bourne).

NEVIN, Mark: Piano Masterpieces for the Young,
   Volume Two (Willis).

OLSON, BIANCHI, BLICKENSTAFF: Repertoire 4B
    (C. Fischer).
PALMER, Willard: Seven Centuries of of Keyboard
    Music (Alfred).
PALMER, Willard: Schumann--The First Book for Young
    Pianists (Alfred).
PALMER, Willard: Schumann--An Introduction to His
    Piano Works (Alfred).
SHEALY, Alexander: Schumann--His Greatest Piano
    Solos (Ashley).
SUZUKI PIANO SCHOOL, Vol. 2 (Summy Birchard).
WELCH, John: Schroeder's First Recital Encores
    (Studio P/R).

The charming simplicity of this <u>Melodie</u> makes it
the perfect opening to the collection.   A clear
expressive single note melody (8 double notes appear) in
quarter note rhythms is accompanied by single eighth
notes. Both voices move in legato two-bar phrases and
both lines are written in the treble clef. This piece has
enjoyed great popularity but it is not without its musical
hazards, mainly bringing out the engaging melody and
not having a "thumpy" thumb.

> Tempo: none indicated
> Length: 20 measures
> Technique: expressive playing, phrasing, hand
>   shifts, fingering, sustained and moving notes
>   in same hand, accents

No. 2 **Soldatenmarsch,**   Advancing Elementary
    G Major (Soldier's March)

ACKERMAN, Gloria: Piano Guide for Third Year
    Students (Belwin-Mills).
AGAY, Denes: From Bach to Bartok, Vol. A (Warner).

AGAY, Denes: Easy Classics to Moderns, Vol. 17
(Consolidated).
ALFRED (Publisher): Schumann--18 of His Easiest
Piano Selections.
ANSON, George: Anson Introduces Schumann, Book One
(Willis).
ANTHONY, George W.: Beethoven to Shostakovich,
Easy, Vol. I (Presser).
BANOWETZ, Joseph: Robert Schumann--An Introduction
to the Composer and His Music (GWM/Kjos).
BASTIEN, James: Easy Piano Classics (Kjos West).
BASTIEN, James: First Piano Repertoire Album
(Kjos West).
BASTIEN, James and Jane: Beginning Piano for Adults
(GWM).
BASTIEN, James and Jane: Intermediate Repertoire I
(Kjos West).
BASTIEN, Jane: Piano Literature, Vol. I (GWM/Kjos).
BIG 3 (Publisher): 79 Renowned Classics, Home
Library Series, Vol. 10.
BRADLEY, Richard: Bradley's Level Three Classics
(Bradley).
BRADLEY, Richard: Easy Teaching Pieces for Piano,
Vol. 2 (Bradley).
BRADLEY, Richard: The Instant Virtuoso (Bradley).
BRADLEY, Richard: Piano Masterworks (Bradley).
BRIMHALL, John: The John Brimhall Piano Method,
Book 4 (Hansen).
BRIMHALL, John: My Favorite Classics, Level One
(Hansen).
BRIMHALL, John: My First Book of Classics--Schumann
(Hansen).
CLARK and GOSS: Piano Literature of the 17th, 18th,
and 19th Centuries, Book 2 (Summy-Birchard).
CURTIS, Helen: Fundamental Piano Series, Book One
(Lyon-Healy).
DANA, Walter: My Favorite Classics, Level Four
(Hansen).
DEXTER, Harry: Selected Piano Works--Schumann
(Hansen).

DEXTER, Harry: The Young Pianist's Schumann (Hansen).

EDISON, June: Peanuts Piano Course, Book Five (Studio P/R).

ETTS, May L.: Beginning to Play Schumann (Schroeder & Gunther).

GLOVER, David Carr: Adult Piano Student, Level Three (Belwin-Mills).

GLOVER and GARROW: Piano Repertoire, Level Four (Belwin-Mills).

HEEREMA, Elmer: Progressive Class Piano (Alfred).

HUGHES, Edwin: Schumann--Master Series for the Young (G. Schirmer).

KAIL, Robert: Easy Schumann Piano Pieces (Columbia #F1035PAX).

KOVATS, Gabor: 300 Years of Piano Music--German Romanticism (Musica Budapest/Boosey & Hawkes).

KREUTZER, Hilde: 42 Favorites for Piano, Book I (Brodt).

LaMAGRA, A.: Master Repertoire Level II, Vol. I (Columbia).

LANNING, Russell: Music by the Masters (Musicord/Belwin).

McGRAW, Cameron: Four Centuries of Keyboard Music, Book 2 (Boston).

MEDLEY, Bill and Pat: The Medley Way for Piano, Book 4 (Hal Leonard).

NEVIN, Mark: Piano Masterpieces for the Young, Vol. Two (Willis).

NIKOLAEV, A.: The Russian School of Piano Playing II (Boosey & Hawkes).

NOONA, Walter and Carol: The Classical Pianist A (Heritage).

NOVIK, Ylda: Young Pianist's Guide to Schumann (Studio P/R).

OLSON, BIANCHI, BLICKENSTAFF: Repertoire 4A (C. Fischer).

OZANIAN, Carole: Piano Album--Romantic and Contemporary Eras, Level 1b (Studio P/R).

PALMER, Willard: Easy Keyboard Music--Ancient to Modern (Alfred).

PALMER, Willard: Schumann--The First Book for Young
 Pianists (Alfred).
PALMER, Willard: Schumann--An Introduction to His
 Piano Works (Alfred).
PALMER and LETHCO: Creating Music for the Piano,
 Book Five (Alfred).
SHEALY, Alexander: Schumann--His Greatest Piano
 Solos (Ashley).

Schumann recollects the theme from the scherzo of
Beethoven's "Spring Sonata," Op. 24, for the violin in
this lively Soldier's March.   An attractive melody is
presented in three and four voice detached chords. The
strong dotted eighth and sixteenth figure at the beginning of each four measure phrase gives the impetus and
zip to this brisk march.
 Tempo: Munter und straff (Brisk and strict)
 Length: 32 measures
 Technique: detached chords, strong rhythm,
  rests, sudden dynamic changes, register
  shifts, ♩. ♬, slight delay of 16th note
  figures to make it "spring to life"

No. 3 **Trällerliedchen,**   Advancing Elementary
 C Major (Humming Song) or "Ditty"

ANSON, George:: Survey of Piano Literature, Level I,
 Book 2: The Romantic Composers (Elkan-Vogel).
ALFRED (Publisher): Schumann--18 of His Easiest
 Piano Selections.
BANOWETZ, Joseph: Robert Schumann--An Introduction
 to the Composer and His Music (GWM/Kjos).
BRADLEY, Richard: Easy Teaching Pieces for Piano,
 Vol. 2 (Bradley).

BRIMHALL, John: My First Book of Classics--Schumann
(Hansen).
DEXTER, Harry: Selected Piano Works--Schumann
(Hansen).
DEXTER, Harry: The Young Pianist's Schumann
(Hansen).
GILES, Allen: Beginning Piano--An Adult Approach
(Presser) B Major.
GLOVER, David Carr: Piano Repertoire, Level Five
(Belwin-Mills).
HUGHES, Edwin: Schumann--Master Series for the
Young (G. Schirmer).
KAIL, Robert: Easy Schumann Piano Pieces
(Columbia #F1035PAX).
PALMER, Willard: Schumann--The First Book for Young
Pianists (Alfred).
PALMER and LETHCO: Creating Music at the Piano,
Book Six (Introduction to the Masterworks) (Alfred).
SCHIRMER (Publisher): Selected Piano Solos by
Romantic Composers, Book I (Vol. 1718).
SHEALY, Alexander: Schumann--His Greatest Piano
Solos (Ashley).
SZAVAI-VESZPREMI: Piano Album, Book I
(Belwin-Mills).
ZEITLIN and GOLDBERGER: Solo Book II
(Consolidated).

The Humming Song was originally entitled
"Kinderstücken" and it employs the same form as
Melodie, Op. 68, No. 1.   In this piece a single-note
melody in quarter note rhythms moves against a steady
eighth note accompaniment which has parallel melodic
lines and occasional contrary motion.   A three-voice
texture is created in the middle section by the addition
of a new voice in the right hand employing repeated
notes.   The accompanimental patterns use the thumb
almost constantly, but they are somewhat easier than
those found in No. 1.

Tempo: Nicht schnell (not fast)
Length: 24 measures
Technique: sustained melody with repeated
    note accompaniment in same hand, long
    melodic lines, fingering, thumb on every
    other note in accompaniment can cause
    problems

No. 4 **Ein Choral**--Freue dich,   Advancing Elementary
o meine Seele, G Major (Chorale--Rejoice, Oh My
Soul) or "A Hymn"

AGAY, Denes: More Easy Classics to Moderns, Vol. 27
    (Consolidated).
ALFRED (Publisher): Schumann--18 of His Easiest Piano
    Selections.
AMSCO (Publisher): It's Easy to Play Classics.
ANTHONY, George W.: Bach to Kabalevsky (Presser).
BANOWETZ, Joseph: Robert Schumann--An Introduction
    to the Composer and His Music (GWM/Kjos).
BRADLEY, Richard: Easy Teaching Pieces for Piano,
    Vol. 2 (Bradley).
BRIMHALL, John My First Book of Classics--Schumann
    (Hansen).
GLOVER, David Carr: Piano Repertoire, Level Five
    (Belwin-Mills).
GRANT, Lawrence: Piano Music by the Great Masters
    (Ashley).
KAIL, Robert: Easy Schumann Piano Pieces
    (Columbia #F1035PAX).
LYKE, ELLISTON, HARTLINE: Keyboard Musicianship,
    Book Two (Stipes).
MEDLEY, Bill and Pat: The Medley Way for Piano,
    Book 4 (Hal Leonard).

PALMER, Willard: Schumann--The First Book for Young
   Pianists (Alfred).
PALMER, Willard: Schumann--An Introduction to His
   Piano Works (Alfred).
ROYAL CONSERVATORY OF MUSIC, Grade III
   (Frederick Harris).
SCHIRMER (Publisher): Selected Piano Solos by
   Romantic Composers, Book I (Vol. 1718).
SHEALY, Alexander: Schumann--His Greatest Piano
   Solos (Ashley).
SZAVAI-VESZPREMI: Piano Album, Book I
   (Belwin-Mills).
WELCH, John: Schroeder's First Recital (Studio P/R).

At the advancing elementary level, this four voice
homophonic hymn in cut time is very difficult to play
well.   However, it is an excellent etude for legato
execution and pedalling. It is also a fine choice to use
for   understanding   basic   harmonic   analysis   as   the
movement and progressions are clear, and the chords
never go beyond the secondary dominant.
        Tempo: no indication
        Length: 32 measures
        Technique: finger legato, sustained, moving,
           and repeated voices within the same hands,
           finger changes on held notes, fermatas,
           legato pedalling

No. 5 **Stückchen,** C Major   Advancing Elementary
   (Little Piece) or "Bagatelle," "Melody,"
   "Canzonetta"

AGAY, Denes: Easy Classics to Moderns, Vol. 17
   (Consolidated).
AGAY, Denes. From Bach to Bartok, Vol. B (Warner).

ANSON, George: Anson Introduces Schumann, Book One (Willis).

BANOWETZ, Joseph: Robert Schumann--An Introduction to the Composer and His Music (GWM/Kjos).

BASTIEN, James: Easy Piano Classics (Kjos West).

BIG 3 (Publisher): 79 Renowned Classics, Home Library Series, Vol. 10.

BRADLEY, Richard: Bradley's Level Three Classics (Bradley).

BRADLEY, Richard: Easy Teaching Pieces for Piano, Vol. 2 (Bradley).

BRIMHALL, John: My First Book of Classics--Schumann (Hansen).

ETTS, May L.: Beginning to Play Schumann (Schroeder & Gunther).

FROST, Bernice: First Classic Collection (J. Fischer/Belwin-Mills).

HERMANN, Kurt: Easy Schubert, Schumann, and Weber (Kalmus #9541/Belwin-Mills).

HUGHES, Edwin: Schumann--Master Series for the Young (G. Schirmer).

KAIL, Robert: Easy Schumann Piano Pieces (Columbia #F1035PAX).

LaMAGRA, Anthony: Master Repertoire Level II, Vol. I (Columbia).

NOONA, Walter and Carol: The Classical Pianist A (Heritage).

OZANIAN, Carole: Piano Album, Romantic and Contemporary Eras, Level 1b (Studio P/R).

PACE, Robert: Music for Piano, Level 3 (Roberts/Schirmer).

PALMER, Willard: Easy Keyboard Music--Ancient to Modern (Alfred).

PALMER, Willard: Schumann--The First Book for Young Pianists (Alfred).

PALMER, Willard: Schumann--An Introduction to His Piano Works (Alfred).

RICHTER, Ada: Great Piano Music, Volume One--Easy (Presser).

SHEALY, Alexander: Schumann--His Greatest Piano Solos (Ashley).

WELCH, John: Schroeder's Favorite Classics,
　　Volume I (Studio P/R).

Similar in style to numbers 1 and 3 of this opus,
number 5 is very straightforward and presents a single
note melody in quarter notes with a moving accompaniment in eighth note rhythms in the left hand. The
accompaniment actually constitutes two independent
voices--a moving low voice and a "pedal point" high
voice so that the piece moves in a three voice texture
throughout.
　　　　Tempo: Nicht schnell (Not fast)
　　　　Length: 24 measures
　　　　Technique: independent voices in same hand,
　　　　　legato playing, hand shifts, high registers,
　　　　　hand independence, careful avoidance of the
　　　　　"thumpy" thumb

No. 6 **Armes Waisenkind,**　　　Advancing Elementary
A Minor (The Poor Orphan) or "The Poor Orphan
Child"

AGAY, Denes: From Bach to Bartok, Vol. C (Warner).
ALFRED (Publisher): Schumann--18 of His Easiest
　　Piano Selections.
ALFRED (Publisher): Schumann--29 of His Most Popular
　　Piano Selections.
BANOWETZ, Joseph: Robert Schumann--An Introduction
　　to the Composer and His Music (GWM/Kjos).
BRIMHALL, John: My First Book of Classics--Schumann
　　(Hansen).
GLOVER, David Carr: Piano Student, Level Six
　　(Belwin-Mills).
HERMANN, Kurt: Easy Schubert, Schumann, and Weber
　　(Kalmus #9541/Belwin-Mills).

KAIL, Robert: Easy Schumann Piano Pieces
(Columbia #F1035PAX).
PALMER, Willard: Schumann--The First Book for Young
Pianists (Alfred).
PALMER, Willard: Schumann--An Introduction to His
Piano Works (Alfred).
SHEALY, Alexander: Schumann--His Greatest Piano
Solos (Ashley).

The pathetic character of this expressive piece is
built on a brief melodic idea which is altered through
rhythm, harmony, and melody to form four-bar phrases
moving in a basically four-voice texture.   There is
constant repetition and without the "Poor Orphan" title
the character could mistakenly be interpreted as a swift
dance or march.   Dotted and undotted rhythms are
frequently interchanged.

> Tempo: Langsam (Slowly)
> Length: 32 measures
> Technique: alternating touches, wide hand
> stretches, independent inner voices, portato
> touch, finger legato, awkward fingering,
> dotted rhythms, double notes requiring a
> relaxed arm

No. 7 **Jägerliedchen,** F Major   Advancing Elementary
(Little Hunting Song) or "Hunting Song"

AGAY, Denes: Easy Classics to Moderns, Vol. 17
(Consolidated).
AGAY, Denes: From Bach to Bartok, Vol. C (Warner).
ANSON, George: Survey of Piano Literature, Level 1,
Book 2, The Romantic Composers (Elkan-Vogel).
BANOWETZ, Joseph: Robert Schumann--An Introduction
to the Composer and His Music (GWM/Kjos).

BASTIEN, James: Easy Piano Classics (Kjos West).
BASTIEN, Jane: Piano Literature, Vol. Two (GWM/Kjos).
BRIMHALL, John: My First Book of Classics--Schumann
    (Hansen).
CLARK and GOSS: Piano Literature of the 17th, 18th,
    and 19th Cent., Book 3-4a-4b (Summy-Birchard).
DEXTER, Harry: Selected Piano Works--Schumann
    (Hansen).
DEXTER, Harry: The Young Pianist's Schumann
    (Hansen).
ETTS, May L.: Beginning to Play Schumann
    (Schroeder & Gunther).
HUGHES, Edwin: Schumann--Master Series for the
    Young (G. Schirmer).
KAIL, Robert: Easy Schumann Piano Pieces
    (Columbia #F1035PAX).
KOVATS, Gabor: 300 Years of Piano Music--German
    Romanticism (Musica Budapest/Boosey & Hawkes).
NOONA, Walter and Carol: The Classical Pianist B
    (Heritage).
PACE, Robert: Music for Piano, Book 5
    (Roberts/Schirmer).
PALMER, Willard: Schumann--The First Book for Young
    Pianists (Alfred).
PALMER, Willard: Schumann--An Introduction to His
    Piano Works (Alfred).
SHEALY, Alexander: Schumann--His Greatest Piano
    Solos (Ashley).

The bright cheeriness of Jagerliedchen is in direct contrast to the pathos of Armes Waisenkind. Hunting and a chase are depicted in this programmatic miniature. These two ideas are represented by energetic single note writing doubled at the octave and staccato broken chords passages with a broken chord accompaniment. A passage in four-voice texture employing the rhythm of the horn call theme concludes the piece.

Tempo: Frisch und fröhlich (Briskly and
  cheerfully)
Length: 28 measures
Technique: rhythmic precision, arpeggios,
  sudden dynamic contrasts, register shifts,
  awkward staccato passages, repeated notes
  in doubled chord outlines, careful fingering,
  important pedalling indications

No. 8 **Wilder Reiter**, A Minor   Advancing Elementary
  (Wild Horseman) or "The Wild Rider"

AGAY, Denes: Easy Classics to Moderns, Vol. 17
  (Consolidated).
AGAY, Denes: From Bach to Bartok, Vol. B (Warner).
ALFRED (Publisher): Schumann--18 of His Easiest
  Piano Selections.
ALFRED (Publisher): Schumann--29 of His Most Popular
  Piano Selections.
ANSON, George: Anson Introduces Schumann, Book One
  (Willis).
BANOWETZ, Joseph: Robert Schumann--An Introduction
  to the Composer and His Music (GWM/Kjos).
BASTIEN, James: Easy Piano Classics (Kjos West).
BASTIEN, James: First Piano Repertoire Album
  (Kjos West).
BASTIEN, James and Jane: Intermediate Repertoire I
  (Kjos West).
BASTIEN, Jane: Piano Literature, Vol. I (GWM/Kjos).
BRADLEY, Richard: Bradley's Level Three Classics
  (Bradley).
BRADLEY, Richard: Easy Teaching Pieces for Piano,
  Vol. 2 (Bradley).
BRADLEY, Richard: Piano Masterworks (Bradley).

BRIMHALL, John: The John Brimhall Piano Method,
Book 5 (Hansen).

BRIMHALL, John: My Favorite Classics, Level One
(Hansen).

BRIMHALL, John: My First Book of Classics--Schumann
(Hansen).

CLARK and GOSS: Piano Literature of the 17th, 18th,
and 19th Cent., Book 3-4a-4b (Summy-Birchard).

DANA, Walter: My Favorite Classics, Level Four
(Hansen).

DEXTER, Harry: Selected Piano Works--Schumann
(Hansen).

DEXTER, Harry: The Young Pianist's Schumann
(Hansen).

EDISON, June: Peanuts Piano Course, Book Five
(Studio P/R).

ETTS, May L.: Beginning to Play Schumann
(Schroeder & Gunther).

FERGUSON, Howard: A Keyboard Anthology, First
Series, Book I (Assoc. Board/Belwin-Mills).

FLETCHER, Leila: The Leila Fletcher Piano Course,
Book Five (Montgomery).

GLOVER, David Carr: Adult Piano Student, Level Three
(Belwin-Mills).

GLOVER and GARROW: Piano Repertoire, Level Four
(Belwin-Mills).

HUGHES, Edwin: Schumann--Master Series for the
Young (G. Schirmer).

KAIL, Robert: Easy Schumann Piano Pieces
(Columbia #F1035PAX).

KOVATS, Gabor: 300 Years of Piano Music--German
Romanticism (Musica Budapest/Boosey & Hawkes).

KREUTZER, Hilde: 42 Favorites for Piano, Book I
(Brodt).

LANNING, Russell: Music by the Masters
(Musicord/Belwin).

LYKE, ELLISTON, HARTLINE: Keyboard Musicianship,
Book Two (Stipes).

McGRAW, Cameron: Four Centuries of Keyboard Music,
Book 2 (Boston).

MEDLEY, Bill and Pat: The Medley Way for Piano,
Book 4 (Hal Leonard).
NAHUM, WOLFE, KOSAKOFF: Piano Classic
(J. Fischer/Belwin-Mills).
NEVIN, Mark: Piano Course, Book Three (Belwin-Mills).
NEVIN, Mark: Piano Masterpieces for the Young,
Vol. Two (Willis).
NOONA, Walter and Carol: The Classical Pianist A
(Heritage).
NOVIK, Ylda: Young Pianist's Guide to Schumann
(Studio P/R).
OLSON, BIANCHI, BLICKENSTAFF: Repertoire 4B
(C. Fischer).
PACE, Robert: Music for Piano, Level 4
(Roberts/Schirmer).
PALMER, Willard: Seven Centuries of Keyboard Music
(Alfred).
PALMER, Willard: Schumann--The First Book for Young
Pianists (Alfred).
PALMER, Willard: Schumann--An Introduction to His
Piano Works (Alfred).
RICHTER, Ada: Great Piano Music, Volume Three
(Presser).
SHEALY, Alexander: Schumann--His Greatest Piano
Solos (Ashley).
SUZUKI PIANO SCHOOL, Volume 3 (Summy-Birchard).
WEYBRIGHT, June: Course for Pianists, Book Five
(American Academy).

This student favorite is harder than it looks or sounds with its single note detached chord accompaniment in the left hand. The middle section (an ABA form) uses the same thematic material in opposite hands, in F Major. The sforzandos give impetus to the "galloping horseman." In one version of Schumann's sketches for this piece, the last four measures employ canonic imitation between the hands, with the left hand repeating the right hand subject one beat later (measures 10-21). This imitation continues to the final cadence.

Tempo: none indicated
Length: 24 measures
Technique: hand independence, careful
melodic fingering in both hands, 2-note
slurs within staccato lines, accents,
quick hand shifts

No. 9 **Volksliedchen,** D Minor   Intermediate
   (Little Folk Song) or "Folk Song"

BANOWETZ, Joseph: Robert Schumann--An Introduction
   to the Composer and His Music (GWM/Kjos).
ETTS, May L.: Beginning to Play Schumann
   (Schroeder & Gunther).
HERMANN, Kurt: Easy Schubert, Schumann, and Weber
   (Kalmus #9541/Belwin-Mills).
KAIL, Robert: Easy Schumann Piano Pieces
   (Columbia #F1035PAX).
SCHIRMER (Publisher): Selected Piano Solos by
   Romantic Composers, Book II (Vol. 1719).

   The ABA form of this folksong features opposing
moods and styles which will be a challenge to a young
performer.   The first A section presents a simple
melody in single and double notes with an improvisatory
chordal accompaniment. The B section, a quick dance,
uses single note writing in the right hand employing
tricky rhythms with chordal accompaniment. The concluding A section presents the theme in a chorale-like
four to six-note texture, with both staves in the treble
clef. Volksliedchen appears in Schumann's sketchbook in
two different versions.
                    Tempo: Im klagenden Ton (Sorrowfully)
                         Lustig (Merry)
                         Wie in Anfang (Same as the Beginning)

Length: 24 measures
Technique: rolled chords, alternating touches,
hand independence, portato, difficult
rhythms, staccato and sustained notes in
same hand, sudden mood changes

No. 10 **Fröhlicher Landmann**   Early Intermediate
von der Arbeitzurückkehrend (The Happy Farmer
returning from work), F Major, or
"The Merry Farmer," "The Merry Peasant"

ALFRED (Publisher): Schumann—18 of His Easiest
  Piano Selections.
ALFRED (Publisher): Schumann—29 of His Most Popular
  Piano Selections.
ANSON, George: Anson Introduces Schumann, Book One
  (Willis).
ANTHONY, George W.: Beethoven to Shostakovich,
  Easy, Vol. I (Presser).
BANOWETZ, Joseph: Robert Schumann—An Introduction
  to the Composer and His Music (GWM/Kjos).
BASTIEN, James: Easy Piano Classics (Kjos West).
BASTIEN, James: First Piano Repertoire Album
  (Kjos West).
BASTIEN, James and Jane: Beginning Piano for Adults
  (GWM).
BASTIEN, James and Jane: Piano—2nd Time Around
  (Kjos West).
BASTIEN, Jane: Piano Literature, Vol. I (GWM/Kjos).
BRADLEY, Richard: Bradley's Level Three Classics
  (Bradley).
BRADLEY, Richard: Easy Teaching Pieces for Piano,
  Vol. 2 (Bradley).
BRADLEY, Richard: Piano Masterworks (Bradley).

BRIMHALL, John: My Favorite Classics, Level One
  (Hansen).
BRIMHALL, John: My First Book of Classics—Schumann
  (Hansen).
CLARK and GOSS: Piano Literature of the 17th, 18th,
  and 19th Cent., Book 3-4a-4b (Summy-Birchard).
CURTIS, Helen: Fundamental Piano Series, Book Two
  (Lyon-Healy).
DANA, Walter: My Favorite Classics, Level Four
  (Hansen).
DEXTER, Harry: Selected Piano Works—Schumann
  (Hansen).
DEXTER, Harry: The Young Pianist's Schumann
  (Hansen).
ETTS, May L.: Beginning to Play Schumann
  (Schroeder & Gunther).
GLOVER and GARROW: Piano Repertoire, Level Four
  (Belwin-Mills).
HUGHES, Edwin: Schumann—Master Series for the
  Young (G. Schirmer).
KAIL, Robert: Easy Schumann Piano Pieces
  (Columbia #F1035PAX).
KREUTZER, Hilde: 42 Favorites for Piano, Book 2
  (Brodt).
LANNING, Russell: Music by the Masters
  (Musicord/Belwin).
McGRAW, Cameron: Four Centuries of Keyboard Music,
  Book 3 (Boston).
MARWICK and NAGY: Creative Keyboard, Level II
  (Columbia).
MOTCHANE, Marthe Morhange: An Introduction to
  Pianistic Styles, Book 3, Romantic (Bourne).
NAHUM, WOLFE, KOSAKOFF: Piano Classic
  (J. Fischer/Belwin-Mills).
NEVIN, Mark: Piano Masterpieces for the Young,
  Vol. Two (Willis).
NOVIK, Ylda: Young Pianist's Guide to Schumann
  (Studio P/R).
PALMER, Willard: Schumann—The First Book for Young
  Pianists (Alfred).

PALMER, Willard: Schumann—An Introduction to His
Piano Works (Alfred).

RUTHARDT, Adolf: Easy Sonatinas and Short Recital
Pieces, Vol. I (Peters No.3195a).

SCHIRMER (Publisher): Selected Piano Solos by
Romantic Composers, Book I (Vol. 1718).

SHEALY, Alexander: Schumann—His Greatest Piano
Solos (Ashley).

SUZUKI PIANO SCHOOL, Volume 2 (Summy-Birchard).

VOGRICH, Max: Schumann Album for the Piano
(G. Schirmer Vol. 100).

WELCH, John: Schroeder's Favorite Classics, Vol. I
(Studio P/R).

The blithe joviality of Fröhlicher Landmann has
made it one of the most popular of the entire set, and a
favorite at recitals. Nevertheless, it is more difficult
than it sounds. A legato single note melody in the left
hand outlines F Major triadic harmonies with an
accompaniment of off-beat chords in the right hand.
Eventually both hands take up the melody while the
detached chord accompaniment continues in the right.
The carefree character of this piece has endeared it to
many generations.

> Tempo: Frisch und munter (Brisk and
> energetic)
> Length: 20 measures
> Technique: awkward hand positions and
> stretches, long melodic line, portato,
> repeated notes and chords, various and
> opposing touches, sustained and moving
> notes, hard to subdue accompaniment

No. 11 **Sicilianisch**, A Minor,   Advancing Elementary
(Sicilian) or "Sicilienne," "Sizilianisch," "Sicilianish"

AGAY, Denes: More Easy Classics to Moderns, Vol. 27
(Consolidated).

BANOWETZ, Joseph: Robert Schumann—An Introduction
to the Composer and His Music (GWM/Kjos).

BASTIEN, James: Easy Piano Classics (Kjos West).

BRIMHALL, John: My First Book of Classics—Schumann
(Hansen).

CURTIS, Helen: Fundamental Piano Series, Book Three
(Lyon & Healy).

DANA, Walter: My Favorite Classics, Level Four
(Hansen).

ETTS, May L.: Beginning to Play Schumann
(Schroeder & Gunther).

GRANT, Lawrence: More Classic to Contemporary
Piano Music (Ashley).

MOTCHANE, Marthe Morhange: An Introduction to
Pianistic Styles, Book 3, Romantic (Bourne).

NOVIK, Ylda: Young Pianist's Guide to Schumann
(Studio P/R).

OZANIAN, Carole: Piano Album—Romantic and
Contemporary Eras, Level 1b (Studio P/R).

PALMER, Willard: Schumann—An Introduction to His
Piano Works (Alfred).

SHEALY, Alexander: Schumann—His Greatest Piano
Solos (Ashley).

SUZUKI PIANO SCHOOL: Vol. 5 (Summy-Birchard).

WELCH, John: Schroeder's First Recital (Studio P/R).

ZIETLIN and GOLDBERGER: The Solo Book III
(Consolidated).

In contrast to most selections in this set, this piece
sounds much harder than it is to perform and is very
accessible. The two contrasting sections of the ABA
form consist of a "roguish" 6/8 meter with a repeated
double note accompaniment. The second section is a
lively tarantella in 2/4 outlining chordal harmonies in
four note groupings with a triadic accompaniment. The
extreme diversity of material exemplifies two separate
movements as indicated by Schumann's sketchbook.

Tempo: Schalkhaft (Roguishly)
Length: 37 measures
Technique: portato, repeated chords, hand
shifts, rapid 16th-note passages, accents,
2-note chordal slurs, hand-wrist-arm
coordination, various articulations within
short phrases need proper tension and
release

No. 12 **Knecht Ruprecht,**   Advancing Elementary
A Minor (Knight Rupert) or "Noisy Claus,"
"Old Bogie"

BANOWETZ, Joseph: Robert Schumann--An Introduction
to the Composer and His Music (GWM/Kjos).
BASTIEN, Jane: Piano Literature, Vol. Four
(GWM/Kjos).
BRIMHALL, John: My Favorite Classics, Level Two
(Hansen).
BRIMHALL, John: My First Book of Classics--Schumann
(Hansen).
DEXTER, Harry: Selected Piano Works--Schumann
(Hansen).
ETTS, May L.: Beginning to Play Schumann
(Schroeder & Gunther).
FLETCHER, Leila: The Leila Fletcher Piano Course,
Book Six (Montgomery).
GRANT, Lawrence: More Classic to Contemporary
Piano Music (Ashley).
KOVATS, Gabor: 300 Years of Piano Music--German
Romanticism (Musica Budapest/Boosey & Hawkes).
LANNING, Russell: Music by the Masters
(Musicord/Belwin).
McGRAW, Cameron: Four Centuries of Keyboard Music,
Book 4 (Boston).

MOTCHANE, Marthe Morhange: An Introduction to Pianistic Styles, Book 3, Romantic (Bourne).

NOVIK, Ylda: Young Pianist's Guide to Schumann (Studio P/R).

PALMER, Willard: Schumann--An Introduction to His Piano Works (Alfred).

SHEALY, Alexander: Schumann--His Greatest Piano Solos (Ashley).

WEYBRIGHT, June: Course for Piano, Book Six (Belwin-Mills).

Knecht Ruprecht is a medieval character of German legend, who appears at Christmas time to berate naughty children. One can easily discern the disapproving knight taking to task a wayward youngster in this impelling piece. The A section of the ABA form presents excited A Minor sixteenth note movement in the low register with constant register shifts upwards to a chordal cadence. The F Major B section provides contrast in *piano* tremolo passagework with minimal melodic activity interspersed with a low register bass melody against the continued tremolo. A literal repeat of the A section concludes the piece. Unfortunately the type of performer who will thoroughly enjoy the A section may become uneasy and lose the tempo in the B section.

Tempo: ♩ = 126

Length: 72 measures

Technique: passagework in both hands, voicing, endurance, sudden dynamic changes, accents, strong rhythm, rapid 16th-note movement, constant register shifts, accented chords, 2-note slurs, melody and accompaniment in same hand

No. 13 **Mai, lieber Mai,**   Advancing Intermediate
  - Bald bist due weider da!, (May, Beautiful
  May, - Soon Thou Art Here Again!) E Major

   This piece in AABB form has light single-note
ornamented melody, characterized by upward intervallic
leaps, which move in sixteenth notes in the upper
register.   The left hand accompaniment is often
imitative and moves in single and double notes. The B
section is stylistically similar to the A section. Much of
the same melodic material appears here, interspersed
with brief new melodic ideas.   This Mendelssohnian
movement has an abundance of thematic and phrase
repetition using sensitivity to nuance to avoid tedium.
         Tempo: Nicht schnell (not fast)
         Length: 52 measures
         Technique: sustained and moving notes in same
              hand, awkward fingerings, large hand
              stretches, grace notes, frequent clef
              changes, simultaneous opposing touches and
              articulations, difficult reading

No. 14 **Kleine Studie,** G Major   Advancing Elementary
   (Little Study) or "Little Etude," "Short Story"

AGAY, Denes: More Easy Classics to Moderns, Vol. 27
   (Consolidated).
ALFRED (Publisher): Schumann--18 of His Easiest
   Piano Selections.

ANSON, George: Anson Introduces Schumann, Book One (Willis).

ANTHONY, George W.: Bach to Kabalevsky (Presser).

BANOWETZ, Joseph: Robert Schumann--An Introduction to the Composer and His Music (GWM/Kjos).

BIG 3 (Publisher): 79 Renowned Classics, Home Library Series, Vol. 10.

BRIMHALL, John: My First Book of Classics--Schumann (Hansen).

ETTS, May L.: Beginning to Play Schumann (Schroeder & Gunther).

HUGHES, Edwin: Schumann--Master Series for the Young (G. Schirmer).

OLSON, BIANCHI, BLICKENSTAFF: Repertoire 4A (C. Fischer).

PACE, Robert: Music for Piano, Level 4 (Roberts/Schirmer).

PALMER, Willard: Schumann--An Introduction to His Piano Works (Alfred).

WELCH, John: Schroeder's First Recital Encore (Studio P/R).

This miniature AAB form is an etude in three-note broken chords alternating from the left to the right hand.   Although this is an easy piece to read, the effective interpretation of tempo and dynamics will produce a musical performance. The B section provides harmonic interest through use of a dominant pedal point. Smaller notes in measures 41, 43, and 63 are the composer's suggestion of an alternate way of playing the left hand. This piece could be played entirely by either hand alone with fingering changes and skillful pedalling.

> Tempo: Leise und sehr egal zu spielen
>   (Play very lightly and evenly)
> Length: 64 measures
> Technique: relaxed legato touch, connecting pedal, awkward hand positions, frequent register shifts, even tone quality, careful rhythm

No. 15 **Frühlingsgesang,** E Major   Intermediate
    (Spring Song)

BANOWETZ, Joseph: Robert Schumann--An Introduction
to the Composer and His Music (GWM/Kjos).

This intimate cameo is in AABAB + coda form. It
employs a delightful 6/8 melody in double notes and
chords characterized by syncopation, dotted rhythms,
and upward intervallic leaps which form the A section.
The B section, in similar style and texture, provides
some contrast in its steady eighth-note movement. The
brief coda makes use of material from both preceding
sections.   Two   distinct   sections   are   marked
"Verschiebung" ("shoving, away," i.e. una corda). This
homophonic piece will attain a beautiful sound in the
hands of a musical performer with good tonal and
rhythmic sense.

       Tempo: Innig zu spielen (To be played
          intimately) ♩. = 56
      Length: 46 measures
      Technique: voicing, phrasing, una corda pedal,
        wide dynamic range, double notes and
        chords, syncopation, awkward fingerings and
        hand positions

No. 16 **Erster Verlust,** E Minor   Advancing Elementary
    (First Loss) or "First Grief," "First Sorrow,"
       "First Disappointment"

AGAY, Denes: An Anthology of Piano Music, Romantic
Period, Volume III (Yorktown),
AGAY, Denes: More Easy Classics to Moderns, Vol. 27
(Consolidated).
ALFRED (Publisher): Schumann--18 of His Easiest
Piano Selections.
ANSON, George: Anson Introduces Schumann, Book One
(Willis).
BANOWETZ, Joseph: Robert Schumann--An Introduction
to the Composer and His Music (GWM/Kjos).
BASTIEN, James: Easy Piano Classics (Kjos West).
BASTIEN, Jane: Piano Literature, Vol. Two (GWM/Kjos).
BRADLEY, Richard: Bradley's Level Four Classics
(Bradley).
BRADLEY, Richard: Easy Teaching Pieces for Piano,
Vol. 2 (Bradley).
BRADLEY, Richard: Piano Masterworks (Bradley).
BRIMHALL, John: My First Book of Classics--Schumann
(Hansen).
CLARK and GOSS: Piano Literature of the 17th, 18th,
and 19th Cent., Book 3-4a-4b (Summy-Birchard).
CURTIS, Helen: Fundamental Piano Series, Book Four
(Lyon-Healy).
ETTS, May L.: Beginning to Play Schumann
(Schroeder & Gunther).
FERGUSON, Howard: A Keyboard Anthology, First
Series, Book II (Assoc. Board/Belwin-Mills).
FROST, Bernice: First Classic Collection
(J. Fischer/Belwin-Mills).
GLOVER David Carr: Piano Repertoire, Level Five
(Belwin-Mills).
HERMANN, Kurt: Easy Schubert, Schumann, and Weber
(Kalmus #9541/Belwin-Mills).
HUGHES, Edwin: Schumann--Master Series for the
Young (G. Schirmer).
LANNING, Russell: Music by the Masters
(Musicord/Belwin).
McGRAW, Cameron: Four Centuries of Keyboard Music,
Book 3 (Boston).
MOTCHANE, Marthe Morhange: An Introduction to
Pianistic Styles, Book 3, Romantic (Bourne).

NOONA, Walter and Carol: Classical Patterns A
(Heritage).

NOVIK, Ylda: Young Pianist's Guide to Schumann
(Studio P/R).

OLSON, BIANCHI, BLICKENSTAFF: Repertoire 4A
(C. Fischer).

PALMER, Willard: Schumann—The First Book for Young
Pianists (Alfred).

PALMER, Willard: Schumann—An Introduction to His
Piano Works (Alfred).

RICHTER, Ada: Great Piano Music, Volume Two
(Presser).

SHEALY, Alexander: Schumann—His Greatest Piano
Solos (Ashley).

SUZUKI PIANO SCHOOL, Volume 5 (Summy-Birchard).

Many sensitive musical, dynamic, and tempo
nuances are incorporated into this piece. A single note
melody featuring downward intervallic "sighs" is
accompanied by an imitative left hand, usually in two
and three-note slurs. The theme is presented twice
followed by an alteration employing similar melodic
material in C Major with double notes and more
extended imitation. Loud, accented chords precede the
final *piano* cadence.

Tempo: Nicht schnell (Not fast)
        Etwas langsamer (Somewhat slower)
Length: 32 measures
Technique: LH sustained and moving notes,
   long melodic lines, chords, hand
   independence

No. 17 **Kleiner Morgenwanderer,**   Intermediate
    C Major (Little Morning Wanderer)

BANOWETZ, Joseph: Robert Schumann--An Introduction
to the Composer and His Music (GWM/Kjos).
HUGHES, Edwin: Schumann--Master Series for the
Young (G. Schirmer).
SHEALY, Alexander: Schumann--His Greatest Piano
Solos (Ashley).

This brisk composition has a light lilt, so that a
ponderous approach is not appropriate. A snappy three-
note motif introduces the descending melodic movement
of the opening theme. The motif is interjected throughout the piece (an ABA form with coda) moving from one
voice to another.   A brief B section continues in the
same style and texture, followed by an alteration of the
A material in which the main theme is presented in
chords and octaves. In the concluding quiet coda one
finds the "wanderer" fading away into the distance,
appropriate to the dynamic direction of "Schwacher"
(softer).

Tempo: Frisch und kräftig
(Brisk and energetic)
Length: 30 measures
Technique: finger facility, descending octave
chords, hand independence, imitation, inner
voices, legato playing, sustained and moving
notes

No. 18 **Schnitterliedchen,** C Major   Elementary
(Little Song of the Reaper) or "Little Reaper's
Song," "The Reaper's Song"

AGAY, Denes: An Anthology of Piano Music, Romantic
Period, Vol. III (Yorktown).
AGAY, Denes: Easy Classics to Moderns, Vol. 17
(Consolidated).

BANOWETZ, Joseph: Robert Schumann--An Introduction
   to the Composer and His Music (GWM/Kjos).
CLARK and GOSS: Piano Literature of the 17th, 18th,
   and 19th Centuries, Book 6b (Summy-Birchard).
DANA, Walter: My Favorite Classics, Level Four
   (Hansen).
ETTS, May L.: Beginning to Play Schumann
   (Schroeder & Gunther).
HUGHES, Edwin: Schumann--Master Series for the
   Young (G. Schirmer).
NOVIK, Ylda: Young Pianist's Guide to Schumann
   (Studio P/R).
SHEALY, Alexander: Schumann--His Greatest Piano
   Solos (Ashley).
WARNER (Publisher): Super Classics for Piano--59 of
   the World's Most Famous Solos.

   This little romance has quite an undercurrent of
passion with long phrasing of the melody. A yearning
minor melody is doubled at the octave and accompanied
by repeated chords in both hands. A brief stormy
outbreak of full sonorous chords interjects twice, each
time answered by material in the style of the opening
melody. With the exception of the quiet staccato
double notes in the coda, the emphasis of this piece is
on legato touch. The selection bears a strong textural
resemblance to a piece of the same name in
Albumblätter, Opus 124, No. 11.
            Tempo: Nicht schnell (Not fast) ♩ = 130
            Length: 20 measures
            Technique: melody and accompaniment in
               both hands simultaneously, chords, awkward
               hand positions and fingering, phrasing

No. 20 **Ländliches Lied,** A Major <u>Intermediate</u>
(Rustic Song)

AGAY, Denes: Classics to Moderns, Intermediate,
Vol. 37 (Consolidated).
ALFRED (Publisher): Schumann—18 of His Easiest
Piano Selections.
ALFRED (Publisher): Schumann—29 of His Most Popular
Piano Selections.
CLARK and GOSS: Piano Literature of the 17th, 18th,
and 19th Centuries, Book 5b (Summy-Birchard).
CURTIS, Helen: Fundamental Piano Series, Book Five
(Lyon-Healy).
ETTS, May L.: Beginning to Play Schumann
(Schroeder & Gunther).
GRANT, Lawrence: Piano Music by the Great Masters
(Ashley).

A light dance-like theme is presented in closely
spaced staccato triads and their inversions, covering a
relatively wide keyboard range. A short section with
broken chord accompaniment provides contrast in its
limited keyboard range. A return of the main fanfare-
like theme concludes this attractive piece.
Tempo: Im mässigen Tempo (Moderato)
Length: 40 measures
Technique: leaps, staccato chords, hand and
register shifts, solid rhythm, voiced chords
to bring out melody

No. 21 *₊*₊*, C Major   Intermediate

BANOWETZ, Joseph: Robert Schumann--An Introduction
to the Composer and His Music (GWM/Kjos).

This untitled work in improvisatory style is based on
a theme from the terzo "Euch werde Lohn in bess'ren
Welten" in Beethoven's "Fidelio."   An impressive
miniature in ABA form, it employs single-note melodic
writing against an off-beat repeated chord accompaniment distributed between the hands.   The work is in
similar style and texture throughout with occasional
countermelodic interest appearing in the left hand. In
the Sketchbook for Opus 68, an additional six measure
coda is found, using left hand melody, imitation, and
extensive legato techniques to vary the theme and
conclude the piece.

Tempo: Langsam und mit Ausdruck zu spielen
     (play slowly and with expression) ♩ = 88
Length: 18 measures
Technique: long melodic line, melody and
     accompaniment in same hand, repeated
     chords, expressive playing, hand
     stretches

No. 22 **Rundgesang,** A Major (Roundelay)   Intermediate
(French rondelet--recurrence of first verse,
     common in 14th century country songs or
     ballads)

Modern editions of the Roundelay may vary due to an error in the original. The engraver misread Schumann's instruction "augestochen" (engraved) for "augestrichen" (taken out) and omitted several measures. A flowing 6/8 melody moves over a simple chordal accompaniment in 8-bar sections of AABABA (suggestive of the 14th century French form). The B section provides contrast through brief tonal excursions in B Minor.

> Tempo: Massig. Sehr gebunden zu spielen
>   (moderato, molto legato) ♩. = 72
> Length: 48 measures
> Technique: inner voices, awkward hand
>   positions, expressive playing, frequent
>   dynamic changes, legato melody, finger
>   legato

No. 23 **Reiterstuck,** D Minor   Intermediate
(Horseman's Piece) or "The Horseman,"
"Horseman's Song," "The Rider's Story"

ANSON, George: Anson Introduces Schumann, Book One (Willis).

BANOWETZ, Joseph: Robert Schumann--An Introduction to the Composer and His Music (GWM/Kjos).

CLARK and GOSS: Piano Literature of the 17th, 18th, and 19th Centuries, Book 6b (Summy-Birchard).

FERGUSON, Howard: A Keyboard Anthology: First Series, Book III (Assoc. Board/Belwin-Mills).

HEINRICHSHOFEN (Publisher): Schumann--Easier Favorites (Peters No.4052).

HUGHES, Edwin: Schumann--Master Series for the Young (G. Schirmer).

KOVATS, Gabor: 300 Years of Piano Music--German Romanticism (Musica Budapest/Boosey & Hawkes).

LANNING, Russell: Music by the Masters
    (Musicord/Belwin).
PACE, Robert: Music for Piano, Book 6
    (Roberts/Schirmer).
SCHIRMER (Publisher): Selected Piano Solos by
    Romantic Composers, Book I (Vol. 1718).

A wonderful character piece, Reiterstuck is not as difficult as it sounds, but is dependent on an exciting performance. A quiet and short broken octave motif gains momentum and breaks out in *fortissimo* chordal style in the major mode. The initial material reappears and the piece winds down through slight variations of the motif and fades away with a *pianissimo* coda of chordal writing in D Major. Emotional and rhythmic drive will tell the story of the horse appearing and then galloping off into the distance.

> Tempo: Kurz und bestimmt (short and precise)
>   ♩. = 100
> Length: 54 measures
> Technique: sudden dynamic changes, chords,
>   strong rhythm, staccato double notes,
>   accents, octaves

No. 24 **Ernteliedchen**, A Major   Intermediate
    (Harvest Song)

CLARK and GOSS: Piano Literature of the 17th, 18th,
    and 19th Centuries, Book 6b (Summy-Birchard).
ETTS, May L.: Beginning to Play Schumann
    (Schroeder & Gunther).
HERMANN, Kurt: Easy Schubert, Schumann, and Weber
    (Kalmus #9541/Belwin-Mills).
PACE, Robert: Music for Piano, Book 6
    (Roberts/Schirmer).

SHEALY, Alexander: Schumann--His Greatest Piano
Solos (Ashley).

This joyful harvest song is built on chordal outlining
of basic I, IV, and V harmonies. Double note figures in
both hands outline these triadic harmonies in a lilting
6/8 meter. Contrasting material presents increased
rhythmic movement in dance-like staccato eighth notes.
The return of the A section (an ABA form) concludes
this light-hearted piece.

> Tempo: Mit fröhlichem Ausdruck (With happy
>   expression)
> Length: 26 measures
> Technique: inner voices, sustained and
>   moving notes, legato double notes and
>   chords, the schneller (↭) "upper mordent"
>   or "inverted mordent" is played A B A G   A,
>   finger and pedal legato, cross-phrasing

No. 25 **Nachklänge aus dem Theater,**   Intermediate
A Minor (Echoes from the Theater) or "Souvenirs
of the Theater," "Reminiscences of the Theater"

ALFRED (Publisher): Schumann--29 of His Most Popular
    Piano Selections.
BANOWETZ, Joseph: Robert Schumann--An Introduction
    to the Composer and His Music (GWM/Kjos).
KOVATS, Gabor: 300 Years of Piano Music--German
    Romanticism (Musica Budapest/Boosey & Hawkes).
LANNING, Russell: Music by the Masters
    (Musicord/Belwin).
PALMER, Willard: Schumann--An Introduction to His
    Piano Works (Alfred).
ROYAL CONSERVATORY OF MUSIC, Grade VIII
    (Frederick Harris).

SHEALY, Alexander: Schumann--His Greatest Piano
Solos (Ashley).

    The agitated tension of a melodrama is expressed by
this dramatic character piece. The driving rhythmic
bass and running sixteenth note melody help to create
an undercurrent of fear and tension. Bombastic octave
chords in dotted rhythms with *forte* and *fortissimo*
dynamics offer contrast to the running sixteenth note
figures. A slight melodic alteration in the return of the
A section in this ABA form concludes the piece.

       Tempo: Etwas agitirt (somewhat agitated)
       Length: 31 measures
       Technique: *p-ff* dynamics, octaves, 4-note
          chords, running staccato 16ths with 2-note
          slurs, repeated chords and octaves, strong
          rhythm, hand coordination

No. 26 * * *, F Major   <u>Intermediate</u>
    or "Leisurely Stroll," "Waltz"

ANTHONY, George W.: Schubert to Shostakovich,
    Intermediate, Volume 2 (Presser).
BANOWETZ, Joseph: Robert Schumann--An Introduction
    to the Composer and His Music (GWM/Kjos).
ETTS, May L.: Beginning to Play Schumann
    (Schroeder & Gunther).
HEINRICHSOFEN (Publisher): Schumann--Easier
    Favorites (Peters N.4052).
HUGHES, Edwin: Schumann--Master Series for the
    Young (G. Schirmer).
SHEALY, Alexander: Schumann-His Greatest Piano
    Solos (Ashley).

The single note singing legato melody that opens this lovely aria appears throughout in different voices with quiet repeated chords as accompaniment. The concluding phrases offer chromatic harmonies and imitative writing in a relatively thick texture. An additional three measures originally added to the ending are found in Schumann's sketchbook.

Tempo: Nicht schnell, hübsch vorzutragen
(Not fast, gracefully)
Length: 22 measures
Technique: expressive playing, legato melody
with detached accompaniment often in the
same hand, finger legato, long melodic
line, iimitation, phrases, connecting pedal

No. 27 **Canonisches Liedchen,** Advancing Intermediate
A Minor (Little Song in Canon Form) or "A Canon,"
"Little Canon," " Kanonisches Liedchen"

A lovely romantic theme and beautiful harmonies enhance this polyphonic ABA form. The four voice texture is an accompanied two voice canon with the subjects appearing in the soprano and tenor voices. The B section provides contrast through key (A Major) and increased rhythmic movement. The canon theme comes in as an inversion in the bass (A section, measure 4).

Tempo: Nicht schnell und mit innigem
Ausdruck (Not fast and with graceful
expression)
Etwas langsamer (Somewhat slower)
Length: 40 measures
Technique: voicing, mastery of canonic
playing, independent voices in legato
4- voice texture, awkward fingering and
hand positions

No. 28 **Erinnerung,** A Major   Intermediate
  (Remembrance) or "In Memoriam," "Souvenir"
  (4. November, 1847)

BANOWETZ, Joseph: Robert Schumann--An Introduction
  to the Composer and His Music (GWM/Kjos).
DEXTER, Harry: Selected Piano Works--Schumann
  (Hansen).
FERGUSON, Howard: A Keyboard Anthology, Second
  Series, Book II (Assoc. Board/Belwin-Mills).
HERRMANN, Kurt: Easy Schubert, Schumann, and
  Weber (Kalmus #9541/Belwin-Mills).
HUGHES, Edwin: Schumann--Master Series for the
  Young (G. Schirmer).
SHEALY, Alexander: Schumann--His Greatest Piano
  Solos (Ashley).

Schumann's memorial to Felix Mendelssohn is
subtitled with the date of his death. Its spirit is closely
linked to Mendelssohn's "Songs Without Words" while re-
maining pure Schumann. A lovely melodic line accompanied by a smooth sweeping bass line incorporates
inner voices, ornamentation, and contrasting touches in
this expressive work. This commemorative piece is one
of an intended series of pieces in the style of, or
arranged from, the works of different composers that is
included in the published version of Opus 68.

      Tempo: Nicht schnell und sehr gesangvoll zu
         spielen (Not fast, in a singing style)
      Length: 23 measures
      Technique: hand and finger independence,
         voicing, LH expansion and contraction in
         arpeggiated figure, expressive playing,
         finger legato, portato, ornaments

No. 29 **Fremder Mann,** <u>Advancing Intermediate</u>
   D Minor (Strange Man) or "The Stranger"

BANOWETZ, Joseph: Robert Schumann--An Introduction
   to the Composer and His Music (GWM/Kjos).
KOVATS, Gabor: 300 Years of Piano Music--German
   Romanticism (Musica Budapest/Boosey & Hawkes).
SCHIRMER (Publisher): Selected Piano Solos by
   Romantic Composers, Book I (Vol. 1718).

<u>Fremder Mann</u> is a lengthy work that contains more
dramatic than harmonic content. Broad chordal writing
unified by a dotted rhythm motif constitutes the
dramatic A section. The B section provides great
contrast in sustained chords followed by *pianissimo*
tremolo figures in Bb Major. A return of the A section
is followed by a concluding coda containing material
from the B section as well as new material. This is a
fine selection to help expand technical and dramatic
skills.

   Tempo: Stark und kräftig zu spielen
      (play strongly and energetically) ♩ = 224
   Length: 107 measures
   Technique: LH octave accompaniment, large
      chords, accents, dotted rhythms, double note
      tremolo, sudden mood changes, important
      rests, quiet chords which are solid and
      precise

No. 30 *⁎⁎⁎*, F Major <u>Advancing Intermediate</u>

FERGUSON, Howard: A Keyboard Anthology, First
  Series, Book IV (Assoc. Board/Belwin-Mills).

This beautiful work in ABBA form is a rewarding
addition to the repertoire of sensitive musicians. A
one-measure motif with countermelodic interest in the
tenor voice dominates the four voice chordal texture of
the A section. The sustained F Minor melody in the B
section is accompanied by a running flow of eighth notes
in the alto voice to be joined by the tenor in chromatic
lines. This middle section is especially lovely.
  Tempo: Sehr langsam (Very slowly)
  Length: 41 measures
  Technique: sustained and moving notes in both
    hands, legato chordal texture, inner voices,
    expressive playing, careful pedal

No. 31 **Kriegslied,** D Major   Advancing Intermediate
  (War Song)

DEXTER, Harry: Selected Piano Works--Schumann
  (Hansen).
SHEALY, Alexander: Schumann--His Greatest Piano
  Solos (Ashley).

Although somewhat similar in character to Opus 68,
No. 29, this piece is a continual unfolding of dynamics.
A trumpet-like motif in octaves opens the march and is
interjected throughout this compound form. Additional
thematic material is found in energetic dotted rhythmic
motives, horn calls, and ascending staccato scales.

Tempo: Sehr kräftig (very energetic) ♩. = 84
Length: 55 measures
Technique: octaves, large chords often in
    staccato passages, leaps, strong rhythm,
    double notes

No. 32 **Sheherazade**, A Minor   Intermediate

ALFRED (Publisher): Schumann--29 of His Most Popular
    Piano Selections.

Sheherazade, in binary form, presents an excellent
etude in right hand facility. Quarter and half note
values in the outer right hand move against a constant
meandering alto line in eighth notes. These are all
against a single note bass line, while style and texture
remain the same throughout.
    Tempo: Ziemlich langsam, leise
        (Rather slowly, gently)
    Length: 46 measures
    Technique: melody and accompaniment in
        same hand, legato playing, rolled chords

No. 33 **Weinlesezeit--"Fröhliche Zeit!"**, Early Advanced
    E Major (Gathering of the Grapes--"Merry Time!")
    or "Vintage Time," "Happy Time"

HEINRICHSHOFEN (Publisher): Schumann--Easier
    Favorites (Peters N.4052).

The tempo indication aptly describes the character of this merry harvest dance. A dance-like motif of detached chords, dotted rhythms, and passages of running sixteenth notes dominates the first two sections of this relatively demanding work. A third section presents new material in the same vein and an appearance of the same motif concludes this playful, scherzo-like piece.

Tempo: Munter (Merry) ♩ = 120
Length: 58 measures
Technique: trills, general facility, wide
   dynamic range, chords, embellishments,
   changing beat divisions (duple and triple),
   double notes in triplets, strong rhythm,
   running 16th notes

No. 34 **Thema,** C Major (Theme)   Intermediate

A one measure motif in four basically independent voices permeates both sections of this ABB form. Voices gain greater independence in the B section, creating constant dialogue. Moving in four bar phrases, the piece remains in similar style and texture throughout, exploring related keys. Harmonic motion, imitative lines, and nonharmonic tones all play important roles in effecting the drama and phrasing. The simple, intimate sound of this musical work belies its compositional complexities.

Tempo: Langsam. Mit inniger Empfindung
(Slowly. With intimate expression) ♪ = 84
Length: 22 measures
Technique: voicing, legato melody, awkward
hand positions and fingering, independent
legato voices, phrasing, dotted rhythms,
tone balance, two melodies in the same
hand, finger control

No. 35 **Mignon,** Eb Major   Intermediate

PALMER, Willard: Schumann--An Introduction to His
Piano Works (Alfred).
PALMER and LETHCO: Creating Music at the Piano,
Book Six (Introduction to the Masterworks--new
title for same book) (Alfred).
SHEALY, Alexander: Schumann--His Greatest Piano
Solos (Ashley).

The broken chord figurations in <u>Mignon</u> are sometimes simple, sometimes difficult, but always delicate.
The patterns bear an undeniable resemblance to Bach's
most familiar C Major prelude. The melodic material is
sparse but lovely. The right hand often carries two
moving voices and a short recitative is found in
measures 17-18. A slowly descending bass line is
accompanied by simple broken chord figurations in the
right hand in this two-part work. The B section
develops an additional right hand voice hinted at in the
A section, adding melodic as well as textural interest.
In Schumann's sketchbook, this piece was originally
titled "Seiltanzerin" or "Tight Rope Dancer."

Tempo: Langsam, zart (Slowly, tenderly)
Length: 33 measures
Technique: two independent voices in the same
    hand, awkward hand positions and fingering,
    tonal and finger control, legato stretches

No. 36 **Lied italienischer Marinari,**   Intermediate
    G Minor (Italian Mariner's Song)
    or "Italian Sailor's Song"

AGAY, Denes: An Anthology of Piano Music, Romantic
    Period, Vol. III (Yorktown).
BANOWETZ, Joseph: Robert Schumann—An Introduction
    to the Composer and His Music (GWM/Kjos).
HUGHES, Edwin: Schumann—Master Series for the
    Young (G. Schirmer).
NOVIK, Ylda: Young Pianist's Guide to Schumann
    (Studio P/R).
SCHIRMER (Publisher): Selected Piano Solos by
    Romantic Composers, Book II (Vol. 1719).

Double note staccato thirds in easy 6/8 meter
against a bouncy single note left hand accompaniment
form the appealing A section of this binary form
tarantella. A big, slow, dramatic tritone and its echo
introduce the piece and also appear in the coda
(followed by two presto bars of A material). The B
section continues in the established style and texture
with ascending scale passages, again in double thirds.

Tempo: Langsam (Slowly); Schnell (fast)
Length: 51 measures
Technique: fluency in staccato 3rds, steady
    rhythm, upper note voicing, well marked
    dynamics and accents

No. 37 **Matrosenlied**, G Minor,   Intermediate
    (Sailor's Song)

PALMER, Willard: Schumann--An Introduction to His
    Piano Works (Alfred).

In contrast to the dance-like Mariner's Song, Sailor's
Song is more of a sea-chanty work song. This is indicated by the downward intervallic motion in the minor of
the opening bars. The second eight bar section in four-
voice texture presents choral style writing. The full
ringing chords in the last section are approached by
wide leaps.

    Tempo: Nicht schnell (Not fast)
    Length: 60 measures
    Technique: legato 3rds, dynamic control,
        chordal writing, ornamentation, wide
        keyboard range, dotted rhythms

No. 38 **Winterzeit I**, C Minor   Advancing Intermediate
    (Wintertime I)

This reflective piece develops through repetition of
a brief motif in four voice texture, featuring descending
melodic motion. The second section further develops
the motif carrying the piece to a *forte*, then winds down
to a quiet close involving moving chromatic voices.

Tempo: Ziemlich langsam (Rather slowly)
Length: 16 measures
Technique: sustained and moving notes in the
same hand, rolled chords, awkward hand
positions and fingering, chordal voicing,
phrasing, wide dynamic variety (pp-f)

No. 39 **Winterzeit II**, C Minor   Advancing Intermediate
(Wintertime II)

In the original edition Wintertime II was given no
number and the following Little Fuge was number 39. It
is possible that the two wintertimes were thus meant to
be performed as one composition. The first C Major
section is derived from the two folk songs from
Papillons, "Sweet Lovers Love the Spring" and later the
"Grandfather's Dance."

On a relatively large scale, this lovely work falls
into three main sections. A cantabile theme outlines
triadic harmonies in C Minor presented in legato single
note unisons (doubled at the octave). The second
contrasting section is a lively dance featuring running
sixteenth notes in the right hand and a steady
accompaniment of two-note slurs. The final section
begins and ends with the opening theme and features a
curious allusion to the "Grossvater Tanz" used in
Papillons and "Grandfather's Dance" from Carnaval.
They are also in J.S. Bach's Peasant Cantata.

Tempo: Langsam (Slowly)
　　　Nach und nach belebter
　　　　(Gradually animated)
Length: 81 measures
Technique: legato, finger facility, leaps,
　　opposing touches, wide range of dynamics
　　and mood, "Verschiebung" pedal indication
　　(una corda) but sustained pedal could be
　　used, change from duple to triple beat
　　divisions

No. 40 **Kleine Fugue,** A Major　　Advancing Intermediate
(Little Fugue)

KAIL, Robert: Easy Schumann Piano Pieces
　(Columbia #F1035PAX).
KOHLER and RUTHARDT: Sonatinen Album
　(Peters N.1233A).

Schumann has treated this prelude in a traditional, contrapuntal manner, but still manages to sound like himself rather than Bach. Three voices are found throughout most of this piece. The perpetual motion prelude features running sixteenth notes often in both hands simultaneously, in scales and broken chord patterns. In binary form with repeats, part one modulates to the dominant, with part two returning to the A Major tonic. The two-measure fugue subject is a rhythmic alteration of the prelude material, in a staccato dance-like 6/8 meter. In a similar style throughout, the texture varies from two to four voices, with three being predominate.

Tempo: Vorspiel (Prelude) no tempo indication
Lebhaft, doch nict zu schnell (Fugue)
(Lively, but not too fast)
Length: Prelude--24 measures
Fugue--52 measures
Technique: finger independence and facility,
contrapuntal voicing, reading problems
because of voice jumping between staves

No. 41 **Nordisches Lied** (Gruss an G),   Intermediate
F Major (Northern Song (Salute to G)) or "Gade,"
"Norse Song," "Greeting to Gade," "Nordic Song
(Homage to Gade)"

AGAY, Denes: Classics to Moderns, Intermediate,
Vol. 37 (Consolidated).
ALFRED (Publisher): Schumann--29 of His Most Popular
Piano Selections.
ANSON, George: Anson Introduces Schumann, Book One
(Willis).
BANOWETZ, Joseph: Robert Schumann--An Introduction
to the Composer and His Music (GWM/Kjos).
BASTIEN, James: Piano Literature, Vol. Three
(Kjos West).
CLARK and GOSS: Piano Literature of the 17th, 18th,
and 19th Centuries, Book 5b (Summy-Birchard).
DEXTER, Harry: Selected Piano Works--Schumann
(Hansen).
DEXTER, Harry: The Young Pianist's Schumann
(Hansen).
ETTS, May L.: Beginning to Play Schumann
(Schroeder & Gunther).
HERRMANN, Kurt: Easy Schubert, Schumann, and
Weber (Kalmus #9541/Belwin-Mills).

KAIL, Robert: Easy Schumann Piano Pieces
    (Columbia #F1035PAX).
LANNING, Russell: Music by the Masters
    (Musicord/Belwin).
ROYAL CONSERVATORY OF MUSIC, Grade V
    (Frederick Harris).
SCHIRMER (Publisher): Selected Piano Solos by
    Romantic Composers, Book II (Vol. 1719).

Neils W. Gade (1817-1890), on whose name the theme is based, was a Danish composer and dear friend of the Schumanns' who incorporated folk songs into his earlier works.

The G-A-D-E motif is presented in a steadily moving homophonic hymn-style in right hand chords and left hand octave accompaniment. The motif begins each of the four bar phrases with each appearance featuring harmonic and dynamic variation.

      Tempo: Im Volkston (In folk song style)
      Length: 20 measures
      Technique: octaves, legato chords, carfeul
         voicing, clear connecting pedal

No. 42 Figurirter Choral,   Advancing Intermediate
    F Major (Figured Chorale)

In this elaboration of the hymn tune Freue dich, o meine Seele, (number 4 of this opus) the right hand carries the melody in octaves as well as an active alto in continuous eighth note movement. Simple tenor and bass voices move in quarter and half note values.

Tempo: no indication
  Getragen (Sostenuto)
Length: 28 measures
Technique: melody and accompaniment in
  same hand, finger independence, voices that
  switch staves

No. 43 **Sylvesterlied,** A Major Advancing Intermediate
 (New Year's Eve) (as conclusion)

  Sylvesternacht (New Year's Eve) is named after
Pope Sylvester I who died December 31, 335. Although
he initially entitled this work "Zum Schluss," Schumann
ultimately decided on the symbolic calender date as the
title to the conclusion of this large opus. It would have
been an especially fitting ending had the collection been
published under the original title of Weihnachtsalbum
(Christmas Album).

  Continuous movement within a homophonic sound
with thoughtful phrasing characterizes this pleasant
piece. The right hand carries legato chords and the
thrice repeated opening theme is an unusual five
measure phrase (four measures with a tag ending). The
third time this theme appears, left hand octaves and
large right hand chords give it a full and final sound as
an appropriate ending. Crescendos and *fp* accents are
important to the overall shape.

  Tempo: Im mässigen Tempo (moderato)
  Length: 21 measures
  Technique: voiced legato chords, octaves

SKETCHES FOR OPUS 68

Note: The following edition contains the Sketches to Opus 68 in their entirety. Other sources are listed with each piece.

DEMUS, Jorg: Robert Schumann Unpublished Pieces from Album for the Young, Op. 68 (G. Ricordi).

No. 1 **Für Ganz Kleine,** C Major   Elementary
(For Smallest Children)

ALFRED (Publisher): Schumann--18 of His Easiest Piano Selections.

This elementary piece is the easiest included in either Opus 68 or the sketches. The right hand stays within the C Major pentachord and uses simple rhythms in detached and connected touches. The left hand employs I, V7 harmonies. Both hands read in the treble clef.

> Tempo: Moderato
> Length: 8 measures
> Technique: sustained and moving notes, one finger substitution

No. 2 **Puppen Schlaffliedchen,** C Major   Elementary
(Doll's Lullaby)

ALFRED (Publisher): Schumann--18 of His Easiest
   Piano Selections.

Although not much more difficult than <u>Fur Ganz
Kleine</u>, this doll's lullaby uses more interesting
rhythms. The left hand carries blocked I and V7
chords. The right hand stays within the C Major penta-
chord. The initial downbeat is marked by an *fp* accent.
This title was also used for the third movement of
Schumann's <u>Clavier-Sonaten für die Jugend</u>, Opus 118,
No. 1.

   Tempo: Schnell (Fast)
   Length: 8 measures
   Technique: dotted rhythms and 16th notes,
      sustained and moving notes

No. 3 **Wilder Reiter,** C Major (Wild Horseman)

   Same as Op. 68, No. 8, except for the ending.
   Tempo: Veloce
   Length: 24 measures

No. 4 **Ein Trinklied von C.M. von Weber,** Intermediate
B Minor (A Drinking Song C.M. von Weber)

A bouncy vivace, this drinking song is difficult for
the level. A good sense of rhythm will keep the trill
figures in time and provide a sense of verve and
excitement.

Tempo: Sehr lebhaft (Very vivacious)
Length: 27 measures
Technique: double notes, chords, scales, leaps
    and jumps, staccato and legato, accents,
    grace notes

No. 5 **Auf der Gondel,** C Major   Advancing Elementary
    (In the Gondola)

ETTS, May L.: Beginning to Play Schumann
    (Schroeder & Gunther).
PALMER, Willard: Schumann--The First Book for Young
    Pianists (Alfred).
PALMER, Willard: Schumann--An Introduction to His
    Piano Works (Alfred).
SCHWERDTNER, Hans-George: Easy Piano Pieces and
    Sonatinas (Schott Ed.6806AP).
SHEALY, Alexander: Schumann-- His Greatest Piano
    Solos (Ashley).

For all around general facility this mild mannered
piece is a good choice. While the right hand is involved
in a variety of legato patterns, the left hand plays
various independent staccato and legato combinations.
Appoggiaturas are played on the beat. Each phrase
encompasses at least four measures.
    Tempo: Nicht schnell (Not fast)
    Length: 21 measures
    Technique: hand coordination, different
        patterns in both hands, melodic voicing of
        double notes, staccato and legato, phrasing

No. 6 * * *

Same as Op. 68, No. 21, except for the ending.
Tempo: Langsam und mit Ausdruck
(Slowly and with expression)
Length: 24 measures

No. 7 * * *

Same as Op. 68, No. 26, except for the ending.
Tempo: Nicht schnell, hübsch vorzutragon
(Not fast, pretty softly)
Length: 28 measures

No. 8 **(Fragment)**, Eb Major   Intermediate

   Most   certainly   a   fragment,   this   partial
representation hops right into the middle of an intimate
movement. The expressive material has a closing or
cadential sound to it. The basic texture is three layers:
melody, broken chords, and bass. Each has its separate
dynamic level with the melody foremost. This texture
is twice interrupted by recitative-like measures that
carry out the intimate, expressive character.

Tempo: Innig (Softly)
Length: 9 measures
Technique: sustained and moving notes,
  trills, appoggiaturas, rolled chord

No. 9 **Gukkuk Im Versteck,** F Major   <u>Elementary</u>
(Cuckoo in Hiding)

AGAY, Denes: The Joy of Classics (Yorktown).
ALFRED (Publisher): Schumann--18 of His Easiest
  Piano Selections.
ETTS, May L.: Beginning to Play Schumann
  (Schroeder & Gunther).
PALMER, Willard: Schumann--The First Book for Young
  Pianists (Alfred).
PALMER, Willard: Schumann--An Introduction to His
  Piano Works (Alfred).
SHEALY, Alexander: Schumann--His Greatest Piano
  Solos (Ashley).

One of the easiest pieces that Schumann wrote, this
hidden cuckoo is a delight. Hands are generally in
unison, with short legato and staccato patterns. A short
contrasting section in the minor mode (measures 9-13)
has an appealing sound. This is an entertaining early
level romantic work that could be incorporated into the
elementary repertoire.

Tempo: Immer sehr very Leise (Always soft)
Length: 21 measures
Technique: important rests and counting,
  finger facility

No. 10 **Haschemann,** D Major   Advancing Elementary
(Playing Tag) or "Blindman's Buff"

AGAY, Denes: The Joy of Classics (Yorktown).
AMSCO (Publisher): It's Easy to Play Classics.

Haschemann is a delightful scherzo with the exemplary and well crafted use of a single motive. This motive begins very simply and grows to include sustained and moving notes and more complicated hand coordination feats. Both hands generally read in the treble clef. This excellent early work is very pianistic and gets easier with each reading.

Tempo: So schnell als möglich
(As fast as possible)
Length: 34 measures
Technique: 3-note phrases, sustained and
moving notes, hand coordination

No. 11 **Lagune in Venedig,**   Advancing Elementary
B Minor, (Lagoon in Venice) or
"At a Venetian Legune"

AGAY, Denes: The Joy of Classics (Yorktown).

A strange sustained mood is projected by this character piece. Phrases are not always symmetrical, being sometimes cut short, sometimes lengthened. A steady tempo and one pulse per measure will "keep the boats from sinking." Clearly marked dynamics help to create a long line and direction.

Tempo: Andante
Length: 27 measures
Technique: solid 3rds and chords, inconsistent
    phrasing, triple and duple division of the
    measures, rolled chord

No. 12 **Kleiner Walzer**, G Major
    (Little Waltz)

This odd little waltz is neither cohesive, pianistic,
nor complete sounding, with occasionally ambiguous
rhythms.   Harmonic progressions are not convincing.
The cross staff notes and double sharps add to reading
problems.

Tempo: Grazioso
Length: 20 measures
Technique: cross staff reading, sustained and
    moving notes

No. 13 **(Preludio)**, A Major
    (Prelude)

Intermediate

This sketch is definitely a prelude in sound and
pattern.   The harmonies are beautiful, but their
direction becomes somewhat vague.   Hands pass from
one line to another causing some reading and technical
problems.   Awareness of bass movement and pedal
points is important.

Tempo: Andante
Length: 20 measures
Technique: sustained and moving notes,
   confusing hand position changes, down beat
   emphasis on 2nd beat

No. 14 **Rebus,** D Minor   Advancing Elementary

This eight measure piece has many enigmatic elements. It has the sound of a prelude or an interlude, and ends on the dominant chord. A strange symbol (as shown above, a "puzzle" of Schumann's own creation) precedes it in Schumann's sketchbook. A mature musicianship and strong rhythmic sense are prerequisites to this piece. Rebus appears in a little manuscript Schumann gave to his daughter Maria for her seventh birthday, September 1st, 1848.

Tempo: Poco lento
Length: 8 measures
Technique: 4 voices, chromatic movement and
   alteration

No. 15 **Bärentanz,** A Minor (Bear's Dance) Elementary

AGAY, Denes: The Joy of Romantic Piano, Book One
   (Yorktown).

This short and engaging sketch is very accessible and would enhance a beginning repertoire. The hands are at opposite extremes of the keyboard, with the left hand taking low open fifths with bagpipe appoggiaturas, and the right hand performing an agile melody. Both repeat marks and a da capo indication are found. This bear dance later became a duet found as number two of Opus 85.

Tempo: Allegro
Length: 12 measures
Technique: drone 5ths, appoggiaturas,
keyboard range, accents

No. 16 **Eine Berühmte Melodie von**   Intermediate
L. van Beethoven, D Major
(A Famous Melody by L. van Beethoven)

Beethoven's "Hymn to Joy" from the Ninth Symphony receives a very musical and pianistic treatment by Schumann. The doubling and registration of each chord are carefully chosen and important to the musical movement. Both staves use the treble clef. Phrasing, touches, and dynamics are explicit and pianistic in this useful arrangement.

Tempo: Kräftig, feierlich (Powerfully, stately)
Length: 17 measures
Technique: chords, phrasing, portato, legato
chords, finger substitution

No. 17 **Ein Stückchen von**   Advancing Elementary
    Mozart, C Major (A Little Piece by Mozart)

Schumann has made a charming, pianistic transcription of a composition by Mozart. The right hand employs double notes, legato and portato touches, appoggiaturas, and trills, while the left hand provides a simple accompaniment. Phrasing is very evenly ordered into four measure groupings. Clarity and elegance mark the character of this delightfully musical look at the classical period.

> Tempo: Nicht schnell (Not fast)
> Length: 33 measures
> Technique: double notes, trills, legato and
>   portato touches, phrasing, appoggiaturas

VIER FUGEN, Opus 72 (Four Fugues) (1845)

The Four Fugues of Opus 72 mark a renewal of Schumann's interest in contrapuntal writing. Numbers one and two were completed in February and March of 1845, when the Schumanns were living in Dresden. The dedication is to Carl Reinecke.

Note: The following editions contain Opus 72 in its entirety.

SAUER, Emil: Complete Works of Robert Schumann, Volume 4 (Peters #2300D).

SCHUMANN, Clara: Piano Music of Robert Schumann, Series II (Dover).

SCHUMANN, Clara: Robert Schumann--Complete Works, Volume 5 (Kalmus #3927/Belwin-Mills).

No. 1, D Minor   Advancing Intermediate

This four-voice fugue begins quietly with the subject revealing a somber tone. A chromatically descending countermelody is given great importance as the fugue progresses. There are many passages containing double thirds and sixths, with suspensions adding to the intensity of the mood. This first fugue ends on the D Major chord.

Tempo: Nicht schnell (Not fast) ♩. = 60
Length: 76 measures
Technique: voicing, double 3rds and 6ths, hand independence, legato, finger substitution

No. 2, D Minor   Advancing Intermediate

The interesting subject, beginning on a whole note, provides this three-voice fugue with much rhythmic vitality. A stream of eighth notes follows, leading to a syncopated countersubject.   The augmentation of the theme at the end provides a good example of the crafts- manship Schumann possessed when writing in this form. The piece ends with large dramatic chords.

Tempo: Sehr lebhaft (Very lively) ♩ = 96
Length: 100 measures
Technique: hand independence, simultaneous
    use of different touches, large chords

No. 3, F Minor   Early Advanced

The creative subject begins a fugue of much inter- est, perhaps the most Schumannesque of the set. Certainly it is the most chromatic, giving rise to much harmonic tension.   The ending shows yet another example of Schumann's writing out contrasting meters.

Tempo: Nicht schnell und sehr ausdrucksvoll
    (Not fast and very expressively) ♩. = 58
Length: 58 measures
Technique: legato, tonal control, double 3rds

No. 4, F Major   Early Advanced

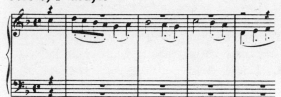

   Schumann has carefully notated the subjects to be
played portamento, thus making the sudden change to
legato at the end a much needed contrast. This fugue is
rather monotonous in its constant use of the theme, a
fault apparent in a lesser degree throughout the opus.
        Tempo: Im mässigen Tempo (In a moderate
            Tempo) ♩ = 104
        Length: 75 measures
        Technique: long melodic line, simultaneous use
            of opposing touches, awkward keyboard
            writing, light touch

VIER MÄRSCHE, Opus 76   Early Advanced
   (Four Marches) (1849)

These romantic and passionate marches were written on Schumann's return to Dresden (from the 12th to
the 17th of June, 1849) after hiding out during the
political uprising. They were composed with patriotic
intent and when they were sent to the publisher
Whistling,   Schumann   requested   that   they   be
immediately published with "Dresden 1849" in large
letters printed on the title page. These marches were
called "the barricade marches" by the Schumanns' closer
friends.

The sectional forms that Schumann liked so much
were   replaced   here   by   simple   ABA   form   with   an
introduction or coda sometimes added. The B sections
offer little contrast or character. All are in common
time and all use duple and compound beat divisions.
They are not really comparable with the early marches
such as the "Davidsbündlermarsch" from Opus 9, or even
Opus 99, No. 11. An additional march was also written
at this time. It ended up as "Geschwindmarsch," No. 14
from Opus 99.   Although technically difficult, these
pieces are much easier to read than many of Schumann's
more advanced works.

Note: The following editions contain Opus 76 in its
      entirety.

SAUER, Emil: Complete Works of Robert Schumann,
      Volume 4 (Peters #2300D).
SCHUMANN, Clara: Piano Music of Robert Schumann,
      Series III (Dover).
SCHUMANN, Clara: Robert Schumann--Complete
      Works, Volume 5 (Kalmus #3927/Belwin).

No. I, Eb Major

The first march combines a large romantic sound with attractive harmonies. A constant juxtaposition of simple and compound beat divisions underlies all parts. The majestic opening is characteristic of this rhythmic complexity. The inner voices are often repeated figures in triplet rhythms. Sometimes these repeated chords build dynamically and harmonically to very dramatic climaxes (measures 29-34 and 81-86). The ABA form basic to these marches is here concluded by an exciting coda. The short B section (measures 35-53) reveals a smoother, slightly more subdued energy and passion. This work is effective at a variety of tempi as long as the martial quality is apparent and the speed does not drag.

> Tempo: Mit grösster Energie
>   (With maximum Energy)
> Length: 96 measures
> Technique: cross-rhythms, large blocked
>   chords, full sound, wide leaps, repeated
>   octaves and chords

No. II, G Minor

The powerful, robust opening and closing sections are contrasted by a middle part that contains the most quiet, peaceful material found in Opus 76. This B section uses delicate legato and portato touches in the Eb Major mode. The form is strictly ABA with the A sections introduced by highly dramatic figures (measures 1-2 and 58-60). The melody is built on chord outlines which are often doubled or tripled strength. The minor mode is essential to the powerful character. Rhythms are similar to those of the first march in that beat divisions alternate and overlap in simple and compound rhythms.

> Tempo: Sehr kräftig (Very powerfully)
> Etwas ruhiger (Somewhat more slowly)
> Erstes tempo (Original tempo)
> Length: 94 measures
> Technique: wide leaps, octaves, repeated
> chords in triplets, cross-rhythms

No. III, **Lager-scene,** Bb Major (Camp scene)

A moderate tempo is indicated in this least flamboyant march of the set. The constant repeated eighth notes combined with a clear and simple melody make this piece very accessible. Crisp dotted rhythms, detached touches, accents, and clear textures add to the martial quality. Rhythms are generally simple and march-like in the A sections, and divided into compound times in the rapid, but smooth middle section. Repeated note figures are carried over even into this contrasting B section, and the melodic material frequently switches hands. The melody often crosses over the accompaniment and both hands are given difficult sustained and moving notes. A quiet, attractive coda concludes this march.

> Tempo: Sehr mässig (Very moderately)
> Length: 81 measures
> Technique: repeated dotted rhythms, quick
> register shifts, repeated triplet chords,
> sudden dynamic changes, staccato and
> legato in same hand

No. IV, Eb Major

    A wide keyboard range covered by leaps and jumps marks this bombastic and fiery march. The fanfare-like chords have a prelude or introductory sound that is almost improvisatory. The middle section employs quieter dynamics and a slightly more sober sound, but the character is changed very little. Unlike the previous marches, triple beat divisions are rarely used. A veiled reference to the "Marseillaise" is found in measures 48-49. The ABA form ends with a very dramatic and lengthy coda (23 measures) that acts as a summary or postlude to the set.

        Tempo: Mit Kraft und Feuer
          (With Strength and Ardor)
        Length: 115 measures
        Technique: wide leaps, jumps, octaves and full
           chords in fast dotted rhythms, awkward
           legato double note passages, solid rhythm,
           solid hand shapes, physical endurance

WALDSCENEN, Opus 82 (Forest Scenes)
or "Waldszenen" (1849)

Soon after the completion of <u>Album for the Young</u>,
Op. 68, Schumann composed these nine pieces within a
nine day span from the 29th of December, 1848 to the
6th of January, 1849.   It was dedicated to Fraulien
Annette Preusser.   Each piece was originally prefaced
with a poem or motto of which only No. 4 remains in
most publications.   The individual movements are
somewhat unequal in importance, but offer good
character and mood contrast.   The key scheme is not
arresting.   Schumann's characterization of the woods
combines the lovely and beautiful with the strange and
ominous.

Note: The following editions contain Opus 82 in its
entirety. Other sources are listed with each piece.

ALFRED (Publisher): Schumann—29 of His Most Popular
Piano Selections.
BOETTICHER, Wolfgang: Schumann Klavierwerke,
Band II (G. Henle).
LIPSKY, Alexander: Robert Schumann Album I for Piano
(Kalmus #3930/Belwin).
SAUER, Emil: Complete Works of Robert Schumann,
Volume 1 (Peters #2300A).
SCHUMANN, Clara: Piano Music of Robert Schumann,
Series II (Dover).
SCHUMANN, Clara: Robert Schumann—Complete
Works, Volume 5 (Kalmus #3927/Belwin).

No. 1 **Eintritt,** Bb Major (Entrance)   <u>Intermediate</u>

GEORGII, Walter: Leichte Klaviermusik, Band I
   (G. Henle Verlag).

> Wir gehn auf tannumzauntem Pfad
> Durch schlankes Gras, durch duft'ges Moos
> Dem grunen Dickicht in den Schoss.
>
> (We go on the fir-bounded path,
> by tall grass and fragrant moss,
> into the heart of the green thicket.)

This invitation to the forest gives little indication of the more ominous aspects of the journey to Waldscenen. The lovely work features changes of dynamic level and tone quality that can be breathtaking. The phrasing is sometimes asymmetrical; the number of measures may be divisible by eight, but the individual phrases contain many subtleties and unusual divisions. This unsettling effect can be used to great advantage in performance. The bass movement, such as in measures 12-16, is especially interesting.

   Tempo: Nicht zu schnell (Not too fast) ♩ = 132
   Length: 45 measures
   Technique: tonal control within soft
      dynamic range, legato chord writing,
      repeated chords, hand independence

No. 2 **Jäger auf der Lauer,**   Advancing Intermediate
   D Minor (Hunter in Ambush)

A successful performance of this exciting work exploits its dramatic flair and driving rhythmic force. Although a well developed general facility is called for, the techniques used are very pianistic. Wide keyboard and dynamic ranges work together for an exciting effect. The figuration varies quite a bit and includes large chords, running triplets, and repeated notes. The lively tempo is characterized by duple and triple beat divisions. Both of the "hunting songs" in Opus 82 are based on Heinrich Laube's poems "Jagdbrevier." The motto which originally preceded this piece described the hunter's expectancy before the hunt. Schumann later used these poems in his Jaglieder, Op. 137, for male chorus and four horns.

> Tempo: Höchst lebhaft (Highest vivaciousness)
> ♩ = 76
> Length: 39 measures
> Technique: leaps, cross-rhythms, full chords,
>   full dynamic range within sudden contrasts

No. 3 **Einsame Blumen,** Bb Major   Intermediate
(Lonely Flowers) or "Solitary Flowers"

DEXTER, Harry: Selected Piano Works—Schumann
    (Hansen).
DEXTER, Harry: The Young Pianist's Schumann
    (Hansen).
GEORGII, Walter: Leichte Klaviermusik, Band I
    (G. Henle Verlag).
HEINRICHSHOFEN (Publisher): Schumann--Easier
    Favorites (Peters N.4052).
KOVATS, Gabor: 300 Years of Piano Music--German
    Romanticism (Musica Budapest/Boosey & Hawkes).
PALMER, Willard: Schumann--An Introduction to His
    Piano Works (Alfred).
ROWLEY, Alec: The Easiest Original Schumann
    (Hinrichsen No.7/Peters).

The tempo indication "Einfach" also describes the character, harmonies, melody, and rhythm of this quiet piece. The similar patterns and somewhat vague harmonic direction could become dull if not played clearly and simply by a sensitive musician. A meandering melody is grouped in long phrases of 8, 10, and 12 measures. The top two voices are often imitative; this is especially clear in measures 27-32. Legato touch is used exclusively. The theme is very similar in melodic outline to a song, "Fruhlingsglauben," by Schubert.

> Tempo: Einfach (Simply) ♩ = 96
> Length: 76 measures
> Technique: 2 independent voices in RH, tonal
>   control in limited dynamic range, LH skips

No. 4 Verrufene Stelle,   Advancing Intermediate
    D Minor (Haunted Spot) or "Place of Evil Fame"

> Die Blumen, so hoch sie wachsen,
> Sind blass hier, wie der Tod;
> Nur eine in der Mitte
> Steht da im dunkeln Roth.
> Die hat es nicht von der Sonne:
> Nie traf sie deren Gluth;
> Sie hat es von der Erde,
> Und die trank Menschenblut.
>
> (The flowers that grow so high are here as pale
>   as death;
> only in the middle grows one
> which gets its dark red not from the sun's glow
> but from the earth which drank human blood.)
>   --F. Hebbel

This dramatic work is based on a ghoulish poem by Hebbel. Schumann originally titled it "Verrufere Ort," meaning "Boycotted Place." The ominous elements of the forest are in full force here. The scope of the piece is large, and there may be some difficulties in making the various parts hang together in a unified fashion. A wide keyboard range is covered smoothly and quickly, and doubly dotted figures abound. This dramatic work is one of Schumann's most successful tone poems, and needs a powerful interpretation.

> Tempo: Ziemlich langsam (Rather slowly)♩ = 60
> Length: 35 measures
> Technique: double dotted rhythms with
> repeated notes in *pp* range, sudden dynamic
> changes, hand independence

No. **5 Freundliche Landschaft,**   Advancing Intermediate
Bb Major (Friendly Landscape) or "Pleasant
Landscape"

AGAY, Denes: Early Advanced Classics to Moderns, Vol.
   47 (Consolidated).
FERGUSON, Howard: A Keyboard Anthology, Second
   Series, Book V (Assoc. Bd./Belwin-Mills).

Although the 2/4 meter is generally divided into triplet figures, duple divisions are occasionally used when drama and dynamics are heightened. These running triplets give a toccata feel to this fast piece. A light, delicate touch is most commonly called for, but a more forceful driving sound is also used. Quick smooth hand shifts are involved. The thematic material is craftily integrated, as what may be an introduction in one place appears as dramatic building material somewhere else. This thematic material and its constant changes give <u>Freundliche Landschaft</u> a fantasy-like air that at a fast tempo appears as a flighty daydream. Schumann originally titled this work "Freier Ausblick" (Free Outlook). The occasional minor discrepancies between Schumann's metronome markings and Clara's "revisions" are quite dramatic. Schumann's original indication was ♩ = 160, and Clara's later change is ♩ = 144.

> Tempo: Schnell (Fast) ♩ = 144
> Length: 56 measures
> Technique: shifting meters, fast register
>   shifts, rapid legato playing, fast 3-note slurs

No. 6 **Herberge,** Eb Major   Intermediate
(The Wayside Inn) or "At the Inn," "Roadside Inn"

AGAY, Denes: An Anthology of Piano Music--Romantic
    Period, Vol. III (Yorktown).
KRAUSE, Annamaria: German Piano Music for the
    Young Musician (Musica Budapest/
    Boosey & Hawkes).
PALMER, Willard: Schumann--An Introduction to his
    Piano Works (Alfred).
PALMER and HALFORD: The Romantic Era--An
    Introduction to the Piano Music (Alfred).

In a straightforward sound, classical harmonies present a gentle, pastoral mood. The metronome marking given in the Clara Schumann edition (♩ = 132) seems a bit fast for the "Massig" tempo indication. <u>Herberge</u>, originally titled "Jagerhaus" (Hunting Lodge), can be quite expressive of the intended, gentle sense if a slower speed is taken. Changing figurations, touches, articulation, tempi, and dynamics keep the performer alert. The leaping figures in ♩. ♪ rhythm are from a theme composed by Clara. The principal theme comes from the melody of Schumann's song setting of a forest poem by Eichendorff. The poem is about a bride who wanders off into the woods and falls prey to a witch.

       Tempo: Mässig (Moderately) ♩ = 132
       Length: 56 measures
       Technique: contrasting musical ideas, leaps, hand independence, wide dynamic and tonal changes, tonal control

No. 7 **Vogel als Prophet,**   Advancing Intermediate
     G Minor (Prophet Bird)

AGAY, Denes: An Anthology of Piano Music--Romantic Period, Volume III (Yorktown).
DEXTER, Harry: Selected Piano Works—Schumann (Hansen).
DEXTER, Harry: The Young Pianist's Schumann (Hansen).
HEINRICHSHOFEN (Publisher): Schumann--Easier Favorites (Peters No.4052).
SCHIRMER (Publisher): Selected Piano solos by Romantic Composers, Lib. Vol. 1720, Book III.
SHEALY, Alexander: Schumann--His Greatest Piano Solos (Ashley).
VOGRICH, Max: Schumann Album for the Piano (G. Schirmer Vol. 100).

"Hüte dich! sei wach und munter" (Take care! Be on your guard!) is the intended motto for this frequently performed piece. The mood is delicate and somewhat unsettling. F.E. Kirby makes an excellent summary by describing the piece as "Pianissimo with piquant dissonances through the use of cross-relations, the fragmentary phrases rising and falling." The asymmet-

rical phrasing is odd and sometimes abruptly fragmented, although it often appears within the classical
four and eight measure divisions. An extremely light
touch is used in most of the broken chord figures. Clara
Schumann's metronome marking seems to be a fitting
tempo. Interesting contrast is offered by a short
homophonic section in measures 19-24. The ending has
an appropriate, unfinished sound to it.

> Tempo: Langsam sehr zart
> (Slowly and softly, tenderly) ♩ = 63
> Length: 42 measures
> Technique: finger independence, register
> shifts, sudden dynamic changes, expanded
> hand positions, rhythmic accuracy

No. 8 **Jagdlied**, Eb Major   Advancing Intermediate
(Hunting Song)

HEINRICHSHOFEN (Publisher): Schumann—Easier
Favorites (Peters No.4052).

Schumann uses all the devices common to hunting
horn imitations, but with fuller, more romantic
harmonies. The ABA format includes long A sections
that employ large chords and repeated notes. These
large chords often span a 9th or a 10th. Dynamics are
not always *forte* even in the big opening and closing
sections. Hand coordination, finger independence, and a
good sense of rhythm are exploited in the odd middle
section. The ♩ ♪ ♫ ♫ rhythmic pattern is an almost
constant element throughout both the A and B
sections. It functions as the rhythm of the theme, of
the horn calls, and of the inner accompanying repeated
notes. The hunting scene described is the fulfillment of
the expectations expressed in Op. 82, No. 2. This large

---

sound is accessible and pleasing.

Tempo: Rasch, kräftig
(Quickly and powerfully) ♩. = 120
Length: 128 measures
Technique: wrist staccato, repeated chords,
full chords, hand independence, hand-
crossings, octaves, 9ths, 10ths, rhythmic
control

No. 9 Abschied, Bb Major   Advancing Intermediate
(Departure)

FERGUSON, Howard: Style and Interpretation, Vol. 4,
Romantic Piano Music (Oxford).
HEINRICHSHOFEN (Publisher): Schumann--Easier
Favorites (Peters No.4052).

Leise dringt der Schatten weiter,
Abendhauch schon weht durchs Tal,
Ferne Hohn nur grussen heiter
Noch den letzten Sonnenstrahl.

(The shadow imperceptibly closes round;
the breath of evening drifts through the valley
only distant peaks salute the last rays of the
sun.)

The final piece of Opus 82 is a gentle, thoroughly romantic farewell that fades ("Immer schwächer") in its last measures. The tempo indication is "Not fast," but a quiet momentum is created by the inner repeated chords. The common time meter is sometimes divided into duple, sometimes triple beat divisions, with frequent two against three rhythms. Each hand often carries two lines that have varying roles and rhythms.

Chromatic movement helps create the lovely romantic
harmonies and flexible rhythmic momentum.

Tempo: Nicht schnell (Not fast) ♩ = 80

Length: 53 measures

Technique: repeated chords as inner voices,
leaps, legato playing, melody against heavy
textured accompaniment, cross-rhythms,
hand coordination

BUNTE BLÄTTER, Opus 99 (Colored Leaves)   Advanced
14 Stucke fur das Pianoforte (1852)

Published by Arnold in 1852, the Bunte Blatter is a
collection of earlier pieces Schumann had not included
in his previous sets. The Opus was dedicated to Fraulein
Mary Potts. Each piece was originally to be issued with
a colored cover indicating its general mood. Many were
written during Schumann's lonely sojourn in Vienna
(1838-1839).

Note: The following editions contain Opus 99 in its
    entirety. Other sources are listed with each piece.

IRMER, Otto von: Schumann Klavierwerke,
    Band I (Henle).
LIPSKY, Alexander: Robert Schumann—Album II for
    Piano (Kalmus #3931/Belwin-Mills).
SAUER, Emil: Complete Works of Robert Schumann,
    Volume 1 (Peters #2300A).
SCHUMANN, Clara: Piano Music of Robert Schumann,
    Series II (Dover).
SCHUMANN, Clara: Robert Schumann—Complete
    Works, Volume 6 (Kalmus #3928/Belwin-Mills).

No. 1 **Drei Stücklein I,** A Major (Three Little Pieces)
    (1839)

HEINRICHSHOFEN (Publisher): Schumann—Easier
    Favorites (Peters No.4052).

Originally intended as a Christmas greeting to
Clara, this inviting piece features a beautiful legato.
The accompanying sixteenth notes serve to produce a
murmuring effect, with long pedals creating the proper

tone color. The *fp* (meaning a stress), fits into the context of the piece.

> Tempo: Nicht schnell, mit Innigkeit
> (Not fast, with deep feeling)
> Length: 17 measures
> Technique: broken chord figurations between the hands, leaps, melody and accompaniment in same hand, tonal control in a limited dynamic range

No. 2 **Drei Stücklein II**, E Minor

Schumann's penchant for writing out opposing meters is ever-present in this stormy piece. Crisp sforzando accents punctuate a taxing figuration. This piece is one of the more difficult of the set.

> Tempo: Sehr rasch (Very quickly)
> Length: 30 measures
> Technique: melody and accompaniment in cross-rhythms in same hand, wide stretches in LH, wide dynamic range

No. 3 **Drei Stücklein III**, E Major

HEINRICHSHOFEN (Publisher): Schumann—Easier Favorites (Peters No.4052).
KOVATS, Gabor: German Romanticism (Musica Budapest/ Boosey & Hawkes).

The boisterous nature of this short piece with its straightforward rhythm makes itself immediately felt. These first three pieces were to have been covered in green.

Tempo: Frisch (Brisk) (Kovats ♩ = 120)
Length: 24 measures
Technique: repeated chords, octaves, hand-crossings, leaps

No. 4 **Albumblätter I**, F# Minor (Album Leaves) (1841)

ALFRED (Publisher): Schumann--18 of His Easiest Piano Selections.

ALFRED (Publisher): Schumann--29 of His Most Popular Piano Selections.

ANSON, George: Anson Introduces Schumann, Book One (Willis).

HERMANN, Kurt: Easy Schubert, Schumann, and Weber (Kalmus #9541/Belwin-Mills).

KAIL, Robert: Easy Schumann Piano Pieces (Columbia #F1035PAX).

KOVATS, Gabor: 300 Years of Piano Music--German Romanticism (Musica Budapest/Boosey & Hawkes).

LYKE, ELLISTON, HARTLINE: Keyboard Musicianship, Book Two (Stipes).

NOVIK, Ylda: Young Pianist's Guide to Schumann (Studio P/R).

PALMER, Willard: Schumann--An Introduction to His Piano Works (Alfred).

ROWLEY, Alec: The Easiest Original Schumann Pieces for the Piano (Hinrichsen, No. 7/Peters).

WEISMANN, Wilhelm: Romantic Masters (Peters No. 5033).

This beautiful piece has been the subject of a set of variations by Brahms and also Clara Schumann. It is extremely well constructed and will be rewarding with good tonal control and a non-percussive touch. The last section makes an ethereal ending.

Tempo: Ziemlich langsam (Somewhat slowly)
Length: 24 measures
Technique: tonal control within limited
dynamic range, inner voices

No. 5 **Allbumblätter II,** B Minor (1838)

This darkly hued piece produces the effect of a whirlwind of sound. The strong, percussive accents on the second beat indicate that this melody note lasts through all the filagree surrounding it. The long pedal at the end creates a pool of sound which makes a striking effect.

Tempo: Schnell (Fast)
Length: 36 measures
Technique: fast figuration broken between
the hands, leaps, dynamic control

No. 6 **Albumblätter III,** Ab Major (1836)

ANTHONY, George W.: Schubert to Shostakovich, Intermediate, Vol. 2 (Presser).
KOVATS, Gabor: German Romanticism (Musica Budapest/Boosey & Hawkes).

This slow, elegant waltz on the theme ASCH is the earliest of the pieces, as it was originally intended to have been part of <u>Carnaval</u>, Op. 9. A successful performance will be achieved through playing in an elegant manner without heaviness, and maintaining a beautiful tone.

> Tempo: Zeimlich langsam (Somewhat slowly)
> Length: 41 measures
> Technique: LH leaps, legato octaves, tonal
>   control within limited dynamic range

No. 7 **Albumblätter IV,** Eb Minor (1838)

The melody of this piece is encased in a thick texture of inner parts. An echo effect is heard at the beginning, though without alteration of the original tempo. The suspensions are another contrapuntal aspect of this writing, contributing to its intense expressiveness.

> Tempo: Sehr langsam (Very slowly)
> Length: 15 measures
> Technique: independent voices in same hand,
>   inner voices, finger independence

No. 8 **Albumblätter V,** Eb Major

FROST, Bernice: Piano Repertoire (J. Fischer/Belwin).
PALMER, Willard: Schumann--An Introduction to His
    Piano Works (Alfred).
ROWLEY, Alec: The Easiest Original Schumann Pieces
    for the Piano (Hinrichsen, No. 7/Peters).

Various changes of harmony produced by the moving
voices distinguish this quiet, reflective piece. The
repeat of the initial phrase could be played *pianissimo*
to produce an echo effect. Again there are many
suspensions, with a portamento helping to create the
hesitating effect called for at the close.
>   Tempo: Langsam (Slowly)
>   Length: 21 measures
>   Technique: inner voices, syncopation, careful
>   pedal, tonal control within limited dynamic
>   range

No. 9 **Novellete**, B Minor (Novellette) (1838)
    or "Novelette"

AGAY, Denes: An Anthology of Piano Music--Romantic
    Period, Volume III (Yorktown).
KAIL, Robert: Easy Schumann Piano Pieces
    (Columbia #F1035PAX).
VOGRICH, Max: Schumann Album for the Piano
    (G. Schirmer Vol. 100).

The capricious nature of this piece is projected
immediately. The outer sections contain a quick
staccato touch without any heaviness, while the middle
section is a moment of repose. Chromatic accompanying figures wind around the melody. This was probably
meant to be part of Novelletten, Op. 21.

Tempo: Lebhaft (Vivacious)
Length: 143 measures
Technique: staccato inner voice with legato
   outer voice in same hand, legato chromatic
   scales, leaps, sudden dynamic changes

No. 10 **Präludium,** Bb Minor (Prelude)

SHEALY, Alexander: Robert Schumann--His Greatest
   Piano Solos (Ashley).

Careful attention to fingering will be a top priority
in this energetic piece, said to be comprised of the
remnants of two fugues. It is not possible to hold the
melody to its full value in many spots without aid of the
pedal. This is one of the more difficult of the set.
   Tempo: Energisch (Energetic, vigorous)
   Length: 21 measures
   Technique: minimal melody above heavily
      textured accompaniment, stretches of 9ths
      and 10ths, syncopation, awkward
      passagework, careful pedal

No. 11 **Marsch,** D Minor (March) (1843)

The sheer length of this somber march in unvarying tempo makes it a challenging piece to play. The many full chords can be played by small hands with careful distribution and rolling of chords. The trio, with its many repeated notes, can be monotonous if not provided with dynamic interest. The chords are lovely.

Tempo: Sehr getragen (Very sustained)

Length: 137 measures

Technique: widely spaced chords, inner voices, careful pedal, dynamic control, fast repeated chords, fast 2-note slurs

No. 12 **Abendmusik,** Bb Major (Evening Music) (1841)

SHEALY, Alexander: Robert Schumann--His Greatest Piano Solos (Ashley).

This pleasant, restrained piece is not taxing technically, the ♪♪♩ ♩ figure with its repeated note being the chief difficulty. The middle section closely resembles the trio of "Grillen" from Op. 12. Rhythmic interest is provided by having the third beat tied over to the first throughout this section. The ear begins to hear the third beat as the first because of this. The entire piece brings to mind the German word "Gemütlichkeit" (comfortable, genial).

Tempo: Im Menuett-Tempo
(In the tempo of a minuet)

Length: 121 measures

Technique: leaps, syncopation, strong rhythmic pulse, *pp* chords in lower register

No. 13 **Scherzo,** G Minor (1841)

This lengthy Scherzo also dates from 1841, for it was originally to be part of the C Minor symphony of that year. The many rapid chords present the major technical difficulty in this long piece. The imitation beginning in measure 27 and the quick dynamic changes in the G Major sections help provide interest. There is a reference to the Carnaval motif in the first trio.

> Tempo: Lebhaft (Vivaciously)
> Length: 243 measures
> Technique: fast staccato chords, leaps, wide
>   hand stretches, sudden dynamic changes

No. 14 **Geschwindmarsch,** G Minor (Fast March) (1849)

This straightforward and humorous march was to have been one of the "Barricade Marches," Op. 76. The grace notes and marked accents help to give it a biting quality. The left hand shifts register frequently, and non-legato octaves produce a direct effect.

Tempo: Sehr markirt (Very marcato)
Length: 161 measures
Technique: wide leaps, octaves in scales, trills,
sudden dynamic changes, strong rhythmic
pulse, sudden character changes

DREI PHANTASIESTÜCKE, Opus 111
(Three Fantasies)

The original title of Opus 111 was "Cyclus fur Pianoforte." It was dedicated to Princess Reuss-Kostritz, nee Countess Castell, and was originally published by C.F. Peters, Leipzig. The entire set is concise and well integrated through key scheme, form, and thematic material. The ultimate title takes its inspiration from Opus 12, and similarities to its namesake are confirmed by the relationship between Opus 12, No. 5, and Opus 111, No. 1. This second set of fantasy pieces is excellent performance material and worthy of more than the relative obscurity it has received.

Note: The following editions contain Opus 111 in its entirety. Other sources are listed with each piece.

BOETTICHER, Wolfgang: Schumann Klavierwerke, Band II (Henle).
SAUER, Emil: Complete Works of Robert Schumann, Volume 4 (Peters #2300D).
SCHUMANN, Clara: Piano Music of Robert Schumann, Series III (Dover).
SCHUMANN, Clara: Robert Schumann—Complete Works, Volume 6 (Kalmus #3928/Belwin).

No. 1, C Minor <u>Advanced</u>

The first of the set is an impassioned free form—an improvisational "fantasia" style. Thematic and harmonic material is generated through broken chord, arpeggiated figurations. These sweep the keyboard in triplet rhythms that ascend and descend chromatically, and are accompanied by constant dynamic swells and diminuendo. The melodic material, presented in asymmetrical phrases, shifts from voice to voice. A direct quotation from "In der Nacht" of Op. 12 finally emerges.

> Tempo: Sehr rasch, mit leidenschaftlichem
> Vortrag (Very fast, played with passion)
> ♩ = 84
> Length: 57 measures
> Technique: awkward rapid chordal figurations
> distributed between the hands, cross-
> rhythms, inner voices, sudden dynamic
> contrasts, tonal control, extreme dynamic
> control, wide leaps

No. 2, Ab Major   Advanced

An "attacca" into the second piece which begins with a lovely cantabile melody with tonal harmonies in chordal writing, provides a sudden and sharp contrast to the previous piece. The middle section of this simple ABA form brings the listener back to the character of the first piece. Its C Minor tonality and arpeggiated triplet rhythms are under a chromatic melodic line. Energetic left hand octaves provide a climax in this section and the piece is brought to a quiet close with the return of the A section.

> Tempo: Ziemlich langsam (Rather slowly)
> ♩ = 72
> Length: 78 measures
> Technique: tonal control, octaves, broken
> chord figuration, cross-rhythms

No. 3, C Minor   Advanced

AGAY, Denes: Early Advanced Classics to Moderns,
   Vol. 47 (Consolidated).

A robust march in an ABA form with a coda
concludes the set. The martial theme in four bar
phrases features dotted rhythms accompanied by off-
beat detached chords. The quiet B section achieves
contrast by inserting florid, often chromatic running
sixteenth note figuration into a texture that retains
something of the established march character. A return
of the initial theme, followed by a coda which uses
melodic material from the B section, closes the piece.

   Tempo: Kräftig und sehr markiert
      (Strong and well marked) ♩ = 96
   Length: 58 measures
   Technique: large chords, LH 16th-note
      figuration, sustained and moving notes in
      same hand, voicing, solid rhythm

DREI CLAVIER-SONATEN FÜR DE JUGEND, Op. 118
(Three Sonatas for the Young) (1853)
(Op. 118a, 118b, 118c)

These three sonatas were written for Schumann's daughters, 118a for Julie who was 8, 118b for Elise who was 10, and 118c for Marie who was 12. Their range of difficulty corresponds to the ages of the three. They contain some "interesting moments" and some Schumannesque writing, but on the whole they tend to be too long and to lack rhythmic originality and substance.

Note: The following editions contain Opus 118 in its entirety. Other sources are listed with each piece.

SAUER, Emil: Complete Works of Robert Schumann, Volume 4 (Peters #2300D).
SCHUMANN, Clara: Piano Music of Robert Schumann, Series II (Dover).
SCHUMANN, Clara: Robert Schumann—Complete Works, Volume 6 (Kalmus #3928/Belwin-Mills).

Sonate No. 1 Julien zur Erinnerung, Early Intermediate
G Major, Opus 118a (For Julie) or "To Julia," "For Juliett," "In Memory of Juliett"

KAIL, Robert: Easy Schumann Piano Pieces (Columbia #F1035PAX).
LIPSKY, Alexander: Schumann—Album I for Piano (Kalmus No.3930/Belwin-Mills).

Allegro

HERMANN, Kurt: Easy Schubert, Schumann, and Weber
(Kalmus #9541/Belwin-Mills).
MOTCHANE, Marthe Morhange: An Introduction to
Pianistic Styles—Book 3--Romantic (Bourne).
PACE, Robert: Music for Piano, Book 5
(Roberts/Schirmer).
PALMER, Willard: Schumann: An Introduction to his
Piano Works (Alfred).
SHEALY, Alexander: Robert Schumann—His Greatest
Piano Solos (Ashley).
WELCH, John: Schroeder's Favorite Classics, Vol. 2
(Studio P/R).

There is a sprightly hymn-like feel to this first
movement in ternary form.   It is appropriate for a
younger performer, being accessible and pianistic.   In
the A section both hands have a parallel melody similar
to "Melody," Op. 68. The B section has joyous two note
slurs of an eighth note, quarter note, and rest.
Tempo: Lebhaft (Vivacious) ♩ = 92
Length: 50 measures
Technique: Alberti bass with independent
voices, syncopation, small skips, contrast in
legato and detached playing

Thema mit Variationen, E Minor
(Theme with Variations)

SZAVAI-VESZPERME: Album for Piano No. 2
(Belwin-Mills).

The theme with its many rests is interesting, but
not inspiring. The variations go from a basic quarter
note beat with portamento touch, to eighths, to triplets,
to an E Major section, and end up in sixteenths. There

is a variety of touches and the left hand has many melody parts. A quick coda in sixteenth notes ties the whole piece together.

Tempo: Zeimlich langsam (Rather slowly)
♩ = 68
Length: 40 measures
Technique: melody and accompaniment in one hand, 2-note slurs, staccato, legato

Puppenwiegenlied, C Major (Doll's cradle song)

HERMANN, Kurt: Easy Schubert, Schumann, and Weber (Kalmus #9541/Belwin-Mills).

This charming movement in ternary form features a similar type of writing to numbers 1, 3, and 5 of Op. 68 with a right hand melody and a left hand countermelody with accompaniment in the same hand. The A section is in eighth notes and the B section in sixteenths with staccato double thirds in the accompaniment.

Tempo: Nicht schnell (Not fast) ♩ = 90
Length: 64 measures
Technique: independent voices using quarter against 8th rhythms in same hand, double 3rds in staccato accompaniment against legato melody

Rondoletto

HUGHES, Edwin: Schumann--Master Series for the
Young (G. Schirmer).

This <u>Rondoletto</u> is the most attractive of the four
movements, with its gay and sprightly air. The first
section has right hand eighths against two-note slurs in
the left hand. The second section is in single
note rhythm. The C section changes to the key of D
Major, and has a more somber mood. It does not
indicate that it is to be slower, but it plays better that
way. The last section of the theme has a canon
feeling. The entire sonata is appealing but not having a
"Clementi" sound may not seem suitable for sonatina
festivals.

> Tempo: Munter (Lively) ♩.= 84
> Length: 208 measures
> Technique: 2-note slurs as accompaniment
> against irregularly slurred melody, register
> shifts, double note passages

No. 2 Sonate, Elisen zum Andenken,   <u>Intermediate</u>
D Major (For Elise) 118b

Allegro

Written for the ten year old Elise, this is a more
difficult work--both of the outer movements are in
sonata form. This movement is very long and
repetitious with a tiresome ♩ ♪♪♪♪ rhythmic motif
throughout. There are a few sprightly passages of
bouncing staccato chords at the end of this rhythmic
figure. The many sixteenth note passages will provide a
workout for the young person studying this piece.

Tempo: Lebhaft (Fast, vivaciously) ♩ = 104
Length: 128 measures
Technique: fast chromatic melodic material,
  independent voices in same hand, leaps,
  skips, cross-rhythms, sudden dynamic
  changes, melody in outer RH with broken
  interval accompaniment in same hand

Canon

ROWLEY, Alec: The Easiest Original Schumann Pieces
  for the Piano (Hinrichsen No. 7/Peters).

As its name indicates, the second movement is a
study in counterpoint. The Canon comes in at one
measure intervals with the left hand having only the
melody line, usually in staccato eighths. The right hand
adds a second part. There is a fast, bright staccato
sound to this straightforward canon.

Tempo: Lebhaft (Vivaciously) ♩ = 96
Length: 62 measures
Technique: staccato melody in both hands,
  LH octave skips, staccato vs. legato (some
  in same hand)

Abendlied (Evening Song)

HERMANN, Kurt: Easy Schubert, Schumann, and Weber
  (Kalmus #9541/Belwin-Mills).

<u>Abendlied</u> presents a gently flowing melody against triplet accompaniment. This is a pretty and welcome respite from the other longer and more "notey" movements.

> Tempo: Langsam (Slowly) ♩ = 50
> Length: 33 measures
> Technique: legato playing, 3-voice texture
>   containing a broken chord accompaniment
>   distributed between the hands, easy
>   2 vs. 3

Kindergesellschaft, D Major (Children's Party)

The fourth movement is the most technically demanding of this sonata, and the most tedious. There are long stretches of incessant sixteenth note passage-work in legato and staccato. The nice bombastic chordal ending will be a big relief to performer and audience alike.

> Tempo: Sehr Lebhaft (Very Lively) ♩ = 102
> Length: 188 measures
> Technique: staccato in both hands, staccato
>   vs. legato, awkward passagework

No. 3 Sonate Marien   Advancing Intermediate
   Gewidmet, C Major, Opus 118c (For Marie)

Allegro

This sonata is obviously for an older student with larger hands and a more mature approach. This first movement is fun to play with its octaves, chords, and running sixteenth note passages. There is a three note motif in a ♪. ♫ ♩ rhythmic pattern which is found throughout the entire movement in various forms and places.

> Tempo: Im Marschtempo
> (Lively, in a march tempo) ♩ = 88
> Length: 105 measures
> Technique: repeated chords, leaps, register
> shifts, syncopation, full dynamic range,
> running 16th note passages

Andante, F Major

The lovely floating sounds of this <u>Andante</u> make it one of the <u>nicest</u> movements of the set. The rhythmic pattern ♫ ♪.♫ prevails throughout. The meaningful dynamics produce the poignant introspective quality characteristic of Schumann.

> Tempo: Ausdrucksvoll (Expressively) ♪ = 132
> Length: 27 measures
> Technique: melody in chordal texture,
> chromatic runs, tonal control

Zigeunertanz, A Minor (Gypsy dance)

ALFRED (Publisher): Schumann--29 of his Most Popular
    Piano Selections.
ROWLEY, Alec: The Easiest Original Schumann Pieces
    for the Piano (Hinrichsen, No. 7/Peters).
SZAVAI-VESZPREME: Album for Piano, Vol. 2
    (Belwin-Mills).

This is a great piece for the "pounder" in our
midst. It doesn't require much musicianship and can be
played with abandoned spirit.   The sixteenth note
triplets and the mad sixty-fourth note dashes will
produce a "Let 'er rip!" effect.
    Tempo: Schnell (Fast) ♩ = 80
    Length: 66 measures
    Technique: legato vs. staccato, frequent
        metrical changes, rapid scales

Traum eines Kindes, C Major (A Child's Dream)

The fourth movement contains some intriguing
ideas, such as quotations from the first movement of
the Sonata, Opus 118a and the horn effects. Otherwise
it is far too long and rhythmically monotonous. It is
interspersed with short classical sounding sections.
Major chords and simple melodies are suddenly
interrupted by staccato "strutting" notes.
    Tempo: Sehr lebhaft (Very vivaciously) ♩. = 130
    Length: 214 measures
    Technique: legato, independent voices, variety
        of touches, syncopation, register changes

ALBUMBLÄTTER, Opus 124 (Album Leaves) (1854)

The Albumblätter, like its predecessor Bunte
Blätter, Op. 99, is a collection of previously unpublished
pieces. Some of these date as far back as 1832.
Schumann prepared the set for publication in 1854. The
Opus was dedicated to Alma von Wasielewski, and was
originally published by A. Furstner, Berlin.

Note: The following editions contain Opus 124 in its
    entirety. Other sources are listed with each piece.

IRMER, Otto von: Schumann Klavierwerke, Band I
    (Henle).
SAUER, Emil: Complete Works of Robert Schumann,
    Volume 1 (Peters #2300A).
SCHUMANN, Clara: Piano Music of Robert Schumann,
    Series III (Dover).
SCHUMANN, Clara: Robert Schumann--Complete
    Works, Volume 6 (Kalmus #3928/Belwin).

No. 1 **Impromptu,** D Minor   Advancing Intermediate
    (1832)

Composed before Chopin began his preludes, this
work is similar in character, style, and size to many of
Chopin's miniatures. A torrent of notes tumble over
each other as swiftly as possible. Backed by a strong
driving force, similar patterns are continuously
repeated, tending to accelerate. Both hands are used
equally. The low register of measures 17-25 makes
clarity and voicing difficult. The left hand is given a
technical challenge by the legato thirds and chromatic
movement. The quiet dynamics of the lovely harmonies
in measures 23-26 are especially effective.

Tempo: Sehr schnell (Very fast)
Length: 34 measures
Technique: rapid figuration with LH double
    3rds, clarity in low register, minimal
    melodic material

No. 2 **Leides Ahnung,** A Minor   Advancing Intermediate
(Premonition of Sorrow) or "Grief's Forebodings"
    (1835)

ROWLEY, Alec: The Easiest Original Schumann
    (Hinrichsen No.7/Peters).
ROYAL CONSERVATORY OF MUSIC, Grade IX
    (Frederick Harris).

Material for this piece comes from some very early
sketches, all unpublished during Schumann's lifetime.
Between 1829 and 1833 Schumann composed 11
variations on a theme of Beethoven taken from the
Allegretto of Symphony No. 7. Of these variations,
found in his "Zwickau Sketchbook IV," the fifth became
Leides Ahnung of this opus. Some of this same material
also shows up in the unpublished "Andante with
variations on an original theme," G Major (measures 78-
83), also written in 1832. An ominous premonition, this
subdued work is almost funereal. A march-like quality
is effected by the detached chords which accompany the
legato melody. The most pervasive motif of this
monothematic piece has a descending melodic outline
befitting the sorrowful character. Both hands carry this
legato melody and the detached accompaniment. The
entire chord is struck, then the accompanimental chords
are released leaving the melody to sound through. *Fp*
accents are often found on the initial note of a phrase,
generally the third beat of the measure.

Tempo: Langsam (Slowly)
Length: 24 measures
Technique: stretches of a 9th, dotted rhythms,
  legato melody with detached chordal
  accompaniment in same hand

No. 3 **Scherzino**, F Major (1832) <u>Advancing Intermediate</u>

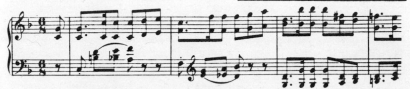

KOVATS, Gabor: German Romanticism
  (Musica Budapest/Boosey & Hawkes).
SHEALY, Alexander: Schumann--His Greatest Piano
  Solos (Ashley).

The material for this impetuous <u>Scherzino</u> was
originally sketched out between 1829 and 1830. It is
found in Schumann's third Zwickau Sketchbook and was
perhaps originally intended for <u>Papillons</u>. The set of
waltzes in which it was sketched later evolved or
expanded to ten pieces entitled "Variationen." Two
sketches were written for the fourth variation, and one
of these eventually became this piece. The lively tempo
indication is especially appropriate in this <u>Scherzino</u>.
The ABA form uses a dance-like scherzo to open and
close the piece, and a legato trio with interesting cross-
rhythms in the middle. These cross-rhythms are very
similar to those found in Opus 12, numbers 1 and 2 ("Des
Abends" and "Aufschwung"). The B section wanders to
and from distant keys by way of accidentals marking
chromatic movement.

Tempo: Rasch (Quickly)
Length: 27 measures
Technique: octaves in scalar passage work,
  syncopation, melody and accompaniment
  in same hand, legato-staccato touch
  contrasts

No. 4 **Walzer,** A Minor (Waltz) (1855)   <u>Intermediate</u>

ALFRED (Publisher): Schumann--18 of His Easiest Piano
  Selections.
ALFRED (Publisher): Schumann--29 of His Most Popular
  Piano Selections.
BRIMHALL, John: My First Book of Classics--Schumann
  (Hansen).
CLARK and GOSS: Piano Literature of the 17th, 18th,
  and 19th Centuries, Book 5b (Summy-Birchard).
DEXTER, Harry: The Young Pianist's Schumann
  (Hansen).
DEXTER, Harry: Selected Piano Works--Schumann
  (Hansen).
ETTS, May L.: Beginning to Play Schumann
  (Schroeder & Gunther).
FLETCHER, Leila: The Leila Fletcher Piano Course,
  Book Six (Montgomery).
HEINRICHSHOFEN (Publisher): Schumann--Easier
  Favorites (Peters No.4052).
KAIL, Robert: Easy Schumann Piano Pieces
  (Columbia #F1035PAX).
KOVATS, Gabor: 300 Years of Piano Music--German
  Romanticism (Musica Budapest/Boosey & Hawkes).
NAHUM, WOLFE, KOSAKOFF: Piano Classic Collection
  (J. Fischer/Belwin-Mills).
NEVIN, Mark: Piano Course, Book Four (Belwin-Mills).
NOVIK, Ylda: Young Pianist's Guide to Schumann
  (Studio P/R).
PALMER, Willard: Schumann--An Introduction to His
  Piano Works (Alfred).
ROWLEY, Alec: The Easiest Original Schumann
  (Hinrichsen No.7/Peters).
SHEALY, Alexander: Schumann--His Greatest Piano
  Solos (Ashley).

LANNING, Russell: Music by the Masters
(Musicord/Belwin).
MOTCHANE, Marthe Morhange: An Introduction to
Pianistic Styles, Romantic (Bourne).
NAHUM, WOLFE, KOSAKOFF: Piano Classic Collection
(J. Fischer/Belwin-Mills).
NOONA, Walter and Carol: The Classical Performer C
(Heritage).
NOVIK, Ylda: Young Pianist's Guide to Schumann
(Studio P/R).
OLSON, BIANCHI, BLICKENSTAFF: Repertoire 5B
(C. Fischer).
ROWLEY, Alec: The Easiest Original Schumann
(Hinrichsen No.7/Peters).
WEISMANN, Wilhelm: Romantic Masters
(Peters No. 5033).

Unrestrained drama is found in the prelude and
interlude which precede a subdued, but passionate
section with its own drama. This piece is similar to the
Opus 124, No. 1 "Impromptu" in that patterns and
figures combine to create a torrential effect. This
impressive dance is very pianistic and easier than it
sounds. The larger sections find a left hand melody
driven by accompaniment patterns and harmonies that
are smooth and rhythmically exciting. This piece was
also rejected from the original sketches of Opus 9. It is
played very fast and impetuously with the dynamics
providing effective contrast.

Tempo: Sehr rasch (Very quickly)
Length: 25 measures
Technique: single note chromatic fragments,
hand independence, legato LH melody with
rapid 2-note slurred figuration as
accompaniment, finger facility

No. 6 **Wiegenliedchen,** G Major   Advancing Elementary
(Cradle Song), or "Little Cradle Song,"
"Little Lullaby" (1843)

ANSON, George: Anson Introduces Schumann, Book One
(Willis).

BRIMHALL, John: My First Book of Classics—Schumann
(Hansen).

DEXTER, Harry: The Young Pianist's Schumann
(Hansen).

ETTS, May L.: Beginning to Play Schumann
(Schroeder & Gunther).

GLOVER and GARROW: Piano Repertoire, Level Four
(Belwin-Mills).

HEINRICHSHOFEN (Publisher): Schumann—Easier
Favorites (Peters No.4052).

HERRMAN, Kurt: Easy Schubert, Schumann, and Weber
(Kalmus #9541/Belwin-Mills).

HUGHES, Edwin: Schumann—Master Series for the
Young (G. Schirmer).

KAIL, Robert: Easy Schumann Piano Pieces
(Columbia #F1035PAX).

KLEINMICHEL, Richard: 32 Sonatinas and Rondos
(Schirmer Vol. 693).

KOVATS, Gabor: 300 Years of Piano Music—German
Romanticism (Musica Budapest/Boosey & Hawkes).

OLSON BIANCHI, BLICKENSTAFF: Repertoire 5B
(C. Fischer).

PACE, Robert: Music for Piano, Book 5
(Roberts/Schirmer).

PALMER, Willard: Schumann—The First Book for Young
Pianists (Alfred).

PALMER, Willard: Schumann—An Introduction to His
Piano Works (Alfred).

ROWLEY, Alec: The Easiest Original Schumann
(Hinrichsen No.7/Peters).

SHEALY, Alexander: Schumann--His Greatest Piano
   Solos (Ashley).
VOGRICH, Max: Schumann Album for the Piano
   (G. Schirmer Vol. 100).

Technically simpler than the first pieces of Opus
124, this cradle song is musically treacherous because of
the bare texture.   An exquisite melody sings over a
subdued accompaniment.   The right hand carries both
melody and broken chord figures while the single line
left hand has a countermelody that adds interest.   Long
melodic lines and tonal variation are basic to the
interpretation of this piece.   The tempo is not
"Langsam" as might be expected, but "Nicht schnell."
Interestingly, the date of this lullaby coincides with the
birth of Schumann's second daughter in 1843.
       Tempo: Nicht schnell (Not fast)
       Length: 48 measures
       Technique: melody and accompaniment in
          same hand, long melodic line, careful
          pedal, legato

No. **7 Ländler**, D Major   Advancing Intermediate
   or "Country Dance" (1836)

ALFRED (Publisher): Schumann--29 of His Most Popular
   Piano Selections.
ROWLEY, Alec: The Easiest Original Schumann
   (Hinrichsen No.7/Peters).
SHEALY, Alexander: Schumann--His Greatest Piano
   Solos (Ashley).

Syncopation, phrasing, and ties all add to the
rhythmic interest in this usually stable dance form.   Of
the three 8-measure phrases, the second with its synco-

pations will flow with an inner sense of rhythm and an assured touch. Accidentals, ties, and notes jumping from one staff to another make reading much harder than playing. Light grace notes and a detached touch at the ending aid the light-hearted character. The <u>Ländler</u> reflects the Schubertian dance influences of the period.

> Tempo: Sehr mässig (Very moderately)
> Length: 26 measures
> Technique: variety of touch contrasts within
> small frame, arpeggiated chords,
> syncopation, 2-note slurs

No. 8 **Lied Ohne Ende,** F Major <u>Advancing Intermediate</u>
(Suffering without end) or "Endless Grief" (1837)

SHEALY, Alexander: Schumann--His Greatest Piano
Solos (Ashley).

A languorous melody is accompanied by broken chord figures that seem to imitate the sound of a harp or a guitar. These two elements combine to create a floating, sustained quality. The rhythm of the melody itself is ambiguous, with many ties over the bar. The shaping of the melody, often indicated by the composer's dynamic markings, provides direction to an improvisatory sound. A short contrasting section is marked "Leidenschaftlicher" meaning "Passionately." The imperfect final cadence with the third in the soprano voices does not give a solid ending sound, thus providing significance to the title.

> Tempo: Langsam (Slowly)
> Length: 50 measures
> Technique: arpeggiation with double note
> figures, careful pedal, p melodic material in
> upper register

No. 9 **Impromptu,** Bb Major   <u>Advancing Intermediate</u>
   (1838)

SHEALY, Alexander: Schumann--His Greatest Piano
   Solos (Ashley).

This very delicate, distant <u>Impromptu</u> has an
extremely thick, four voice texture that is both
homophonic and linear at the same time. The
descending melody, recalling the so-called "Clara
motive," is fragmented among its layers. These
important lines are distributed among the soprano, alto,
and tenor voices. Constructed from two different four
measure phrases, this <u>Impromptu</u> is very repetitive. The
appearance of these two phrases is symmetrical:
AABAABAA. The melodic material of the B phrase is
directly derived from the A material. The bass of the A
sections is an F pedal point. Rhythm is almost wholly
ambiguous; the time signature is 3/4, but it is extremely
difficult to hear the music in this pulse. Visually, the
notes barred together often suggest a 6/8 meter, but
accents and emphasis of the weak beats even disguises
this plan. Articulation is minutely marked and will aid
voicing. The initial character indication is translated
"with delicate execution." This work requires a more
advanced musicianship than its technical level calls for.
>Tempo: Mit zartem Vortrag
>   (To be played Tenderly)
>Length: 32 measures
>Technique: 4 voice texture with independent
>   inner voices in contrasting touches,
>   syncopation, 2-note slurs, clarity in heavy
>   texture with limited dynamic range

No. 10 **Walzer,** Eb Major   Advancing Intermediate
(Waltz) (1838)

KOVATS, Gabor: German Romanticism
(Musica Budapest/Boosey & Hawkes).
NAHUM, WOLFE, KOSAKOFF: Piano Classic Collection
(J. Fischer/Belwin-Mills).

Predating Brahm's Opus 39 waltzes by almost 50
years, this large romantic waltz contains many of the
sounds typical of Brahms. Octaves and chords with a
strong, powerful sound comprise the texture. The
melody is generated from the harmonies and the chordal
movement. Chords often span ninths and tenths, and
the hands are in an open, stretched position
throughout. Apart from the open position of the hands,
the hardest technical challenge is elaboration of the
opening theme in octaves and larger chords. Dynamics
stay in the *mf-ff* range.

> Tempo: Mit Lebhaftigkeit (With vivacity)
> Length: 40 measures
> Technique: large chordal texture in 2-note
> slurs, 9ths, expanded hand positions, octave
> passagework

No. 11 **Romanze,** Bb Major   Advancing Intermediate
(Romance) (1835)

The sectional nature of this romance gives it a
fantasia-like, improvisatory feel. The symmetrical

form involves three different themes. An odd, but lovely two measure fragment both opens and closes the work. The major portion of the piece has driving offbeat accompaniments that propel the unison legato melodies. Both texture and character strongly resemble "Kleine Romanze," No. 19 of Opus 68. This piece was rejected from Opus 9 and its first theme, following the introduction, presents the ASCH motive in octaves. Another tie to Carnaval lies in the similar middle sections and key schemes of "Reconnaissance," Opus 9.

> Tempo: Nicht schnell (Not fast)
> Length: 36 measures
> Technique: legato melodic line with detached
> accompaniment in same hand in both hands
> simultaneously, careful pedal, wide dynamic
> range, expressive playing, hard to subdue
> dynamics

No. 12 **Burla**, F Minor (1832)   Advanced

Although Schumann has a "tendency to invent monotonous sequential texture" (Kathleen Dale--"The Piano Music" from Schumann, A Synposium, edited by Gerald Abraham), he has put some variety into this limited material. This presto is built entirely on a ♩♪♩ rhythmic figure. Chromatic movement using sustained and moving notes in both hands is found throughout. The basic ABA form includes a dramatic middle section that offers an excursion first away from and then back to the main theme. Bass movement in measures 34-40 is of interest. The main opening and closing sections present the theme twice each time. The top two voices move in chromatically descending lines. Bringing out a different voice upon the repetition of the theme will provide variety.

> Tempo: Presto
> Length: 66 measures
> Technique: legato melody and detached
> accompaniment in same hand, long melodic
> line, repeated rhythmic motive, octaves,
> contrasting inner voices

No. 13 **Larghetto,** F Minor   Advancing Intermediate
(1832)

    This odd little nine measure interlude fits well into the overall scheme of the set. It lies between two very fast and busy works, and provides a welcome contrast. Of the four voices, the top two are generally in unison, an octave apart, with the bass providing a different, yet parallel voice. The hovering between the major and minor modes is reminiscent of the handling of tonality found in Nachtstücke, Op. 23.

> Tempo: Larghetto
> Length: 9 measures
> Technique: legato octaves, melody in 4-voice
> texture, dynamic and tonal control, careful
> pedal, phrasing

No. 14 **Vision,** F Major   Advanced

    This very fast, impetuous piece moves quickly between sections and characters in an ABA form. Overall dynamics range from *piano* to *pianissimo* and help create an effective mood. Fast repeated chords and double notes are found in both sections, but appear first in a light staccato touch (A), and then in a more passionate legato (B). The unusual pedal marking in measures 1 and 2 of the Henle edition might give an indication as to how the damper pedal might be employed throughout. "Verhallend" in the penultimate measure indicates a fading away of the sound. The piece is framed by low *pianissimo* F's and F Major chords marked with fermatas.

> Tempo: Sehr rasch (Very quickly)
> Length: 16 measures
> Technique: fast staccato figuration with
> repeated chords and octaves in *pp* range

No. 15 **Walzer,** Ab Major   Advancing Intermediate
 (Waltz) (1832)

HEINRICHSHOFEN (Publisher): Schumann—Easier Favorites (Peters No.4052).

An airy, sustained quality is projected in this dolce waltz. The main theme involves a lilting pulse to be projected by the performer as the third beat is tied over the bar line, and no notes are struck on the downbeat. In the middle section (measures 9-17), improvisatory, recitative-like lines use wide leaps for dramatic contrast. A sudden echo dynamic that begins in measure 21 can be very effective in maintaining the sustained, floating quality. This lovely waltz was originally intended for inclusion in Carnaval, Op. 9, although it has no ASCH ties. It was written at a time when Schumann was writing variations on Schubert's "Sehnsuchtwalzer."

Tempo: none indicated
Length: 26 measures
Technique: leaps, double note figuration,
  syncopation, tonal control, careful pedal

No. 16 **Schlummerlied,**   Advancing Intermediate
Eb Major, (Slumber Song) or "Berceuse" (1841)

DEXTER, Harry: Selected Piano Works--Schumann
  (Hansen).
DEXTER, Harry: The Young Pianist's Schumann
  (Hansen).
KLEINMICHEL, Richard: 32 Sonatinas and Rondos
  (Schirmer Vol. 693).
LIPSKY, Alexander: Robert Schumann Album I for Piano
  (Kalmus #3930/Belwin-Mills).
SHEALY, Alexander: Schumann--His Greatest Piano
  Solos (Ashley).
VOGRICH, Max: Schumann Album for Piano
  (G. Schirmer Vol. 100).

This long allegretto is styled as a lilting lullaby.
Basically melody and accompaniment, the texture is
thin and transparent.   A favorite of sentimental
musicians, this work is accessible, pianistic, and fun to
play. Though generally composed around one theme and
texture, a short contrasting section (measures 41-52)
offers a lovely change of character and mode with left
hand ninths. Dynamics never reach above *mf*. This
lullaby was written the year of Schumann's daughter
Marie's birth.

Tempo: Allegretto
Length: 99 measures
Technique: expanded hand positions, legato
    playing, cross-rhythms, chordal texture in
    lower register, tonal control, careful pedal

No. 17 **Elfe**, Ab Major   Advancing Intermediate
(The Elf) (1835)

AGAY, Denes: Early Advanced Classics to Moderns, Vol.
    47 (Consolidated).
FROST, Bernice: Piano Repertoire
    (J. Fischer/Belwin-Mills).
ROYAL CONSERVATORY OF MUSIC, Grade IX
    (Frederick Harris).
SHEALY, Alexander: Schumann--His Greatest Piano
    Solos (Ashley).

This character piece is a brisk etude in light touches
and advanced drop-lift technique. The main theme
begins in basic classical harmonies which evolve into
chromatic movement. Dynamics range from *piano* to
pianissimo. At top speed, this elf should appear as a
brief, light breath of air. Elfe was originally part of an
early set of ten pieces, probably written between 1829
and 1832 and found in Zwickau Sketchbook III. It was
adapted in 1835 for use in Opus 9, but was eventually
placed here in Opus 124. It uses the ASCH motif, but
its appearance is somewhat obsured by its division
between the hands.

Tempo: So rasch als möglich
    (As quickly as possible)
Length: 28 measures
Technique: rapid leaps in *p* dynamic range,
    finger facility, pedal

No. 18 **Botschaft,** E Major   <u>Advancing Intermediate</u>
    (Message) (1838)

HEINRICHSHOFEN (Publisher): Schumann--Easier
    Favorites (Peters No.4052).

   The plaintive, speaking qualities of this message are
especially apparent when the right hand changes from a
chordal texture into an eighth note melody. The
consistent return of the E Major A section in this
ABABA form is reassuring and settling. Both sections
are derived from the same theme. "Mit zartem Vortag"
indicates a delicate expression. The strange harmonic
progression at the final cadence seems to call for a
ritard, but there is none indicated whereas they are
explicitly marked elsewhere.
    Tempo: Mit zartem Vortrag
        (To be played tenderly)
    Length: 42 measures
    Technique: melody in heavy chordal texture,
        widely spaced arpeggiated chords, limited
        dynamic range, LH spans of a 10th

No. 19 **Phantasiestück,** A Major   <u>Advanced</u>
    (Fantasy) (1839)

   This carnival music generally has more spirit than
merit. Schumann calls for a graceful quality, but the
speed is not indicated. Intertwined hands, chromatic
accidentals, and syncopated notation all add up to hor-

rendous reading difficulties. The right hand alternates between syncopated legato double notes and legato single line melody. The left hand accompaniment is bouncy with staccato leaps throughout. Technical demands are much diminished when the right hand takes the upper left hand note.

> Tempo: Leicht, etwas graziös
> 　(Lightly, somewhat gracefully)
> Length: 62 measures
> Technique: wide leaps involving awkward hand
> 　placements, syncopation, legato double note
> 　melodic material with staccato
> 　accompaniment

No. 20 **Canon,** D Major　　　　　Advancing Intermediate
　(1845)

The "discovery" of Bach by many romantic composers led to such excursions as this canon. Although it appears to be written for pedal piano or organ with the lowest voice too far away from the others to be reached, this cannot be determined. Direct, linear imitation is found between the soprano and tenor voices, although the sound is very homophonic. Nonharmonic tones are sometimes startling. This canon was written in the same year that Schumann composed Six Studies for Pedal Piano, Op. 56, Four Sketches for Pedal Piano, Op. 58, and Six figures on Bach for Organ or Pedal Piano, Op. 60.

> Tempo: Langsam (Slowly)
> Length: 16 measures
> Technique: 4-voice texture, awkwardly spaced
> 　chords, legato playing, tonal control, inner
> 　voices

SIEBEN STÜCKE IN FUGHETTEN FORM, Opus 126
(Seven Pieces in Fughetta Form) (1853)

These pieces were written after Schumann had suffered a paralytic stroke. The Opus was dedicated to Rosalie Leser and published by Furstner of Berlin. Though there is evidence that the composer was not quite comfortable in the contrapuntal form, the set offers much artistic interest and is gratifying to perform.

Note: The following editions contain Opus 126 in its entirety. Other sources are listed with each piece.

SAUER, Emil: Complete Works of Robert Schumann, Volume 4 (Peters #2300D).
SCHUMANN, Clara: Piano Music of Robert Schumann, Series III (Dover).
SCHUMANN, Clara: Robert Schumann—Complete Works, Volume 4 (Kalmus #3926/Belwin).

I. A Minor   Advancing Intermediate

ROWLEY, Alec: The Easiest Original Schumann (Hinrichsen No.7/Peters).

This pleasant, uncomplicated three voice fughetta is much easier to read than most contrapuntal pieces of the level. A delicate legato touch and minimal pedalling are appropriate for the simplicity of this work. The 6/8 meter subject is four measures long and entrances occur precisely every four measures with the exception of a short episode in measures 13-20. The compound beat division is interrupted only once by simple division (ms. 39-40). The piece ends in A Major.

Tempo: Nicht schnell, leise vorzutragen
(Not fast, to be played softly) ♩.= 50
Length: 53 measures
Technique: tonal control within limited soft
    dynamic range, cross-rhythms, legato
    playing, important fingering

II. D Minor   Advanced

A full sound is generated by the four voices of this
fughetta.   Because the texture is fairly thick, the
subject needs to be brought out for clarity.   The *fp*
accents mark all subject entrances, both complete and
fragmentary.   Non-harmonic tones create a more
interesting harmonic structure than is found in most of
this opus.   Reading is made difficult through instances
of the hands having to take notes on both staves.   One
of the few occurences of stretto is found in measure 19
between the tenor and bass voices.   The final D Minor
chord sounds odd after the frequent use of F# in the
final measures.

Tempo: Mässig (Moderately) ♩ = 66
Length: 26 measures
Technique: voicing in heavy texture, widely
    spaced hand positions, sustained and moving
    notes in wide hand stretches

III. D Minor   Advanced

The tempo and character of this fughetta are more intense than most pieces of this opus. The four voices enter every two measures. In measures 9-12, incomplete subjects enter more rapidly, at a rate of one per measure. The piece seems to build toward a dynamic climax, which then pulls back into a lovely two measure sequence that quiets the mood. An unusual C pedal point is found in measures 26-31.

  Tempo: Ziemlich bewegt (Rather agitatedly)
  ♩ = 68
  Length: 37 measures
  Technique: finger independence, voicing,
    heavy texture, sustained and moving notes

IV. D Minor   Advanced

The subject and sounds of this exciting piece are very baroque. Compared with others of this opus, the scope is large and dramatic, but possibly too long for Schumann's treatment of the material. The three measure subject appears in four voices. Accents and detached touches are specifically marked to prevent a muddled sound. A short modulation to Bb Major occurs in measures 16-27. In the final measures, a stretto of subject fragments leads to an exciting climax.

  Tempo: Lebhaft (Vivaciously) ♩ = 80
  Length: 46 measures
  Technique: finger independence in heavy
    texture, legato and staccato in same hand,
    expanded hand positions, predominantly in
    16th notes

V. A Minor   Early Advanced

    This fughetta contains the most expressive possibilities of the set. A delicate legato touch is used within a slow tempo. The simple four measure subject appears in four voices with soft dynamics throughout. Near the ending a *pianissimo* marking along with an A pedal point causes a sudden dramatic effect. Adding the una corda pedal can heighten this feeling. The simple rhythms of the beginning become somewhat complex when triple beat divisions are interspersed among the duple divisions. The triplet figures which embellish the main material use the so-called "Clara's motive," a descending minor pentachord.

    Tempo: Ziemlich langsam, empfindungsvoll
       vorzutragen (To be played rather slowly and
       with sentiment) ♪ = 54
    Length: 45 measures
    Technique: tonal control, voicing, finger
       independence, phrasing, careful rests,
       sensitive performance

VI. F Major   Early Advanced

    A fast 12/16 meter divides the sixteenth notes into groups of three. The effect is a bouncy, almost gigue-like sound. The subject contains a clear chord outline which is marked by ∧ accents. Although there are three voices, generally only one at a time carries the running sixteenth note figures. There are short episodes where the subject does not appear and the final eight measures do not contain the complete subject. Interesting bass movement provides a contrast in sound.

> Tempo: Sehr schnell (Very fast) ♪ = 122
> Length: 44 measures
> Technique: rapid 16th notes played with a finger staccato, independent voices in opposing touches in same hand, leaps

VII. A Minor   Early Advanced

This slow, expressive piece is reminiscent of number 5 of this set, but does not have the interest or beauty. The four voices offer a clarity of texture that is similar to that of the first fughetta. The subject uses syncopated rhythms, but its treatment does not quite live up to the interest it should provide. Occasionally the subject appears in two voices simultaneously. Closely aligned entrances (stretto) occur between measures 18 and 28.

> Tempo: Langsam, ausdrucksvoll
>   (Slowly, expressively) ♪ = 96
> Length: 32 measures
> Technique: legato playing, voicing, legato 6ths and double note passages, tonal control, wide hand stretches

GESÄNGE DER FRÜHE, Opus 133
(Songs of the Morning) or "Morning Songs" (1853)

<u>Gesänge der Frühe</u>, Schumann's last completed piano work, was written during a final period of creativity, October 15th to the 18th, 1853, when Brahms was on his first visit to the Schumann household. It was "dedicated to the lofty poetess Bettina Brentano von Armin" and originally published by A. Furstner of Berlin. The set was not composed at the piano, which may explain the unpianistic elements found throughout. The quality of craftsmanship varies widely and the "harmonic and polyphonic elements are never convincingly integrated," (K. Dale). Schumann's manuscript was inscribed with "An Diotima," a reference to Holderlin's poems. These programmatic pieces are cyclic in subject and key scheme. Schumann describes them as "characteristic pieces which depict the emotions on the approach and advance of morning, but more as an expression of feeling than painting."

Note: The following editions contain Opus 133 in its entirety. Other sources are listed with each piece.

SAUER, Emil: Complete Works of Robert Schumann, Volume 4 (Peters #2300D).

SCHUMANN, Clara: Piano Music of Robert Schumann, Series III (Dover).

SCHUMANN, Clara: Robert Schumann--Complete Works, Volume 6 (Kalmus #3928/Belwin).

I. D Major   Advanced

The sustained, tranquil mood of this prelude is supported by beautiful and odd harmonies. Phrasing is irregular although a nine measure grouping (four plus five measures) is found throughout much of the piece. This grouping presents the theme four times on different tonal centers. The fullness and motion build until the final presentation of the theme. It begins with thick chords at a *forte* dynamic, and leads into the stretto ending. The writing of individual parts in this polyphonic piece is awkward and unpianistic. Some of the wider spans can be broken, but others cannot be played even by a large hand. The beautiful, building character of this piece gives a lovely, sustained feeling of dawn.

> Tempo: Im ruhigen tempo (In a calm tempo)
>   ♩ = 73
> Length: 39 measures
> Technique: tonal and dynamic control,
>   extended hand positions, legato playing,
>   careful pedal, register shifts, large hand
>   stretches, voicing

II. B Minor   Advanced

This short animated work offers an excellent contrast to the opening piece. A more overt passion is expressed through the driving rhythms and the busy textures. This rhythmic drive is the most prominent element and seems to control all aspects of the work. The beat is generally divided by three, but duple dotted rhythms are juxtaposed over these triple figures in some very complex composite rhythms. Figuration and textures change swiftly and quite often for such a short piece. The fragmentary melody is a minimal element, but it sometimes adds to the driving force. As the writing is not very pianistic, the hands work together intricately. The left hand covers a large range and helps in dividing up the various figures. Written when Brahms was visiting the Schumanns, this work and No. 4 of this opus reflect Schumann's influence on Brahm's style.

> Tempo: Belebt, Nicht zu rasch
> (Animatedly, not too quickly) ♪ = 190
> Length: 35 measures
> Technique: leaps, cross-rhythms, octaves, wide
> hand stretches, staccato chordal passages,
> figuration distributed between the hands

III. A Major   Advanced

This lively fanfare depicting morning at its height employs sturdy chords and octaves in monotonous dotted rhythms. Bombast is not given free rein as many of the dynamics are quiet. The harmonies are unsuccessful and not well integrated, and the rhythmic and melodic elements are uninteresting. The ending builds to a large climax, but diminishes quickly in the final measure to a *piano* level. The overall effect of this piece is disappointing.

> Tempo: Lebhaft (Vivaciously) ♩ = 93
> Length: 63 measures
> Technique: repeated octaves and chords,
> chordal texture with quick hand position
> shifts, register shifts, staccato chords,
> leaps, awkward hand-crosses, endurance,
> solid hand shapes, 64th note passage, trills
> need a large hand

IV. F# Minor   <u>Advanced</u>

    The agitated character of this passionate piece involves a firm and beautiful tone with rhythmic drive. A high register melody is driven forward by cascading thirty-second note broken chord figures. The *forte* dynamics marked over the melody line indicate its supremacy. Figuration and dynamics are consistent throughout until the final measures when the broken chords descend to the lower registers, and diminish to a closing *pianissimo.*

         Tempo: Bewegt (Agitatedly)♪ = 72
         Length: 53 measures
         Technique: melody in upper register, rapid
            broken chord figuration distributed between
            the hands, leaps, legato playing, legato and
            staccato within same hand

V. D Major   <u>Advanced</u>

    This beautiful piece begins with a calm, homophonic introduction that leads into the most lengthy section. This consists of trill figures and constant sixteenth notes that create a shimmering effect. The opening melody is found throughout. The final section is in a lovely, sustained mood using legato broken chords. Harmonic and figurative elements give this romantic piece much of its motion. The trill figures are taken by both hands, and all combinations of fingers. The final indication is "fading away little by little," and the piece ends at a *pianissimo* level. The overall effect can be quite magical if the right touch and character are projected.

Tempo: Im Anfange ruhiges, im Verlauf bewegtes Tempo (Calm Tempo at the beginning, agitated tempo as the piece continues) ♩ = 68

Length: 40 measures

Technique: RH 4th and 5th finger tremolo with held chords in same hand, sudden dynamic changes, arpeggiation, leaps, tonal control, careful fingering and division of hands

KANON ÜBER "AN ALEXIS", WoO 4, Ab Major
(Canon to Alexis)

The Kanon über "An Alexis send' ich dich" is based
on a song, popular during the first half of the 19th
century, by the influential opera composer Friedrich
Heinrich Kimmel (1765-1814). The exact date at which
Schumann composed the work is unknown, but the Kanon
was first published as a supplement to the Deux
Fantasies mignonnes de Salon pour Piano, Op. 30 of
Julius Knorr (1807-1861), a colleague of the composer
who served as initial editor of the Neue Zeitschrift fur
Musik. This publication was issued by the Leipzig firm
of C.F. Kahnt in 1858/59. Though later printed by
Peters, the enigmatic Kanon remains one of the least
familiar of Schumann's works.

Note: The following edition contains the Kanon in its
    entirety.

SAUER, Emil: Complete Works of Robert Schumann,
    Volume 4 (Peters #2300D).

An extremely complex contrapuntal texture of from
four to six parts is featured in this elaborate little
canon.   A decorated motivic fragment of Himmel's
melody is woven into a dense polyphonic web. Against
the tortured intertwinings of this material Schumann
superimposes a new and engaging countermelody, first
as a soprano voice with octave doubling, and later as a
closing bass line.   In spite of the brevity of this
miniature, it reveals an accomplished mastery of
romantic counterpoint at its most dissonantly intense.
The technical demands are not great, but a large hand
will facilitate both the essential voicing and the wide
intervals. When prefaced by a transcription of Himmel's

quaint Lied, the <u>Kanon</u> possesses a unique and ingratiating charm.

Tempo: Andantino
Length: 21 measures
Technique: contrapuntal textures, voicing,
sustained and moving notes, wide intervals

THEME IN Eb MAJOR (no opus number)   <u>Intermediate</u>

On the night of February 17, 1854, Schumann, who was in a rapidly deteriorating mental state, claimed to have had a vision in which Schubert and Mendelssohn dictated the theme to him.   Actually the melody was not an original one; it stems from the main theme of the slow movement of Schumann's own <u>Violin Concerto</u>.

The theme was followed by <u>five variations</u> which were not published until 1939. Brahms had chosen not to publish them, choosing to include only the theme in the supplement of the complete works.   The five variations that Schumann completed reveal his exhausted mental state. None of the variations contain writing which is innovative. While they may be said to possess a certain naive charm, it is clear that they do not rank among the major works of Schumann.   The work was never completed. It has been published only recently. It is interesting to note that Brahms used the theme for his own "Variations," Op. 23.

Note: The following edition contains the Theme in Eb Major with 5 variations.

GEIRINGER, Karl: Schumann Variations on an Original Theme (Hinrichsen No.70/Peters).

The following editions contains the theme only.

ANTHONY, George W.: Schubert to Shostakovich, Intermediate (Presser).
SCHUMANN, Clara: Piano Music of Robert Schumann, Series III (Dover).
ZIETLIN and GOLDBERGER: The Solo Book IV (Consolidated).

Theme

This hymn-like theme is the longest variation theme that Schumann composed. The second section is marked with repeats. A gently moving melody in the right hand is supported by a simple bass line predominantly in octaves.

> Tempo: Moderato
> Length: 28 measures
> Technique: RH chords, LH leaps, singing tone

Variation 1

The melody remains virtually unchanged throughout this variation, now supported by triplet figures.

> Tempo: none indicated
> Length: 28 measures
> Technique: melody and accompaniment in
>   same hand, 2 vs. 3 in one hand, double notes

Variation 2

The melody is presented in canon form between the soprano and tenor voices. The voices are primarily one beat apart in the first section and two bars apart in the second section.

> Tempo: none indicated
> Length: 28 measures
> Technique: leaps, melody and accompaniment
>   in same hand, voicing

Variation 3

The left hand is assigned the melody throughout most of this sprightly variation. The accompanying figures sometimes have grace notes and double thirds, and are more difficult and more fun than in the previous variations.

> Tempo: Poco piu mosso
> Length: 28 measures
> Technique: leaps, repeated notes, voicing,
>   variety of touches

Variation 4

The theme is transposed to the key of G Minor. The variation is chordal in nature and sounds like a dirge.

> Tempo: none indicated
> Length: 28 measures
> Technique: chords, legato octave voicing

Variation 5

The theme appears in its most altered form against a stream of thirty-second notes. There are discordant intervals between the melody and the accompaniment throughout.

> Tempo: none indicated
> Length: 32 measures
> Technique: melody and accompaniment in same hand, accompaniment divided between the hands, leaps

ETÜDEN IN FORM FREIER VARIATIONEN ÜBER EIN THEMA VON BEETHOVEN

According to the Schumann scholar Werner Schwarz, these etudes exist as a set of four groups of variations based on the sixteen bar theme of the second movement of Beethoven's "Seventh Symphony." The variations are interrelated, as some of the etudes appear in more than one set.

The Henle edition of the etudes is based on these autographs. Autograph A contains a set of eleven etudes, the ninth and eleventh being incomplete. Autograph B contains nine studies, with the third, sixth, and eighth left unfinished. Autograph C contains seven etudes, only two of which are actually new, the others being derived from the first two autographs.

The third autograph is the basis for the first group of etudes in the Henle edition. Following these etudes are four studies from the first autograph and four studies from the second.

Throughout the variations it is apparent that Schumann is more interested in experimenting with pianistic figuration than in exploring harmonic alteration of the theme. This results in a monotony which does not exist in the bolder Etudes Symphoniques, Op. 13.

The performer can choose to intersperse the eight etudes from the first two autographs among the seven variations of the third autograph. The Henle edition offers suggestions for the order of performance in the Preface.

Note: The following edition contains these etudes in their entirety.

MÜNSTER, Robert: Robert Schumann--Exercises Etuden in Form Freier Variations uber Ein Thema von Beethoven (G. Henle).

The main technical features of each variation are:

I. Seven etudes based on the Autograph C
1. broken chords and melody in same hand.
2. arpeggiated figures and broken chords.
3. broken chords and leaps (this variation is closely related to the sixth etude of <u>Etudes Symphoniques</u>, Op. 13).
4. quiet figurations containing repeated notes (very similar to the third etude in <u>Etudes Symphoniques</u>, Op. 13).
5. a five part choral motet containing problems of voicing and distribution of notes between the hands.
6. delicate passagework divided between the hands
7. tremolo.
II. Four etudes from the First Autograph (Autograph A)
1. broken chords, leaps, correct articulation of touches.
2. broken thirds, independence of fingers.
3. complicated figuration in right hand against octaves in the left.
4. combination of metrical units, good finger legato, tremolo.
III. Four Etudes from the second autograph
1. syncopated accompaniment figures against melody in same hand.
2. staccato and legato touch in same hand (This variation was later to become the piece <u>Leides Ahnung</u>, No. 2 of the <u>Albumblatter</u>, Op. 124).
3. broken chord figuration combining different metrical units.
4. leaps in left hand, syncopation, widely spaced arpeggiated melody in the right hand.

BIBLIOGRAPHY

Chissell, Joan. Schumann. London: J.M. Dent and Sons, 1948.

Dale, Kathleen. "The Piano Music." Schumann: A Synopsium. edited by Gerald Abraham. New York: Oxford University Press, 1952.

Gillespie, John. Five Centuries of Keyboard Music. New York: Dover Publications, Inc. 1965.

Grove, Sir George. The New Grove Dictionary of Music and Musicians. edited by Stanley Sadie. London: Macmillan, 1980.

Lang, Paul Henry. Music in Western Civilization. New York: Norton, 1941.

Oppers, Kurt. Notes on Music Ideas and History. Arthur Lewis, editor. 1975.

Plantinga, Lean B. Schumann as Critic. New Haven: Yale University Press, 1967.

Schauffler, Robert Haven. Florestan: The Life and Work of Robert Schumann. New York: Dover, 1963.

Schumann, Robert. On Music and Musicians. New York: Pantheon, 1946.

Robert Schumann: The Man and His Music. Alan Walker, editor. London: Burrie and Jenkins, 1972.

GERMAN INDEX

Abegg Vartiationen, Op. 1, 1
Abendlied, Op. 118b, 287
Abendmusik, Op. 99, 277
Abschied, Op. 82, 268
Albumblätter, I, II, III, IV, V, Op. 99, 272
Albumblätter, Op. 124 (20 Pieces), 291
Allegro, B Minor, Op.8, 45
Allegro, Bb Minor, Op. 26, 164
Am Camin, Op. 15, 118
Arabeske, Op. 18, 136
Arlequin, Op. 9, 50
Armes Waisenkind, Op. 68, 202
A.S.C.H. - S.C.H.A. (Lettres Dansantes), Op. 9, 54
Auf der Gondel, Sketches Op. 68, 245
Aufschwung, Op. 12, 78
Aveu, Op. 9, 59

Barentanz, Sketches Op. 68, 250
Bittendes Kind, Op. 15, 114
Blumenstück, Op.19, 138
Botschaft, Op. 124, 307
Bunte Blätter, Op. 99 (14 Pieces), 270
Burla, Op. 124, 302

Canon, B Minor, Op. 118b, 287
Canon, D Major, Op. 124, 308
Canonisches Liedchen, Op. 68, 229
Carnaval, Op. 9, 47
Chiarina, Op 9, 55
Chopin, Op. 9, 55
Clavierstücke für die Jugend, Op. 68 (43 Pieces), 191
Coquette, Op. 9, 52
Curiose Gerschichte, Op. 15, 113

Davidsbündler Achtzehn Charakterstücke, Op. 6, 30
Der Dichter Spricht, Op. 15, 121
Des Abends, Op.12, 77
Drei Clavier-Sonaten für de Jugend, Op. 118, 283
Drei Phantasiestücke, Op. 111, 280
Drei Romanzen, Op. 28, 171
Drie Stücklein, Op.99, 270
Dritte Grosse Sonata, No. 3, Op. 14, 100

Ein Choral--Freue dich, o meine Seele, Op. 68, 199
Eine Berühmte Melodie von L. van Beethoven, Sketches Op. 68, 251
Einsame Blumen, Op. 82, 262
Ein Stückchen von Mozart, Sketches Op. 68, 251
Ein Trinklied von C.M. Von Weber, Sketches Op. 68, 244
Eintritt, Op. 82, 260
Elfe, Op. 124, 306
Ende von Lied, Op. 12, 82
Erinnerung, Op. 68, 230
Ernteliedchen, Op. 68, 226
Erster Verlust, Op. 68, 217
Estrella, Op. 9, 56
Etüden in Form Freier Variationen, über ein Thema von Beethoven, 325

Etüden in Form von Variationen, Op. 13 (12 sections), 85
Anhang zu Op. 13, 96
Eusebius, Op. 9, 51
Fabel, Op. 12, 81
Faschingschwank aus Wien, Op. 26 (5 pieces), 163
Fast zu Ernst, Op. 15, 119
Figurirter Choral, Op. 68, 241
Finale, Op. 26, 169
Florestan, Op. 9, 52
(Fragment) Sketches, Op. 68, 246
Fremder Mann, Op. 68, 231
Freundliche Landschaft, Op. 82, 264
Fröhlicher Landmann, Op. 68, 209
Frühlingsgesang, Op. 68, 217
Fughette, G Minor, Op. 32, 177
Fürchtenmachen, Op. 15, 120
Für Ganz Kleine, Sketches Op. 68, 243

Gesänge der Frühe, Op. 133, 314
Geschwindmarsch, Op. 99, 278
Gigue, G Minor, Op. 32, 176
Gluckes Genug, Op. 15, 115
Grillen, Op. 12, 79
Grosse Sonata, No. 1, Op. 11, 69
Gukkuk Im Versteck, Sketches, Op. 68, 247

Haschemann, Sketches Op. 68, 248
Hasche-Mann, Op. 15, 114
Herberge, Op. 82, 265
Humoreske, Op. 20, 140

Impromptu, No. 1, D Minor, Op. 124, 291
Impromptu, No. 9, Bb Major, Op. 124, 300
Impromptus Über ein Thema von Clara Wieck (10 variations), Op. 5, 23
In Der Nacht, Op. 12, 80
Intermezzi, Op. 4 (6 Pieces), 18
Intermezzo, Eb Minor, Op. 26, 168

Jagdlied, Op. 82, 267
Jäger auf der Lauer, Op. 82, 261
Jägerliedchen, Op. 68, 203

Kanon über "An Alexis," WoO 4, 319
Kindergesellschaft, Op. 118b, 288
Kinderscenen, Op. 15 (13 Pieces), 111
Kind im Einschlummern, Op. 15, 121
Kleine Fuge, Op. 68, 239
Kleine Romanze, Op. 68, 221
Kleiner Morgenwanderer, Op. 68, 219
Kleiner Waltzer, Sketches Op. 68, 249
Kleine Studie, Op. 68, 215
Knecht Ruprecht, Op. 68, 213
Kreisleriana, Op. 16 (8 Pieces), 123
Kriegslied, Op. 68, 232

Lager-scene, Op. 76, 258
Lagune in Venedig, Sketches Op. 68, 248
Ländler, Op. 124, 298
Ländliches Lied, Op. 68, 223

Larghetto, Op. 124, 303
Leides Anhung, Op. 124, 292
Lied italienischer Marinari, Op. 68, 236
Lied Ohne Ende, Op. 124, 299

Mai, lieber Mai, - Bald bist due
  weider da!, Op. 68, 215
Marche des Davidsbündler contre
  les Philistines, Op. 9, 60
Marsch, Op. 99, 276
Matrosenlied, Op. 68, 237
Melodie, Op. 68, 192
Mignon, Op. 68, 235

Nachklänge aus dem Theater, Op. 68, 227
Nachtstücke, Op. 23 (4 Pieces), 159
Nordisches Lied, Op. 68, 240
Novellete, Op. 99, 275
Novelletten, Op. 21 (8 Pieces), 142

Paganini, Op. 9, 58
Paganini Capricen, Op. 3 (6 Pieces), 13
Pantalon et Colombine, Op. 9, 57
Papillons, Op. 2 (12 Pieces), 5
Papillons, Bb Major, Op. 9, 54
Pause, Op. 9, 60
Phantasie, C Major, Op. 17 (3 Pieces) 129
Phantasiestücke, Op. 12 (8 Pieces), 76
  Supplement to Fantasiestücke, Op. 12, 84
Phantasietanz, Op. 124, 295
Präludium, Op. 99, 276
Preambule, Op. 9, 49
(Preludio), Sketches Op. 68, 249
Promenade, Op.9, 59
Puppen Schlaffliedchen, Sketches Op. 68, 243
Puppenwiegenlied, Op. 118a, 285

Rebus, Sketches Op. 68, 250
Reconnaissance, Op. 9, 56
Reiterstück, Op. 68, 225
Replique, Op. 9, 53
Ritter von Steckenpferd, Op. 15, 119
Romanze, G Minor, Op. 26, 167
Romanze, D Minor, Op. 32, 176
Romanze, Bb Major, Op. 124, 301
Rundgesang, Op 68, 224

Scherzino, Bb Major, Op. 26, 168
Scherzino, F Major, Op. 124, 293
Scherzo, Bb Major, Op. 32, 175
Scherzo, G Minor, Op. 99, 278
Schlummerlied, Op. 124, 305
Schnitterliedchen, Op. 68, 220
Sechs Concert-Etuden nach Capricen
  von Paganini, Op. 10, 62
Sechs Fugen über den Namen BACH, Op.68, 186
Sheherazade, Op. 68, 233
Sicilianisch, Op. 68, 211
Sieben Stücke in Fughetten Form, Op. 126, 309
Sketches for Op. 68 (17 Pieces), 243
Soldatenmarsch, Op. 68, 194

Sonate, Elisen zum Andenken, Op. 118b, 286
Sonate Julien zur Erinnerung, Op. 118a, 283
Sonate Marien gewidmet, Op. 118c, 288
Sphinxes, Op. 9, 53
Stückchen, Op. 68, 200
Studien fur den Pedal-Flügel, Op. 56, 178
Studien nach Capricen von Paganini, Op. 3, 13
Sylvesterlied, Op. 68, 242
Symphonische Etüden, Op.13, 85
  Anhang zu Op. 13, 96

Thema, Op. 68, 234
Thema mit Variationen, Op. 118a, 284
Theme in Eb Major (5 Variations), 321
Toccata, Op. 7, 43
Trällerliedchen, Op. 68, 197
Traum eines Kindes, Op. 118c, 290
Traumes Wirren, Op. 12, 81

Valse Allemande, Op. 9, 58
Valse Noble, Op. 9, 51
Variationen uber den Namen Abegg, Op. 1, 1
Verrufene Stelle, Op. 82, 263
Vier Clavierstucke, Op. 32, 175
Vier Fugen, Op. 72, 253
Vier Märsche, Op. 76, 256
Vier Skizzen fur den Pedal-Flügel, Op. 58, 183
Vision, Op. 124, 303
Vogel Als Prophet, Op. 82, 266
Volksliedchen, Op. 68, 208
Von Fremden Landern und Menschen, Op. 15, 112

Waldscenen, Op. 82 (9 Pieces), 260
Walzer, No. 4, A Minor, Op. 124, 294
Walzer, No. 10, Eb Major, Op. 124, 301
Walzer, No. 15, Ab Major, Op. 124, 304
Warum?, Op. 12, 79
Weinlesezeit--"Fröhliche Zeit!," Op. 68, 233
Wichtige Begebenheit, Op. 15, 116
Wiegenliedchen, Op. 124, 297
Wilder Reiter, Op. 68, 205
Winterzeit I, Op. 68, 237
Winterziet II, Op. 68, 238

Zigeunertanz, Op. 118c, 289
Zweite Sonate, No. 2, Op. 22, 148
  Anhang zu Op. 22, 155

* *, Op. 68, No. 21, 224
 *

* *, Op. 68, No. 26, 228
 *

* *, Op. 68, No. 30, 231
 *

* *, Supplement to Op. 12, No. 9, 84
 *

ENGLISH INDEX

Abegg Variations, Op. 1, 1
Album for the Young, Op. 68 (43 Pieces), 191
Album Leaves, No. I, II, III, IV, V, Op. 99, 272
Album Leaves, Op. 124 (20 Pieces), 291
Allegro, B Minor, Op. 8, 45
Allegro, Bb Major, Op. 26, 164
Almost Too Serious, Op. 15, 119
Arabesque, Op. 18, 136
Arlequin, Op. 9, 50
A.S.C.H.-S.C.H.A. (Dancing Letters), Op. 9, 54

Bear's Dance, Sketches Op. 68, 250
Burla, Op. 124, 302
Butterflies, Op. 2 (12 Pieces), 5
Butterflies, Op. 9, 54
By The Fireside, Op. 15, 118

Camp Scene, Op. 76, 258
Canon, D Major, Op. 118b, 287
Canon, D Major, Op.124, 308
Canon on "To Alexis", WoO 4, 319
Caprices from Paganini Caprices (6 Pieces), 13
Carnaval, Op. 9 (21 Pieces), 47
Carnival Jest from Vienna, Op. 26 (5 Pieces) 163
Catch Me, Op. 15, 114
Chiarina, Op. 9, 55
Child Falling Asleep, Op. 15, 121
Children's Party, Op. 118b, 288
(A) Child's Dream, Op. 118c, 290
Chopin, Op. 9, 55
Chorale--Rejoice, Oh My Soul, Op. 68, 199
Colored Leaves, Op. 99 (14 Pieces), 270
Confession, Op. 9, 59
Coquette, Op. 9, 52
Country Dance, Op. 124, 298
Cradle Song, Op. 124, 297
Cuckoo in Hiding
Curious Story, Op. 15, 113

Davidsbundler Eighteen Character Pieces, Op. 6, 30
Departure, Op. 82, 268
Disturbing Dreams, Op. 12, 81
Doll's Cradle Song, Op. 118a, 285
Doll's Lullaby, Sketches Op. 68, 243
Dreaming, Op. 15, 116
(A) Drinking Song, Op. 68, 244

Echoes from the Theater, Op. 68, 227
(The) Elf, Op. 124, 306
(The) End of the Story, Op. 12, 82
Endless Grief, Op. 124, 299
Entrance, Op. 82, 260
Entreating Child, Op. 15, 114
Estrella, Op. 9, 56
Etudes in the Form of Variations (Symphonic Etudes)
(12 Sections), Op. 13, 85
Supplement to Op. 13, 96
Etudes in the Form of Variations on a
Theme by Beethoven, 325
Eusebius, Op. 9, 51
Evening Music, Op. 99, 277
Evening Song, Op. 118b, 287

Fable, Op. 12, 81
(A) Famous Melody by L. van Beethoven
Sketches Op. 68, 251
Fantasy, Op. 17 (3 Pieces), 129
Fantasy, A Major, Op. 124, 295
Fantasy Dance, Op. 124, 295
Fantasy Pieces, Op. 12 (8 Pieces), 76
Supplement to Fantasy Pieces, Op. 12, 84
Fast March, Op. 99, 278
Figured Chorale, Op. 68, 241
Finale, Op. 26, 169
First Grand Sonaa, Op. 11, 69
First Loss, Op. 68, 217
Florestan, Op. 9, 52
Flower Piece, Op. 19, 138
Forest Scenes, Op. 82 (9 Pieces), 260
For Smallest Children, Sketches, Op. 68, 243
Four Fugues, Op. 72, 253
Four Marches, Op. 76, 256
Four Pieces, Op. 32, 175
Four Sketches for Pedal-Piano, Op. 58, 183
(Fragment), Sketches Op. 68, 246
Friendly Landscape, Op. 82, 264
Frightening, Op. 15, 120
Fughette, Op. 32, 177

Gathering of the Grapes--"Merry Time", Op. 68, 233
Gigue, G Minor, Op. 32, 176
Gypsy Dance, Op. 118c, 289

(The) Happy Farmer, Returning from Work,
Op. 68, 209
Harvest Song, Op. 68, 226
Haunted Spot, Op. 82, 263
Horseman's Piece, Op. 68, 225
Humming Song, Op. 68, 197
Humoresque, Op. 20, 140
Hunter in Ambush, Op. 82, 261
Hunting Song, Op. 82, 267

Important Event, Op. 15, 116
Impromptu, D Minor, Op. 124, 291
Impromptu, Bb Major, Op. 124, 300
Impromptus on a Theme by Clara Wieck
(10 Variations), Op. 5, 23
Intermezzi, Op. 4 (6 Pieces), 18
Intermezzo, Eb Minor, Op. 26, 168
In the Gondola, Sketches Op. 68, 245
In the Night, Op. 12, 80
Italian Mariner's Song, Op. 68, 236

Knight of the Rocking Horse, Op. 15, 119
Knight Rupert, Op. 68, 213
Kreisleriana, Op. 16 (8 Pieces), 123

Lagoon in Venice, Sketches Op. 68, 248
Larghetto, F Minor, Op. 124, 303
Little Folk Song, Op. 68, 208
Little Fugue, Op. 68, 239
Little Hunting Song, Op. 68, 203
Little Morning Wanderer, Op. 68, 219
(A) Little Piece by Mozart, Sketches Op. 68, 251
Little Romance, Op. 68, 221

Little Song in Canon Form, Op. 68, 229
Little Song of the Reaper, Op. 68, 220
Little Study, Op. 68, 215
Little Waltz, Sketches Op. 68, 249
Lonely Flowers, Op. 82, 262

March, Op. 99, 276
March of the Davidsbundler against
    the Philistines, Op. 9, 60
May, Beautiful May,--Soon Thou Art
    Here Again, Op. 68, 215
Melody, Op. 68, 192
Message, Op. 124, 307
Mignon, Op. 68, 235

New Year's Eve, Op. 68, 242
Night Pieces, Op. 23 (4 Pieces), 159
Northern Song, Salute to Gade, Op. 68, 240
Novelette, B Minor, Op. 99, 275
Novelettes, Op. 21 (8 Pieces), 142

Of Strange Lands and People, Op. 15, 112

Paganini, Op. 9, 58
Paganini Caprices, Set I, Op. 3 (6 Pieces), 13
Paganini Etudes, Op. 10 (6 Pieces), 62
Pantalon et Colombine, Op. 9, 57
Papillons, Op. 2 (12 Pieces), 5
Papillon, Op. 9, 54
Pause, Op. 9, 60
Perfect Happiness, Op 15, 115
Pierrot, Op. 9, 49
Playing Tag, Sketches Op. 68, 248
(The) Poet Speaks, Op. 15, 121
(The) Poor Orphan, Op. 68, 247
Preambule, Op. 9, 49
Prelude, Sketches Op. 68, 249
Prelude, Op. 99, 276
Premonition of Sorros, Op. 124, 292
Promenade, Op. 9, 59
Prophet Bird, Op. 82, 266

Rebus, Sketches Op. 68, 250
Reconnaissance, Op. 9, 56
Remembrance, Op. 68, 230
Reply, Op. 9, 53
Romance, Op. 26, 167
Romance, D Minor, Op. 32, 176
Romance, Bb Major, Op. 124, 301
Rondoletto, Op. 118a, 224
Roundelay, Op. 68, 224
Rustic Song, Op. 68, 223

Sailor's Song, Op. 68, 237
Scenes from Childhood, Op. 15 (13 Pieces), 111
Scherzino, Op. 26, 168
Scherzino, Op. 124, 293
Scherzo, Bb Major, Op. 32, 175
Second Sonata, Op. 22, 148
    Supplement to Op. 22, 155
Sheherazade, Op. 68, 233
Seven Pieces in Fughetta Form, Op. 126, 309
Sicilian, Op. 68, 211

Six Concert Etudes based on
    Caprices of Paganini, Op. 10, 62
Six Etudes in Canon
    (for the Pedal Piano) Op. 56, 178
Six Fugues on BACH (for Pedal-Piano) Op. 60, 186
Sketches for Album for the Young (17 Pieces), 243
Slumber Song, Op. 124, 305
Soaring, Op. 12, 78
Soldier's March, Op. 68, 194
Sonata No. 1, Op. 11, 69
Sonata No. 2, Op. 22, 148
    Supplement to Sonata No. 2, Op. 22, 155
Sonata No. 3, Op. 14, 100
    Supplement to Sonata No. 3, Op. 14, 109
Sonatas (Three Sonatas for the Young), Op. 118, 283
    Sonata for Julie, Op. 118a, 283
    Sonata for Elise, Op. 118b, 286
    Sonata for Marie, Op. 118c, 288
Songs of the Morning, Op. 133, 314
Sphinxes, Op. 9, 53
Spring Song, Op. 68, 217
Strange Man, Op. 68, 213
Studies on Paganini Caprices, Set I, Op. 3
    (6 Pieces), 13
Suffering without End, Op. 124, 299
Symphonic Etudes, Op. 13, 85
    Supplement to Symphonic Etudes, Op. 13, 96

Theme, C Major, Op. 68, 234
Theme in Eb Major with Five Variations, 321
Theme with Variations, Op. 118a, 284
Third Great Sonata, Concerto Without
    Orchestra, Op. 14, 100
    Supplement to Op. 14, 109
Three Fantasies, Op. 111, 280
Three Little Pieces, Op. 99, 270
Three Romances, Op. 28, 171
Three Sonatas for the Young, Op. 118, 283
Toccata, Op. 7, 43

Valse Allemande, Op. 9, 58
Valse Noble, Op. 9, 51
Variations on the Name Abegg, Op. 1, 1
Vision, Op. 124, 303

Waltz, A Minor, Op. 124, 294
Waltz, Eb Major, Op. 124, 301
Waltz, Ab Major, Op. 124, 304
War Song, Op. 68, 232
Wayside Inn, Op. 82, 265
Whims, Op. 12, 79
Why?, Op. 12, 79
Wild Horseman, Op. 68, 205
Wintertime I, Op. 68, 237
Wintertime II, Op. 68, 238

* *, Supplement to Op. 12, No. 9, 84
* *, Op. 68, No. 21, 224
* *, Op. 68, No. 26, 228
* *, Op. 68, No. 30, 231

OTHER MAXWELL MUSIC EVALUATION PUBLICATIONS

HAYDN: SOLO PIANO LITERATURE: Edited by Carolyn Maxwell and Charles Shadle.
HAYDN provides the musician with an invaluable guide to the important, yet often neglected keyboard music of Franz Joseph Haydn (1732-1809). It contains thematics and reviews of all the works for solo piano and Musical Clock, graded according to level of difficulty. ($9.00)

MAXWELL MUSIC EVALUATION FILE, Edited by Carolyn Maxwell.
This comprehensive file is composed of over 3000 index cards fulfilling the need for an all-purpose reference aid in piano instruction Now, student needs can be matched with recommended music, and piano music can be ordered with assurance of quality and level of difficulty. ($190.00)

ENSEMBLE PIANO LITERATURE NOTEBOOK, including: *Duets
*Duet Collections   *Two-Piano   *Two Piano Collections
*Three or More at One or Two Pianos   ($10.00)

CONTEMPORARY PIANO LITERATURE NOTEBOOK, including:
*Contemporary Solo Literature   *Contemporary Collections
*Definitions of Contemporary Devices   ($10.00)

Both Notebooks are edited by Carolyn Maxwell and include EVERY CARD in the Maxwell Music Evaluation File about Ensemble and Contemporary Piano Literature respectively, with yearly updates if desired, and an extensive set of cross-referencing indexes.

MAXWELL MUSIC EVALUATION
1245 KALMIA
BOULDER, COLORADO, 80302   (303) 443-1603/ 449-1435

Please send the Maxwell Music Evaluation publications checked above. Enclosed is $_____ or please charge to VISA or MASTERCARD #_____
Exp_____ (These prices include postage and handling)

NAME_____

ADDRESS_____

CITY_____ STATE_____

ZIP CODE_____

DO YOU DESIRE UPDATES?_____

HOW DID YOU FIRST HEAR OF US?_____
----

13 00 BB